B A Z I N   A T   W O R K

BAZIN AT WORK

MAJOR ESSAYS & REVIEWS
FROM THE FORTIES & FIFTIES

ANDRÉ BAZIN

*Translated from the French by Alain Piette
and Bert Cardullo*

Edited by Bert Cardullo

ROUTLEDGE / NEW YORK AND LONDON

Published in 1997 by

Routledge
29 West 35th Street
New York, NY 10001

Published in Great Britain by

Routledge
11 New Fetter Lane
London EC4P 4EE

Cataloging-in-Publication Data available from the Library of Congress.

CONTENTS

ACKNOWLEDGMENTS

Alain Piette and Bert Cardullo would like to thank Mme Janine Bazin, as well as the following journals and publishers, for permission to print English translations of André Bazin's work: *Esprit, Cahiers du Cinéma,* and *Éditions du Cerf.* They would also like to thank William Germano of Routledge for his belief in this project and his long-suffering patience with its editor; Dudley Andrew of the University of Iowa for his encouragement and help with the bibliography; and John Mosier of Loyola University in New Orleans for giving them the confidence to undertake a translation of this magnitude. Bert Cardullo would like in addition to remember here Raymond Beirne, under whose inspiring tutelage at the University of Florida he first became interested in the study of film, and whose modesty-cum-simplicity, yet courageous catholicity of taste and spirit, matched Bazin's own.

INTRODUCTION

André Bazin was born on April 18, 1918, in the city of Angers in north-west France, but moved with his family to the western seaport of La Rochelle when he was five years old. Since he wanted to become a teacher, he studied first at the École normale of La Rochelle (1936) and the École normale of Versailles (1937–38), then at the École normale supérieure of Saint-Cloud (1938–41). Bazin graduated from Saint-Cloud with the highest honors (after he was called up for military service in 1939, then demobilized in mid-1940) but was disqualified from teaching in French schools because of a stutter. The failed teacher quickly turned into a missionary of the cinema, his passion for which was part of his general passion for culture, truth, and moral or spiritual sensibility.

In 1942, during the German Occupation, Bazin became a member of an organization in Paris—the Maison des Lettres—that was founded to take care of young students whose regular scholastic routine had been disturbed by the war. There he founded a cinema club where he showed politically banned films in defiance of the Nazi authorities and the Vichy government. During World War II, in 1943, Bazin also worked at the Institut des hautes études cinématographiques (I.D.H.E.C.), the French film school, to which he was appointed director of cultural services after the war. After the Liberation, he was in addition appointed film critic of a new daily newspaper, *Le Parisien libéré.* Thus began his formal life as a public critic and with it the development of a new type of movie reviewing—one of Bazin's singular achievements was his ability to make his insights understood to readers on all levels without any concessions to popularizing.

From the postwar period on, Bazin became a more or less permanent contributor to numerous French periodicals that covered most of the political spectrum: *L'Écran Français* (liberal), *France-Observateur* (socialist), *Esprit* (left-wing Catholic monthly), *Radio-Cinéma-Télévision* (Catholic and slightly less left-wing; today called *Télérama*), *L'Education Nationale* (non-religious and state-run), and the more and more conservative *Le Parisien libéré*. In addition, he wrote for two notable, specialized monthlies: *La Revue du Cinéma*, which Bazin started in 1947 but which collapsed in 1949; and *Les Cahiers du Cinéma*, which he founded in 1951 with Lo Duca and Jacques Doniol-Valcroze and which grew under his direction into Europe's most influential, and one of the world's most distinguished, film publications. As if all this writing and editing were not enough, Bazin contributed to foreign magazines (mainly Italian), was active in film societies and cultural associations (popular ones, like *Travail et Culture*), and attended film conferences and festivals (such as Venice and Cannes). He maintained all these activities (plus a family consisting of his wife, Janine, and a son, Laurent) despite a long and painful illness, leukemia, which he contracted in 1954 and from which he died at Bry-sur-Marne on November 11, 1958. Perhaps because of his fatigue, he grew attached toward the end of his life to television viewing, becoming one of that medium's first perceptive critics. At the time of his death, he was even working on a film script commissioned by the producer Pierre Braunberger, *Les Églises romanes de Saintonge*, which he probably would have directed himself had he lived.

As Bazin's biographer, Dudley Andrew, has argued, "André Bazin's impact on film art, as theorist and critic, is widely considered to be greater than that of any single director, actor, or producer in the history of the cinema. He is credited with almost single-handedly establishing the study of film as an accepted intellectual pursuit," as well as with being the spiritual father of the French New Wave. Seeking a new and revivified cinema, such men as François Truffaut, Jean-Luc Godard, Jacques Rivette, and Claude Chabrol wrote under Bazin's tutelage at *Cahiers du Cinéma*. As critics, these individuals contributed significantly to the development of theory, particularly the *auteur* theory, which was derived from Bazin's ideas and which argued that since a film is a work of art necessarily stamped with the personality of its creator, it is the director above all who gives the film its distinctive quality. As filmmakers, Truffaut and company comprised the first generation of cinéastes whose work was thoroughly grounded in film history and theory, and thus they contributed heavily to

Bazin's effort to get the cinema recognized as a serious and important field of study rather than merely as an avenue of escape from the pressures of life.

Unlike nearly all the other authors of major film theories—and he was the realist among them—André Bazin was a working or practical critic who wrote regularly about individual films. He never left a systematic book of theory; instead he preferred to have implicit theoretical dialogues with filmmakers and other critics through his critical writing in a number of journals. It has been suggested that the best of his criticism has been lost because it occurred in the form of oral presentations and debates at such places as I.D.H.E.C. That may be the case; however, the most important of his essays—some sixty of them—were collected in the posthumously published *Qu'est-ce que le cinéma?* (1958–62); the rest lie scattered in the various magazines enumerated above. Then there are his books on Jean Renoir, Orson Welles, and Charlie Chaplin, all published after his death, like the four volumes of *Qu'est-ce-que le cinéma?*. See the bibliography for details on these works and translations in addition to those contained here.

Bazin based his criticism on the films actually made rather than on any preconceived aesthetic or sociological principles; and film theory for the first time became a matter not of pronouncement and prescription, but of description, analysis, and deduction. "While the fragmentary method of his writing may have prevented him from organizing a fully elaborated system like Siegfried Kracauer's in *Theory of Film*," in the words of Andrew,

> it gives to his criticism a density of thought and a constructive dependence on examples that are absent from Kracauer's work. Bazin's usual procedure was to watch a film closely, appreciating its special values and noting its difficulties or contradictions. Then he would imagine the kind of film it was or was trying to be, placing it within a genre or fabricating a new genre for it. He would formulate the laws of this genre, constantly reverting to examples taken from this film and others like it. Finally, these "laws" would be seen in the context of an entire theory of cinema. Thus Bazin begins with the most particular facts available, the film or films before his eyes, and through a process of logical and imaginative reflection, he arrives at a general theory.

Every movie, even a bad one, is an opportunity for him to develop an historical or sociological hypothesis, or to postulate about the manner of artistic creation. Bazin founds his critical method on the fecundity of para-dox—dialectically speaking, something true that seems false and is all the truer for seeming so. Starting from the most paradoxical aspect of a film, he demonstrates its utter artistic necessity. Bresson's *Diary of a Country Priest* and Cocteau's *Les Parents terribles*, for example, are all the more cin-ematic for the former's scrupulous faithfulness to its novelistic source and the latter's to its dramatic antecedent; thus for Bazin they are ideal instances of "impure" or "mixed" cinema. He even anticipates decon-structive analysis by justifying the shortcomings or anomalies of so-called masterpieces, arguing that they are as necessary to the success of these works as their aesthetic qualities. The deconstructionists, of course, like the structuralists, semioticians, Marxists, and other such fellow travelers of the left, are the ones who revile André Bazin today with lethal epithets like "bourgeois idealist," "mystical humanist," and "reactionary Catholic." But their analysis is reductive and partial, for Bazin's formalist and spiritualist enterprise aimed less at discovering a conservative synthesis, communion, or unity in art as in life than at freeing aesthetic pleasure from dramatur-gical exigency alone, at implicating the viewer in an active relationship with the screen, and at freeing cinematic space and time from slavery to the anecdotal. As such, Bazin was, if anything, a species of transcendental-ist, a kind of cinematic Hegel, who proposed to discover the nature of filmic reality as much by investigating the process of critical thought as by examining the artistic objects of sensory experience themselves.

Bazin's criticism, then, is not remotely doctrinal in its Catholicism, but is fundamentally holistic; its source lies elsewhere than in aesthetic dissection. His true filmmaker attains his power through "style," which is not a thing to be expressed but an inner orientation enabling an outward search. This spiritual sensitivity and its enablement through film are cen-tral to Bazin's view of film as obligated to God, to honor God's universe by using film to render the reality of the universe and, through its reali-ty, its mystery-cum-musicality. This led Bazin to certain specific espousals—Italian neorealism, the technique of deep focus, and more—but these were all secondary consequences for him of the way that film could best bear witness to the miracle of the creation. Éric Rohmer, who became a filmmaker in the Bazinian tradition but who was in the 1950s a critical-editorial colleague of Bazin's, has said: "Without a doubt, the whole body of Bazin's work is based on one central idea, an affirmation of the objectivity of the cinema."

Bazin's general idea was to discover in the nature of the photographic image an objectively realistic feature, and, as Rohmer points out, the concept of objective reality as a fundamental quality of the cinematic shot in fact became the key to his theoretical and critical work. For Bazin, the photographic origin of film explains the novelty of and the fascination with the cinema. The picture is a kind of double of the world, a reflection petrified in time, brought back to life by cinematic projection; in other words, everything that is filmed once *was* in reality. A rapt Bazin thus speaks of the ontological realism of the cinema, and according to him, naturally, the camera is the objective tool with which to achieve it. He granted the camera a purifying power and an impassiveness that restored the virgin object to the attention and love of the viewer. He saw almost perfect examples of this "brute representation" of the cinema in documentary and scientific films, in which the filmmaker interferes or tampers very little with nature. Bazin saw such brute representation as well in the deep-focus *mise en scène* of William Wyler's films, which tended toward a neutrality or objectivity that was eminently moral and liberal, hence perfectly characteristic of American freedom and democracy. For him, only ontological realism of this type was capable of restoring to the object and its setting the density of their being.

The critic Stanley Kauffmann has explained that Bazin's basic position cannot be understood except as a strong reaction against principles of filmmaking that had prevailed before then: of subjectivity, of an arrangement and interpretation of the world—what might be called Eisenstein-Pudovkin principles (different though those two men were) in editing. Bazin was opposed to such an approach as "self-willed" and "manipulative," as the imposition of opinion where the filmmaker should try, in effect, to stand aside and reveal reality. By contrast, the first line of Pudovkin's *Film Technique* is: "The foundation of film art is *editing*." Bazin upheld *mise en scène* against editing or *montage* because, to him, the former represented "true continuity" and reproduced situations more realistically, leaving the interpretation of a particular scene to the viewer rather than to the director's viewpoint through cutting. Consistent with this view, he argued in support of both the shot-in-depth and the long or uninterrupted take, and commended the switch from silent to talking pictures as one step toward the attainment of total realism on film—to be followed by such additional steps as widescreen cinematography, color, and 3-D.

The Russians themselves had derived their methods from American films, especially those of D. W. Griffith, and American films had continued in the "editing" vein. In Hollywood pictures and, through their example, in most pictures everywhere, the guiding rule was to edit the film to conform to the flow of the viewer's attention, to anticipate and control that attention. The director and editor chose the fraction of space that they thought the viewer would be most concerned with each fraction of a second: the hero's face when he declares his love, then the heroine's reaction, then the door when someone else enters, and so on, bit by bit. The Russians' use of montage had much more complex aims, aesthetic and ideological, than presumed audience gratification, but technically it, too, was a mosaic or discontinuous approach to reality.

Bazin disagreed strongly and, one can legitimately say, religiously. Possibly the best example of his disagreement is in his essay "The Technique of *Citizen Kane*," in particular his analysis of Susan Alexander Kane's attempted suicide:

> We get [the suicide attempt] in a single shot on a level with the bed. In the left-hand corner, on the night table, are the enormous glass and the teaspoon. A little farther back, in shadow, we sense rather than see the woman's face. The presence of drama and its nature, already suggested by the glass, are revealed to us on the soundtrack: by a raspy groan and the snore of a drugged sleeper. Beyond the bed: the empty room, and completely in the background, even farther away because of the receding perspective created by the wide-angle lens: the locked door. Behind the door, we hear on the soundtrack Kane's calls and his shoulder bumping against the wood....The door gives way and Kane appears and rushes to the bed.

Again, all of this in one shot.

Traditional editing, the five or six shots into which all the above could be divided, would give us, according to Bazin, "the illusion of being at real events unraveling before us in everyday reality. But this illusion conceals an essential bit of deceit because reality exists in continuous space and the screen presents us in fact a succession of fragments called 'shots.'" Instead, Welles presents the experience whole, in order to give us the same privileges and responsibilities of choice that life itself affords. In "The Evolution of the Language of Cinema" Bazin says further that "*Citizen Kane* is unthinkable shot in any other way but in depth. The

uncertainty in which we find ourselves as to the spiritual key or the interpretation we should put on the film is built into the very design of the
image." The best director, then—Welles, Rossellini, Renoir, and Murnau
rank high for Bazin—is the one who mediates least, the one who exercis-
es selectivity just sufficiently to put us in much the same relation of regard
and choice toward the narrative as we are toward reality in life: a director
who thus imitates, within his scale, the divine disposition toward man.

The Eisenstein-Bazin "debate" is of course not decisively settled in
film practice. Other than such an anomalous director as Miklós Jancsó, to
whom one reel equals one shot, most good modern directors use the reality of the held, "plumbed" shot as well as the mega-reality of montage.
One need look no further than the work of Bazin's venerator Truffaut for
an example of this. And such a balance between montage and *mise en scène*
doesn't smugly patronize Bazin: no one before him had spoken up so fully
and influentially for his side of the question.

Truly mourned by many—among them filmmakers like Renoir,
Truffaut, Visconti, and Bresson—André Bazin died, as Dudley Andrew
describes,

> just ahead of the movement that placed cinema in university class-
> rooms. He did his teaching in film clubs, at conferences, and in
> published articles. Yet while many people now make their livings
> teaching film (and far better livings than Bazin ever enjoyed), some
> teachers look back with longing to that era when reflection about
> the movies took place in a natural arena rather than in the hothouse
> of the university. Film theory as well as criticism is for the most
> part now an acquired discipline, not a spontaneous activity, and the
> cinema is seen as a field of "research" rather than as a human reali-
> ty. Current film scholars, including those hostile to his views, look
> in wonder at Bazin, who in 1958 was in command of a complete,
> coherent, and thoroughly humanistic view of cinema.

More than once he has been called the Aristotle of film for being the first
to try to formulate principles in all regions of this then unexplored field.
Today, however, the cinema is considered so large a subject that the crit-
ic-theorist can at best carve out for study only a small portion of it.

Bazin ambitiously and innocently tried to tackle all of it, and *Bazin at
Work* presents some of the very best of his work from 1946 until his death
in 1958. Included in this collection are previously untranslated essays and
reviews from the four volumes of *Qu'est-ce que le cinéma?* as well as from

such important periodicals as *Cahiers du Cinéma, Esprit,* and *France-Observateur. Bazin at Work* addresses such significant subjects as the paradox of realism, filmic adaptation, CinemaScope, Stalinist cinema, and religious film; such prominent filmmakers as Rossellini, Eisenstein, Pagnol, De Sica, and Capra; and well-known films like *La Strada, Citizen Kane, Forbidden Games, The Bridge on the River Kwai,* and *Scarface.* The book is extensively illustrated and, in addition to its faithful yet not literal translations—uniquely executed by a native speaker of French in collaboration with a working film critic, features explanatory notes, a helpful index, and a comprehensive Bazin bibliography. It is aimed, as Bazin would want, not only at scholars, teachers, and critics of film but also at educated or cultivated moviegoers and students of the cinema at all levels. In his modesty and simplicity André Bazin considered himself such a student, such an "interested" filmgoer, and it is to the spirit of his humility before the god of cinema, as well as to the steadfastness of his courage in life, that this book is dedicated. Long may his work, and the memory of the man, live.

Bert Cardullo

PART ONE

BAZIN ON DIRECTORS AND ON CINEMA

CHAPTER 1

William Wyler, or the Jansenist of Directing[1]

When studied in detail, William Wyler's directing style reveals obvious differences for each of his films, both in the use of the camera and in the quality of the photography. Nothing is stranger to the form of *The Best Years of Our Lives* (1946) than the form of *The Letter* (1940). When one recalls the major scenes in Wyler's films, one notices that their dramatic material is extremely varied and that the editing of it is very different from one film to another. When one considers the red gown at the ball in *Jezebel* (1938); the dialogue in the scene in *The Little Foxes* (1941) where Herbert Marshall gets a shave, or the dialogue in his death scene in the same film; the sheriff's death in *The Border Cavalier* (1927); the traveling shot at the plantation at the beginning of *The Letter*; or the scene in the out-of-use bomber in *The Best Years of Our Lives*, it becomes clear that there is no consistent motif in the work of Wyler. One can find such a motif, however, in the chase scenes of John Ford's westerns; the fist fights in Tay Garnett's films; or in the weddings or chases in René Clair's work. There are no favorite settings or landscapes for Wyler. At most, there is an evident fondness for psychological scenarios set against social backgrounds. Yet, even though Wyler has become a master at treating this kind of subject, adapted either from a novel like *Jezebel* or a play like *The Little Foxes*, even though his work as a whole leaves us with the piercing and rigorous impression of a psychological analysis, it does not call to mind sumptuously eloquent images suggesting a formal beauty that would demand serious consideration. The style of a director cannot be defined, however, only in terms of his predilection for psychological analysis and social realism, even less so here since we are not dealing with original scripts.

And yet, I do not think that it is more difficult to recognize the signature of Wyler in just a few shots than it is to recognize the signatures of Ford, Fritz Lang, or Hitchcock. I would even go so far as to say that the director of *The Best Years of Our Lives* is among those who have least often employed the tricks of the trade at the expense of genuine style. Whereas Capra, Ford, or Lang occasionally indulges in self-parody, Wyler never does so: when he goes wrong, it is because he has made a bad choice. He has occasionally been inferior to himself, his taste is not absolutely to be trusted, and he seems to be capable sometimes of being a sincere admirer of Henry Bernstein[2] or the like, but he has never been caught in the act of cheating on the form. There is a John Ford style and a John Ford manner. Wyler has only a style. That is why he is proof against parody, even of himself. Imitation of Wyler by other directors would not pay off, because Wyler's style cannot be defined by any precise form, any lighting design, any particular camera angle. The only way to imitate Wyler would be to espouse the kind of directing ethic to be found in its purest form in *The Best Years of Our Lives*. Wyler cannot have imitators, only disciples.

If we were to attempt to define the directing in this film and if we took its form as a starting point, we would have to give a negative definition. The whole tendency of the *mise en scène* is to efface itself. The alternative, positive definition would be that, when this self-effacement is at its extreme, the story and the actors are at their clearest and most powerful. The aesthetic sense of this kind of asceticism will perhaps be clearer if we locate it in *The Little Foxes*, because it is seemingly pushed there to the point of paradox. Lillian Hellman's play has undergone almost no adaptation: the film respects the text almost completely. In this regard, one can easily understand why there are no exterior scenes of movement in the film—the sorts of scenes that most directors would have deemed necessary in order to introduce a little "cinema" into this theatrical mass. Indeed, a good adaptation usually consists of "transposing" into specifically cinematic terms everything that can be freed from the literary and technical restraints of the theater. If you were told that Mr. Berthomieu,[3] for instance, had just filmed the latest play by Mr. Henry Bernstein without changing a single line, you would start worrying. If the bringer of bad tidings added that nine-tenths of the film was set in the same living room that was used in the theater, you would think that you still had a lot to learn about the impudence of the makers of filmed theater. But if on top of all that the messenger announced that the film does not include more than ten different camera angles and that the camera is mostly stationary in front of the actors, your opinion of the film would be final. "Now I have seen everything!" Yet, it is upon these paradoxical premises that Wyler has built one of the most purely cinematic works ever.

The majority of the action takes place on the same, totally neutral set, the ground-floor living room of a huge colonial house. At the back, a staircase leads to the first-floor bedrooms: Bette Davis's and Herbert Marshall's, which adjoin each other. Nothing picturesque adds to the realism of this somber place, which is as impersonal as the setting of classical tragedy. The characters have a credible, if conventional, reason for confronting one another in the living room, whether they come from outdoors or from their bedrooms. They can also linger there. The staircase at the back plays exactly the same role as it would in the theater: it is purely an element of dramatic architecture, which will be used to situate the characters in vertical space. Let's take as an example the central scene of the film, the death of Herbert Marshall, which indeed takes place both in the living room and on the staircase. An analysis of this scene will clearly reveal the essential secrets of Wyler's style.

Bette Davis is sitting in the middle ground facing the viewers, her head at the center of the screen; very strong lighting further underlines the brightness of her heavily made-up face. In the foreground, Marshall is sitting in three-quarter profile. The ruthless exchanges between husband and wife take place without any cutting from one character to the other. Then comes the husband's heart attack: he begs his wife to get him his medicine from the bedroom. From this instant, the whole drama resides, as Denis Marion[4] has very aptly observed, in the immobility of Bette Davis and the camera. Marshall is obliged to stand up and go get the medicine himself. This effort will kill him on the first steps of the staircase.

In the theater, this scene would most likely have been staged in the same manner. A spotlight could also have been focused on Bette Davis, and the spectator would have had the same sense of horror regarding her criminal inaction, the same sense of anguish at the sight of her staggering victim. Yet, despite appearances, Wyler's *mise en scène* makes as extensive a use as possible of the means offered him by the camera and the frame. Bette Davis' position at the center of the screen endows her with privilege in the geometry of the dramatic space. The whole scene revolves around her, but her frightening immobility takes its full impact only from Marshall's double exit from the frame, first in the foreground on the right, then on a third plane on the left. Instead of following him in this lateral movement, as any less intelligent eye would naturally have done, the camera remains imperturbably immobile. When Marshall finally enters the frame for the second time and climbs the stairs, the cinematographer Gregg Toland (acting at Wyler's request) is careful not to bring into focus the full depth of the image, so that Marshall's fall on the staircase and his death will not be perfectly visible to the viewer. This artificial blurriness augments our feeling of anxiety: as if over the shoulder of Bette Davis, who faces us and has her back toward her husband, we have to discern in the distance the outcome of a drama whose protagonist is nearly escaping us.

We can see here everything that the cinema adds to the means of the theater, and we can also see that, paradoxically, the highest level of cinematic art coincides with the lowest level of *mise en scène*. Nothing could better heighten the dramatic power of this scene than the absolute immobility of the camera. The slightest movement, which a less skillful director would have deemed the right cinematic element to introduce, would have decreased the dramatic tension. Here, furthermore, the camera does not follow the path of the average viewer's eyes by cutting from one character to the other. It is the camera itself that organizes the action by means of the frame and the ideal coordinates of its dramatic geometry.

In my school days, when I was studying mineralogy, I remember being struck by the structure of certain fossil shells. Although the limestone was arranged in the living animal in thin parallel layers at the surface of the valves, a slow process in the dead animal had rearranged the molecules into thin crystals perpendicular to the initial direction of the layers. Apparently, the shell was intact; one could still discern perfectly the original stratification of the limestone. But, when the shell was cracked, the fracture revealed that the perpendicular external pattern was completely contradicted by the parallel interior architecture. I apologize for this comparison, but it illustrates well the invisible molecular process that affects the deep aesthetic structure of Lillian Hellman's play, and that at the same time respects with a paradoxical fidelity its superficial theatrical appearance.

In *The Best Years of Our Lives* the problems were of a totally different order from those encountered in *The Little Foxes*. The film had an almost original script. The novel in [blank] verse by MacKinlay Kantor (*Glory for*

Me), from which Robert Sherwood drew his screenplay, has certainly not been respected as Hellman's play was.[5] The nature of the subject, its relevance, its seriousness, its social usefulness, demanded first and foremost an extreme meticulousness, a quasi-documentary accuracy. Samuel Goldwyn and Wyler wanted to create a civic good work in this film as much as to create a work of art. The task was to expose through a story—romanticized, to be sure, but credible and even exemplary in its details—one of the most crucial and distressing social problems of postwar America, and to do so with the necessary breadth and subtlety. In a certain sense, *The Best Years of Our Lives* is still related to American wartime propaganda films, to the didactic mission of the film unit of the American army, from which unit Wyler had just been discharged. The war and the particular view of reality that it engendered have deeply influenced the European cinema, as we all know; the war's consequences were less strongly felt in Hollywood. Yet, several American filmmakers took part in the war, and some of the horror, some of the shocking truths, with which it overwhelmed the world, could be translated by them as well into an ethic of realism. "All three of us (Capra, Stevens, and Wyler) took part in the war. It had a very strong influence on each of us. Without that experience, I couldn't have made my film the way I did. We have learned to understand the world better. . . . I know that George Stevens has not been the same since he saw the corpses at Dachau. We were forced to realize that Hollywood has rarely reflected the world and the time in which people live." These few lines of Wyler's sufficiently illuminate his purpose in making *The Best Years of Our Lives*.

We know how much care he devoted to the making of this, the longest and probably the most expensive film in his career. Yet, if *The Best Years of Our Lives* were only a propaganda film, it would not deserve very much attention, no matter how skillful, well-intended, moving, and useful it was. For instance, the script of *Mrs. Miniver* (1942) is not so inferior to that of *The Best Years of Our Lives*: but *Mrs. Miniver* is marked by pedestrian direction and does not move toward any particular style. The result is rather disappointing. By contrast, in *The Best Years of Our Lives* Wyler's ethical reverence for reality found its aesthetic transcription in the *mise en scène*. Indeed, nothing is more fallacious and absurd than to contrast "realism" and "aestheticism," as was frequently done in reference to the Russian or the Italian cinema. In the true sense of the word, there is no film more "aesthetic" than *Paisan* (1946). Reality is not art, but a truly "realistic" art can create an aesthetic that is incorporated in reality. Thank God, Wyler was not satisfied merely to be faithful to the psychological and social truth of the action (which truths, by the way, did not come off so well). He tried to find aesthetic equivalents for psychological and social truth in the *mise en scène*. I will mention these equivalents in the order of their importance.

First, there is the realism of the set, built in its entirety to realistic dimensions (which drastically complicated the shooting, as one might expect, since the walls had to be removed to give the camera mobility). The actors and actresses were wearing the same clothes that their characters would have worn in reality, and their faces were not made up more than they would have been in everyday life. Granted, this quasi-superstitious faithfulness to the truth of daily life is particularly strange in Hollywood, but its actual significance lies perhaps not so much in the guarantee of verisimilitude it gave to the viewer as in the revolution it unmistakably implied for the art of *mise en scène*: lighting, camera angle, the directing of the actors. It is not on the basis of meat hanging down onstage or on the basis of André Antoine's[6] real trees that realism defines itself, but through the means of expression that a realistic subject allows the artist to discover. The "realistic" tendency in the cinema has existed since Louis Lumière and even since Marey and Muybridge.[7] It has known diverse fates, but the forms it has taken have survived only in proportion to the aesthetic invention or discovery (conscious or not, calculated or naive) that it allowed. There is not one realism, but several realisms. Each period looks for its own, the technique and the aesthetics that will capture, retain, and render best what one wants from reality. On the screen, technique naturally plays a much more important role than in the novel because the written word is more or less stable, whereas the cinematic image has undergone deep modifications since its creation. Lighting, sound, and color have wrought true transformations of the image. The syntax that organizes the vocabulary of cinema has also undergone change. "Associational montage," which is identified mainly with the period of silent film, has been succeeded almost totally by the logic of cutting and by narrative editing. Changes are undoubtedly due in part to fashion, which exists in the cinema as it does everywhere else, but all the changes that have a real significance and that add to film heritage are closely connected with cinematographic technique: and such technique is the infrastructure of film.

To want one's film to look true, to show reality, the whole reality and nothing but reality, may be an honorable intention. As it stands, however, this does not go beyond the level of ethics. In the cinema, such an intention can result only in a *representation* of reality. The aesthetic problem begins with the means of that representation. A dead child in close-up is not the same as a dead child in medium shot is not the same as a dead child in color. Indeed, our eyes, and consequently our minds, have a way of seeing a dead child in real life that is not the way of the camera, which places the image within the rectangle of the screen. "Realism" consists not only of showing us a corpse, but also of showing it to us under conditions that re-create certain physiological or mental givens of natural perception, or, more accurately, under conditions that seek equivalents for these givens. The classical approach to editing ("psychological montage"), which divides a scene into a certain number of elements (the hand on the telephone or the door knob that slowly turns), implicitly corresponds to a particular natural mental process that makes us accept the sequence of shots without being conscious of the cutter's hand at work. Indeed, in real life our eye, like a lens, focuses spatially on the aspects of an event that interest us most. The eye proceeds through successive investigations: in scanning the space in which an event takes place, it introduces a kind of additional temporalization to that event, which itself is occurring in time.

The first camera lenses were not varied. Their optical characteristics naturally created a large depth of field that suited the cutting, or rather the near absence of cutting, of the films of that time. It was absolutely out of the question back then to divide a scene into twenty-five camera placements and at the same time to keep the lens focused on the actors. Progress in optics is closely linked with the history of editing, being at the same time its cause and consequence.

To consider a different method of filming, the way Jean Renoir did as early as 1933 and Orson Welles did a little later, one had to have discovered that analytical cutting or classical editing was founded on the illusion of psychological realism. Although it is true that our eye changes its focus continually according to what interests or attracts it, this mental and psychological adjustment is done after the fact. The event exists continuously in its entirety, every part of it demands our undivided attention; we are the ones who decide to choose this or that aspect, to select this instead of that according to the bidding of our feelings or our thinking. Someone else, however, would perhaps make a different choice. In any case, we are *free* to create our own *mise en scène*: another "creation" or cutting is always possible that can radically modify the subjective aspect of reality. Now the director who does the cutting for us also does the selecting that we would do in real life. We unconsciously accept his choices, because they conform to the seeming laws of ocular attraction; but they deprive us of a privilege that is well grounded in psychology and that we give up without realizing it: the freedom, at least the potential one, to modify at each instant our method of selection, of "editing."

The psychological, and in addition aesthetic, consequences of this are significant. The technique of analytical cutting tends[8] to destroy in particular the ambiguity inherent in reality. It "subjectivizes" the event to an extreme, since each shot is the product of the director's bias. Analytical cutting implies not only a dramatic, emotional, or moral choice, but also, and more significantly, a judgment on reality itself. It is probably excessive to bring up the controversy over the "universals" in regard to Wyler. Even if the philosophical dispute over nominalism and realism (at the basis of which is the controversy over the definition of "universals" or abstract terms) has its equivalent in film in the opposition between formalism and realism, formalism and realism are not defined only on the basis of a director's shooting and cutting method. It is certainly not a coincidence, however, that Renoir, André Malraux, Welles, Roberto Rossellini, and the Wyler of *The Best Years of Our Lives* come together in their frequent use of depth of field, or at least of "simultaneous" *mise en scène*, of action occurring simultaneously on different planes. It is not an accident that, from 1938 to 1946, their names are attached to everything that really matters in cinematic realism, the kind of realism that proceeds from an aesthetics of reality.

Thanks to depth of field, at times augmented by action taking place simultaneously on several planes, the viewer is at least given the opportunity in the end to edit the scene himself, to select the aspects of it to which he will attend. I quote Wyler:

> I had long conversations with my cameraman, Gregg Toland. We decided to strive for a realism that would be as simple as possible. Gregg Toland's talent for keeping the different planes of the image simultaneously in focus allowed me to develop my own style of directing. Thus I could follow an action to its end without cutting. The resulting continuity makes the shots more alive; more interest-

ing for the viewer, who can choose of his own will to study a partic-ular character and who can make his own cuts.

The terms used by Wyler above plainly show that his concern was drastically different from that of Welles or Renoir. Renoir used simulta-neous, lateral *mise en scène* mostly to underline the connections between plots, as is clearly visible in the feast at the castle in *The Rules of the Game* (1939).[9] Welles sometimes aims toward a tyrannical objectivity à la Dos Passos, sometimes toward a kind of systematic extension in depth of real-ity, as if that reality were sketched on a rubber band that he would take pleasure first in pulling back to scare us, second in letting go right into our faces. The receding perspectives and the low-angle shots of Welles are fully extended slingshots. Wyler's method is completely different from Welles's and Renoir's. We are still talking about integrating into the overall structure and the individual image a maximum of reality, about making the set and the actors totally and simultaneously present, so that action will never be an *abstraction*. But this constant accretion of events on the screen aims in Wyler at perfect neutrality. The sadism of Welles and the ironic anxiety of Renoir have no place in *The Best Years of Our Lives*. The purpose in this film is not to harass the viewer, to break him upon the wheel and to quarter him. Wyler wants only to allow him to: (1) see everything; (2) make choices "of his own will." This is an act of loyalty toward the viewer, a pledge of dramatic honesty. Wyler puts his cards on the table. Indeed, it seems that the use of classical editing in *The Best Years of Our Lives* would have been somewhat deceptive, like a never-ending magic trick. "Look at this," the camera would say, "and now at that." But what about in between shots? The frequency of depth-of-focus shots and the perfect sharpness of the backgrounds contribute enormously to reas-suring the viewer and to giving him the opportunity to observe and to make a selection, and the length of the shots even leaves him time to form an opinion, as we will see later. Depth of field in Wyler aims at being lib-eral and democratic, like the consciences both of the American viewers and of the characters in *The Best Years of Our Lives*.

THE STYLELESS STYLE

The depth of field of Wyler is more or less the film equivalent of what André Gide and Roger Martin du Gard[10] have deemed the ideal of com-position in the novel: the perfect neutrality and transparency of style, which must not interpose any filter, any refractive index, between the reader's mind and the story. In consonance with Wyler, then, Toland has used in *The Best Years of Our Lives* a technique distinctly different from the one he used in *Citizen Kane* (1941). First the lighting: Welles preferred chiaroscuro lighting, that is, lighting that is harsh and subtle at the same time; he wanted large areas of semidarkness penetrated by rays of light with which he and the actors could skillfully play. Wyler asked Toland only for lighting as neutral as possible, which would not be artistic or even dramatic, but simply honest light that would sufficiently illuminate the actors and the surrounding set. It is a comparison between the lenses Toland used, however, that will enable us to understand better the difference between the two techniques. The wide-angle lenses of *Citizen Kane*, on the one hand, strongly distort perspective, and Welles exploits the resulting receding quality of the set. The lenses used in *The Best Years of Our Lives*, on the other hand, conform more to the optics of normal vision and tend because of deep focus to foreshorten the image, that is to say, to spread it out on the surface of the screen. Wyler thus deprives himself, once again, of certain technical means at his disposal so that he can respect reality better. This requirement of Wyler's seems, by the way, to have complicated Toland's task; deprived of optical means, he had to "diaphragm" (to regulate the amount of light entering the lens of the camera) far more, it seems, than had ever been done on any film in the world.

Sets, costumes, lights, and above all photography, each of these tends now to neutrality. This *mise en scène* seems to define itself through its absence, at least in the aspects we have studied. Wyler's efforts systematically work toward the creation of a film universe that not only rigorously conforms to reality, but also is as little modified as possible by cinematic optics. Paradoxically, even though enormous technical skill was necessary to shoot scenery built to realistic dimensions and to "diaphragm" a lot, Wyler obtains (and wants) on the screen only a picture that resembles as closely as possible, despite the inevitable formal elements required to create it, the spectacle that an eye could see if it looked at reality through an empty framing device.[11]

This experiment could not take place without a change in editing as well. First, for rather evident technical reasons, the average number of shots in a film diminishes as a function of their realism, of the long take with its respect for continuous time and unfragmented space. We know that talking films have fewer shots than silent films. Color in turn further diminished the number of shots, and Roger Leenhardt,[12] adopting one of

Georges Neveux's[13] hypotheses, could maintain with some credibility that the cutting of the 3-D film would naturally recover the number of scenes in Shakespeare's plays: around fifty. One understands indeed that the more the image tends to resemble reality, the more complex the psycho-technical problem of editing becomes. Sound had already created problems for "associational montage," which, in fact, was almost completely replaced by analytical editing; depth of field has made of each change in camera placement a technical *tour de force*. It is in this sense that we must understand Wyler's esteem for his cameraman. Indeed, Toland's talent does not lie in a particularly deep knowledge of the properties of the film stock itself, but above all in an ability to maintain a consistent flow from image to image, besides his sense of framing, about which I will speak again later. Toland maintains a consistent flow not only in the sense that he creates a sharp surface in the conventional shots, but also because he creates the same surface even when he must encompass the entire mass of set, lights, and actors within a virtually unlimited field.

But the determinism of this technique perfectly suited Wyler's purposes. The composition of a scene into shots is an operation that is necessarily artificial. The same aesthetic calculation that made Wyler choose depth-of-focus shooting was bound to lead him in his mind to reduce to a minimum the number of shots necessary to convey the narrative clearly. As a matter of fact, *The Best Years of Our Lives* does not have more than 190 shots per hour, which is approximately 500 shots for a film of two hours and 40 minutes. Let us recall here that contemporary films have an average of 300 to 400 shots per hour, in other words, more or less double that of this film. Let us remember in addition that *Antoine and Antoinette* (1947, dir. Jacques Becker), which undoubtedly represents the absolute opposite in technique from Wyler's film, has some 1,200 shots for one hour and 50 minutes of projection time. Shots of more than two minutes in duration are not infrequent in *The Best Years of Our Lives*, without even the slightest reframing to compensate for their stasis. In fact, there is no trace of "associational montage" in such a *mise en scène*. Even classical editing, which is the aesthetic of the relationship between shots, is drastically reduced: the shot and the sequence tend to fuse. Many of the scenes in *The Best Years of Our Lives* have the unity or discreteness of a Shakespearean scene and are shot as a result in a single long take. Here again, a comparison of this film with the films of Welles clearly shows different aesthetic intentions, although these intentions are based upon techniques that are in part similar. Because of its realistic quality, depth-of-focus shooting was bound to lead the director of *Citizen Kane* to also identify shot with sequence. Remember, for instance, the scene where Susan takes poison, the scene of the falling out between Kane and Jed Leland, and, in *The Magnificent Ambersons* (1942), the admirable love scene in the carriage with the endless tracking shot that the final reframing reveals to have been an actual one and not a traveling matte. Another example in the same film is the scene in the kitchen where young George stuffs himself with cake while talking with Aunt Fanny. But Welles uses depth of field for purposes of extreme contrast. The deep-focus shots correspond in his aesthetics to a certain way of rendering reality, to which other ways of rendering it are opposed, such as those of the "March of Time" newsreel[14] and, above all, the compressed time of the several series of lap dissolves that sum up long portions of the story. The rhythm and the structure of events are thus modified by the dialectics of Welles's narrative technique. Not so with Wyler. The aesthetic of each shot remains constant; the narrative method aims only at a maximum of clarity and, through this clarity, at a maximum of dramatic efficiency.

At this point in my analysis, the reader may wonder where the *mise en scène* is in *The Best Years of Our Lives*. It is true that all my analysis so far has attempted to demonstrate its absence. But before considering finally the concrete aspects of so paradoxical a technique, I would like to avoid another misunderstanding. Even though Wyler has systematically sought to create a perfectly neutral dramatic universe, sometimes creating in the process technical problems never before encountered in film, it would be naive to mistake this neutrality for an absence of art. Just as the respect for dramatic form and theatrical representation in the adaptation of *The Little Foxes* conceals subtle aesthetic modifications, so the arduous yet skillful achievement of neutrality implies here the advance neutralization of numerous film conventions. Whether it be the nearly unavoidable technical devices (which also carry with them almost inevitably certain aesthetic conventions), or editing methods imposed by custom, courage and imagination were needed if the director wanted to do without them. It is rather common to praise a writer for the austerity of his style, and Stendhal is after all admired for writing in the unadorned manner of the French Civil Code: he is never suspected of intellectual laziness for doing so.[15] Earlier I compared Wyler's concern to achieve a perfect neutrality and transparency of style with Gide's and

Martin du Gard's concern to define the ideal style for the novel. It is true that this preliminary "stripping away," in film as in the novel, takes its full meaning and value only from the artwork that it makes possible and for which it paradoxically provides the necessary grounding. But I still have to demonstrate this.

In the article from which I quoted above, Wyler did not hide the confidence he had in Toland to compose shots on the set. What is more, he confirmed this in person to me, and it is easy to believe him when we carefully examine the shots. The happy collaboration of the two men on this film, which would be exceptional in a French studio, can be accounted for by the fact that they had already made six films together. Consequently, since he relied on his cameraman's judgment and on their artistic concurrence, Wyler did not use a shooting script. Each scene had to find its technical solution on the set. A lot of preparatory work was done before the photographing of each scene, but this work had nothing to do with the actual shooting. The *mise en scène* in this film, then, concentrated wholly on the actors. The space filled by the individual actor, already cut off and limited by the frame of the screen, was additionally robbed by Wyler of significance in and of itself, so that the entire dramatic spectrum polarized by the actors would attract the focus. Almost all Wyler's shots are built like an equation, or perhaps better, like a dramatic mechanism whose parallelogram of forces can almost be drawn in geometrical lines. This may not be an original discovery on my part: to be sure, every true director organizes the movement of his actors within the coordinates of the screen according to laws that are still obscure but whose spontaneous perception is part of his talent. Everyone knows, for instance, that the dominant character must be higher in the frame than the dominated one.

But, aside from the fact that Wyler knows how to give his implicit stagings an exceptional clarity and strength, his originality lies in the discovery of a few laws that are his own and, above all, in the use of depth of field as an additional coordinate. My analysis of Marshall's death in *The Little Foxes* clearly reveals how Wyler can make a whole scene revolve around one actor. Bette Davis at the center of the screen is paralyzed, like a hoot owl by a spotlight, and around her the staggering Marshall weaves as a second, this time mobile, pole, whose shift first out of the frame and then into the background, draws with it all the dramatic attention. In addition, this creates tremendous suspense because it is a double disappearance from the frame and because the focus on the staircase at the back is imperfect. One can see here how Wyler uses depth of field. The intention in *The Best Years of Our Lives* was always to keep the depth of field continuous within the frame, but Wyler did not have the same reason for using this method of shooting in *The Little Foxes*. The director elected to have Toland envelop the character of the dying Marshall in a certain haziness, to have his cinematographer, as it were, befog the back of the frame. This was done to create additional anxiety in the viewer, so much anxiety that he would almost want to push the immobile Bette Davis aside to have a better look. The dramatic development of this scene does indeed follow that of the dialogue and of the action itself, but the scene's cinematic expression superimposes its own evolution upon the dramatic development: a second action that is the very story of the scene from the moment Marshall gets up from his chair to his collapse on the staircase.

Now here is, from *The Best Years of Our Lives*, a dramatic construction built around three characters: the scene of the falling out between Dana Andrews and Teresa Wright. This scene is set in a bar. Fredric March has just convinced Andrews to break off with his daughter and urges him to call her immediately. Andrews gets up and goes toward the telephone booth located near the door, at the back of the room. March leans on a piano in the foreground and pretends to get interested in the musical exercise that the crippled sailor (Harold Russell) is learning to play with his hooks. The field of the camera begins with the keyboard of the piano large in the foreground, includes March and Russell in an "American" shot,[16] encompasses the whole barroom, and distinctly shows in the background a tiny Andrews in the telephone booth. This shot is clearly built upon two dramatic poles and three characters. The action in the foreground is secondary, although interesting and peculiar enough to require our keen attention since it occupies a privileged place and surface on the screen. Paradoxically, the true action, the one that constitutes at this precise moment a turning point in the story, develops almost clandestinely in a tiny rectangle at the back of the room—in the left corner of the screen.

The link between these two dramatic areas is provided by March, who, with the viewer, is the only one that knows what is going on in the telephone booth and who, according to the logic of the scene, is impressed, like us, by the musical prowess of the crippled seaman. From time to time, March turns his head slightly and glances across the room, anxiously scrutinizing the behavior of Andrews. Finally, the latter hangs the telephone up and, without turning to the men at the piano, suddenly disappears into the street. If we reduce the real action of this scene to its essence, we are left with Andrews' telephone call. This telephone conversation is the only thing of immediate interest to us. The one character whose face we would like to see in close-up is precisely the person whom we cannot clearly discern because of his position in the background and because of the glass surrounding the booth. His words themselves are of course inaudible. The true drama occurs, then, far away in a kind of little aquarium that reveals only what appear to be the trivial and ritual gestures of an ordinary phone call. Depth of field is used here for the same purpose it was used in Marshall's death scene in *The Little Foxes*. The position of the camera is such that the laws of perspective produce the same effect created by the haziness enveloping the staircase in the background: even as we felt anxiety because we couldn't view the dying Marshall clearly on the stairs, we feel anxiety because we cannot distinctly see Andrews in the phone booth at the back, nor can we hear him.

The idea of situating the telephone booth at the back of the room, thereby obliging the viewer to figure out what is happening there and obliging him to participate in March's anxiety, was in itself an excellent directorial device. However, Wyler immediately felt that by itself it destroyed the spatial and temporal balance of the shot. He therefore set out at once to counterbalance and to reinforce the action in the phone booth. Hence the idea of a diverting action *in the foreground*, secondary in itself, whose spatial prominence would be conversely proportional to its dramatic significance. The action in the foreground is secondary, not insignificant, and the viewer cannot ignore it because he is also interested in the fate of the crippled sailor and because he doesn't see someone play the piano with hooks every day. Forced to wait for Andrews to finish his call in the phone booth and unable to see him well, the viewer is obliged furthermore to divide his attention between this same booth and the scene at the piano. Thus Wyler killed two birds with one stone: first, the diversion of the piano allows him to extend as long as possible a shot that would otherwise have seemed endless and consequently monotonous; second, and more important, this parasitic pole of attraction organizes the image dramatically and spatially. The real action at the phone booth is juxtaposed against the action at the piano, which directs the attention of the viewer almost against his will to itself, where it is supposed to be, for as long as it is supposed to be there. Thus the viewer is induced actively to participate in the drama planned by the director.

I should mention, for the sake of accuracy, that this scene is interrupted twice by close-ups of March glancing toward the phone booth. Wyler probably feared that the viewer might become too absorbed in the piano playing and gradually forget the action in the background. He therefore cautiously took a few "safety shots"—the close-ups of March—which focus completely on the main action: the dramatic line between March and Andrews. The editing process probably revealed that two interpolated shots were necessary and sufficient to recapture the diverted attention of the viewer. This degree of caution, by the way, is characteristic of Wyler's technique. Welles would have placed only the telephone booth in the frame, filmed it in deep focus, and would have let the booth forcefully call attention to itself through its position in the background; he would also have held the shot as long as necessary. The thing is that, for Welles, depth of field is in itself an aesthetic end; for Wyler, depth of field is subject to the dramatic demands of the *mise en scène*, and in particular to the clarity of the narrative. The two interpolated shots amount to a sort of attention-getter: a rerouting of the viewer's eye.

Wyler particularly likes to build his *mise en scène* on the tension created in a shot by the coexistence of two actions of unequal significance. This is clearly discernible once again in a shot from the last sequence of *The Best Years of Our Lives*. The characters grouped on the right, in the middle ground, apparently constitute the main dramatic pole, since nearly everyone is assembled here for the wedding of the crippled sailor and his long-time sweetheart. In fact, however, since their marriage is now to be taken for granted, the attention of the viewer focuses on Teresa Wright (in white in the third plane) and Dana Andrews (on the left in the foreground), who meet for the first time since their breakup. During the entire wedding scene, Wyler skillfully directs his actors in order gradually to isolate from the wedding party Andrews and Wright, who, the viewer feels, cannot stop thinking about each other. The still normally reproduced corresponds to the intermediary stage between the entrance of the wedding party into the room and the coming together of Andrews and Wright. These two characters have not yet reunited, but the shift of the wedding party to the right of the frame, which seems so natural but is actually contrived by Wyler, clearly reveals their connection. Wright's white dress, which is located almost in the middle of the image, constitutes a dramatic boundary between the two components of the action. The two lovers are the only ones in the scene to be spatially, and logically, set apart on the left side of the screen.

We should also notice in this shot the importance of the looks the characters direct at one another. These always constitute with Wyler the foundation of the *mise en scène*.[17] The viewer has only to follow these looks as if they were pointed index fingers in order to understand exactly the director's intentions. One could easily trace the paths of the characters' eyes on the screen and thereby make visible, as clearly as iron filings make visible the field of a magnet, the dramatic currents that flow across the image. All of Wyler's pre-production work consists, as I have suggested, of simplifying to a maximum the technical aspects of the *mise en scène*, so as to free him to compose each shot as clearly and effectively as possible. In *The Best Years of Our Lives* he reaches an almost abstract austerity. All the dramatic joints are so conspicuous that a few degrees' shift in the angle of a glance would not only be clearly visible even to the most obtuse viewer, but would also be capable of causing an entire scene to lose its symmetry, as if this shift in the angle of glance were extra weight added to a perfectly balanced scale.

Perhaps one of the distinctive qualities of a skillful "scientist" of *mise en scène* is that he avoids proceeding from a preestablished aesthetics. Here again Wyler is at the opposite end from Welles, who came to the cinema with the declared intention of creating certain aesthetic effects out of it. For a long time Wyler labored on obscure Westerns whose titles nobody remembers. It is through this work on Westerns, work not as an aesthetician but as a craftsman, that he became the recognized artist whom *Dodsworth* (1936) had already revealed. When he speaks of his directing, it is always in regard to the viewer: his one and only concern is to make the viewer understand the action as precisely and fully as possible. Wyler's immense talent lies in this "science of clarity" obtained through the austerity of the form as well as through equal humility toward his subject matter and his audience. There is in him a sort of genius about his profession, about all things cinematic, which allowed him to stretch an economy of means so far that, paradoxically, he invented one of the most personal styles in contemporary cinema. To attempt to describe this style, however, we had to pretend first that it was an absence of style.

Cinema is like poetry. It would be foolish to imagine cinema as an isolated element that one could capture on celluloid and project on a screen through a magnifying lens. Such pure cinema can be combined as much with a sentimental drama as with the colored cubes, i.e., the abstractions, of Fischinger.[18] The cinema is not any kind of independent matter, whose molecules have to be isolated at any cost. Rather, cinema is that matter once it has achieved an aesthetic state. It is a means for representing a narrative-spectacle. Experience proves sufficiently that one should be careful not to identify the cinema with any given aesthetic or, what is more, with any style, any concrete form that the director must absolutely use, as he would salt and pepper. Cinematic "purity" or values or, more accurately in my opinion, the cinematic "coefficient" of a film, must be calculated on the basis of the effectiveness of the *mise en scène*.

Paradoxically, insofar as Wyler has never attempted to hide the novelistic or theatrical nature of most of his scripts, he has made all the more apparent the cinematic phenomenon in its utmost purity. Not once has the *auteur* of *The Best Years of Our Lives* or *Jezebel* said to himself a priori that he had to have a "cinematic look"; still, nobody can tell a story in cinematic terms better than he. For him, the action is expressed first by the actor. Like a director in the theater, Wyler conceives of his job of enhancing the action as beginning with the actor. The set and the camera are there only to permit the actor to focus upon himself the maximum dramatic intensity; they are not there to create a meaning unto themselves. Even though Wyler's approach is also that of the theater director, the latter has at his disposal only the very limited means of the stage. He can manipulate his means, but no matter what he does, the text and the actor constitute the essence of theatrical production.

Film is not at all, as Marcel Pagnol naively would have it, magnified theater on screen, the stage viewed constantly through opera glasses. The size of the image or unity of time has nothing to do with it. Cinema begins when the frame of the screen and the placement of the camera are used to enhance the action and the actor. In *The Little Foxes*, Wyler has changed almost nothing of the drama, of the text, or even the set: one could say that he limited himself to directing the play in the way that a theater director would have directed it, and furthermore, that he used the frame of the screen to conceal certain parts of the set and used the camera to bring the viewer closer to the action. What actor would not dream of being able to play a scene, immobile on a chair, in front of 5,000 viewers who don't miss the slightest movement of an eye? What theater director would not want the spectator in the worst seat at the back of the house to be able to see clearly the movements of his actors, and to read with ease his intentions at any moment in the action? Wyler didn't choose to do anything other than realize on film the essence of a theatrical *mise en scène* that would not use the lights and the set to ornament the actor and the text. Nevertheless, there is probably not a single shot in *Jezebel, The Little Foxes,* or *The Best Years of Our Lives* that is not pure cinema.[19]

William Wyler, or the Jansenist of Directing

This essay first appeared in *Revue du Cinéma* in 1948, and appeared in Volume 1 ("Ontologie et langage"), pp. 149–173, of Bazin's four-volume *Qu'est-ce que le cinéma?* (Paris: Éditions du Cerf). Volume 1 was published in 1958, Volumes 2–4 in 1959, 1961, and 1962, respectively. "William Wyler, or the Jansenist of Directing" was not included by Hugh Gray in his selected two-volume translation of Bazin's work entitled *What is Cinema?* (Berkeley: University of California Press, 1967 and 1971).

1. Editor's note: Axel Madsen comments on the title of Bazin's essay:

   > Jansenism in contemporary French thought refers less to the theological princi-
   > ples of Cornelius Jansen, the seventeenth-century Dutch churchman con-
   > demned [by the Catholic Church] as heretical (for maintaining that human
   > nature is incapable of good and for emphasizing predestination over free will),
   > than to René Descartes's desire for austerity and ordered, if slightly subversive,
   > behavior. [Jansenism inspired aspects of the work of Descartes's contemporary,
   > the philosopher Pascal, and of the work of the playwright Racine.] By calling
   > Wyler a directorial Jansenist, Bazin meant to qualify him as a filmmaker of
   > stern virtues [austerity and self-denial among them], order, and a certain artistic
   > hauteur. (*William Wyler* [New York: Thomas Y. Crowell, 1973], p. 273, note.)

   The title in French of this essay is "William Wyler ou le Janséniste de la *mise en scène*." *Mise en scène* literally means "putting on stage," and has been taken over into cinema from the theater, where it refers to the act or art of directing, especially of actors as they interpret the script. In film it refers less to such directing than to the following components, all of which the director is ultimately responsible for: visual style (created by the lighting, color, and decor); editing style; movement and place-ment of the camera; and movement and placement of the actors.

2. Editor's note: Henry Bernstein (1876–1953) was a French dramatist who had com-mercial success in London and on Broadway with *La Rafale* (*The Whirlwind*, 1906) and *Le Voleur* (*The Thief*, 1907), but whose attempts at profundity in such later plays as *Le Secret* (1913), *Judith* (1922), and *Le Venin* (1927) were heavy-handed.

3. Editor's note: André Berthomieu (1903–1960) was one of the most prolific of French film directors, a competent technician with no artistic pretense. He entered films in 1924 as an assistant to Julien Duvivier and three years later began a busy career as the director of some seventy commercially viable but none too significant films, the most interesting of which is said to be *La Femme idéale* (*The Ideal Woman*, 1934).

4. Editor's note: Denis Marion collaborated with André Malraux on the original screen-play for *Espoir* (1939, released 1945; also known as *Days of Hope*, *Man's Hope*), also directed by Malraux (his only film). *Espoir* was an anti-fascist film that used surviving combatants of the Spanish Civil War to re-create events in it. Denis Marion is in addition the author of *André Malraux* (1970).

5. Editor's note: MacKinley Kantor (1904–) had been commissioned by the producer, Samuel Goldwyn, to write a story about returning war veterans. He submitted this story in the form of *Glory for Me*, the novel in blank verse that Robert Sherwood (1896–1955), himself a playwright, adapted into the screenplay of *The Best Years of Our Lives*.

6. Editor's note: André Antoine (1858–1943) was a pioneer of naturalism in the French theater. As the director of the Théâtre Libre (1887–1894), the Théâtre Antoine (1897–1906), and the Odéon (1906–1914), he produced works by Ibsen, Strindberg,

Hauptmann, Brieux, and many others. Antoine sought to reproduce the environment onstage in every detail. Real trees figured in several of his productions between 1902 and 1906; in *The Butchers* (1888), he hung real carcasses of beef on the stage. Through his belief in the importance of environment, Antoine helped to establish the principle that each play requires its own setting quite distinct from that of any other work. Antoine was also influential in the development of a realistic acting style. He coached his mostly amateur actors carefully, directing them to behave as if there were no audience, discouraging conventionalized movement and declamatory speech, and always seeking natural behavior from them.

7. Editor's note: Etienne-Jules Marey (1830–1904), a French physician and physiologist, took an early interest in the study of animal motion. He developed the chronophotograph camera (1882) and patented a camera using celluloid film (1890). His research inspired Eadweard Muybridge (1830–1904), the British-born American photographer, to begin his famous experiments in which he photographically recorded the successive phases of animal locomotion; these studies were an essential step towards the development of motion pictures as we know them today. Muybridge invented the Zoopraxiscope, a primitive form of film projector.

Louis Lumière (1864–1948) was a French inventor and pioneer director. In 1894, he invented the Cinématographe, a combination camera-projector into which he incorporated the ideas and inventions of such predecessors as Marey, Muybridge, and Thomas Edison; this development led to the first public, commercial screenings (1895). The typical Lumière films (or rather, brief film clips), such as *The Arrival of a Train at the Station* (1895) and *Workers Leaving the Factory* (1895), recorded real life and current events; they were the predecessors of the newsreel and documentary traditions. The evolution of the art of film is often seen as having proceeded along two distinctive lines that eventually merged into one: the tradition of reality, originating in the films of Lumière, and the tradition of fantasy, originating in the films of Georges Méliès (1861–1938).

8. Bazin's note: I say "tends" because it is nevertheless possible to use this technique in such a way that it compensates for the psychological mutilation implied in its principle. Hitchcock, for instance, excels in suggesting the ambiguity of an event while decomposing it into a series of close-ups.

9. Bazin's note: In *The Rules of the Game* Renoir actually made more use of the simultaneity of actions happening at the same time in the same shot than of depth of field. But the goal and the effect of these two techniques are the same. We could almost call simultaneous *mise en scène* a lateral depth of field. A psychological paradox must be noted here. The depth of focus of the lens ostensibly permits us to view clearly a cross-section of reality. Granted, this clarity seems at first to be the clarity of reality itself: a chair is not blurry just because our eye doesn't focus on it; therefore it is right that this chair should stay in focus on the screen. But an event taking place in reality has three dimensions: it would be physiologically impossible in reality, for example, to see at the same time, with the same clarity, the glass of poison in the foreground on Susan Alexander Kane's night table and the door to her bedroom in the background. We would have to re-direct the focus of our crystalline lens from the night table to the door, as Henri Calef (French director, b. 1910) re-directs the focus of his lens during the municipal council scene in *Jéricho* (1946; this film aimed to capture the psychological and social aspect of the Resistance). One could maintain, then, that the true representation of reality is achieved with analytical cutting. But this would be to disregard the mental factor in perception, which is more important here than the physio-

logical one. Despite the fact that our attention shifts, that our eyes move from one object to another, we perceive the event or the space of which these objects are a part in a continuous manner.

Moreover, the adjustments of the eye to new objects, with the resulting "angle shifts," are so swift that they amount, through an unconscious summation in the viewer's mind, to the reconstitution of a complete mental image; they do so almost in the same way that the scanning of the fluorescent screen by the cathodic beam gives the television viewer the illusion of a continuous and constant image. One may even add that the viewer of a deep-focus shot continuously trains his eye on the screen and thus necessarily and constantly perceives an event in all its sharpness *without being permitted* a physiological way out (by watching from a closer point or from farther away); in this way the continuity of the event (its ontological unity, which precedes its dramatic unity) is made evident to him.

The slight cheating or "special effect" implied in a cinematic image in deep focus does not work against realism, then, but on the contrary reinforces it, confirms it, and is true to its ambiguous essence. A shot in deep focus gives concrete form to the metaphysical affirmation that all reality exists *on the same plane*. The slight physical effort of ocular adjustment often masks, in our perception of the world, the corresponding mental operation that is the only one that matters. On the other hand, in the cinema, as in the portraits of the *quattrocento* where the landscape is as clear as the human faces, the mind cannot escape the purity of the one choice open to it, ocular reflexes are destroyed, and attention becomes a function of the responsibility of the conscience.

10. Editor's note: Roger Martin du Gard (1881–1958) was a French novelist who won the Nobel Prize in 1937. His reputation was made by, and rests on, *Les Thibault* (1922–1940), one of the outstanding *romans-cycles* of twentieth-century French fiction (in seven parts). It exemplifies his ideal of composition: it is a strictly objective or impersonal and unsparingly realistic narrative.

11. Bazin's note: Compare the kaleidoscopic *Prisunic* of *Antoine and Antoinette* to the drug-store of *The Best Years of Our Lives*, where one can always see simultaneously all the items for sale (and nearly the price tags, too) and all the customers, as well as the manager perched in his glass booth far in the background.

12. Editor's note: Roger Leenhardt (1903–1985) was an influential film critic for a number of French publications who began making documentary shorts in the mid-1930s. These covered a wide range of cultural subjects and gained him a reputation for excellence. His series of biographical studies of prominent personalities in literature and the arts has also been of special interest. In between dozens of shorts, he directed two feature films of some quality: *Les Dernières Vacances* (1948) and *Le Rendezvous de Minuit* (1962). See chapter 16, this volume.

13. Editor's note: Georges Neveux (1900–1983) was the writer of the original screenplay for *Mademoiselle Docteur (Fräulein Doktor)*, directed by G.W. Pabst in 1936. Marcel Carné's *Juliette ou la Clef des Songes* (1951) is based on Neveux's work of the same name.

14. Editor's note: *The March of Time* was a monthly film magazine of current affairs, produced by Louis de Rochemont from 1935 to 1951. It combined archive material and stock shots with fresh documentary footage and staged scenes that utilized professional actors. *Citizen Kane* parodies *The March of Time* under the title *News on the March*, the newsreel of Kane's life that is screened by reporters early in Welles's film.

15. Editor's note: The French Civil Code was promulgated by Napoleon Bonaparte in

1804. In straightforward language, it set out the legal rights and responsibilities of the citizen and the state in post-revolutionary France.

16. Editor's note: A common European term for the Academy aperture two-shot (a two-shot is one composed with two characters; in the scene that Bazin refers to, the "shot" of Fredric March and Harold Russell occupies only the foreground of the deep-focus image), which is more intimate and involving than the widescreen two-shot.

17. Bazin's note: To the real looks the actors direct at one another, one must add the virtual "look" of the camera with which our own identifies. Wyler excels in making us sensitive to his camera's gaze. Jean Mitry has noticed in *Jezebel* the low-angle shot that clearly points the lens directly at Bette Davis's eyes looking down at the white cane that Henry Fonda holds in his hand with the intention of using it. We thus follow the dramatic line between the character and the object much better than we would have if, by the rules of conventional cutting, the camera had shown us the cane from the point of view of Bette Davis herself.

   A variation on the same principle: in *The Little Foxes*, in order to make us understand the thoughts of the character who notices the small steel box in which the stolen bonds were locked and whose absence from the box is going to indicate theft, Wyler placed it in the foreground with the camera being this time at eye level and at the same distance from the box as the eyes of the character. Our eyes no longer meet the character's eyes directly through the beheld object, as in the above-mentioned scene from *Jezebel*, but as if through a mirror. The angle of incidence of our own view of the object is, as it were, equal to the angle of reflection of the character's view, which angle takes us to this person's eyes. In any case, Wyler commands our mental vision according to the rigorous laws of an invisible dramatic optics.

18. Editor's note: Oskar Fischinger (1900–1967) was a German avant-garde painter who had begun toying with the idea of creating abstract visual interpretations of poetry and music at the age of 19 and became involved in film animation in the course of diagramming the emotional movements in a Shakespeare play. He made his first animated shorts in 1920 with the help of a wax-cutting machine of his own design. In 1926 he presented the first of a series of "absolute film" shorts, which he named *Study 1*, *Study 2*, etc. In 1933 he began exploring color with a special process he had helped develop and in 1935 won a prize at the Venice Festival for his *Komposition in Blau* (*Composition in Blue*). He won the Grand Prix at the Brussels Exhibition of 1949 for his *Motion Painting No. 1*, in which he used intricate designs and geometric forms to the accompaniment of Bach's *Brandenburg Concerto* no. 3.

19. Bazin's note: After re-reading this ten-year-old article, I feel the need to readjust my judgment for the reader of 1958, and I also feel the need to do so because of my current opinions. If I had not thought that the analyses contained in this essay retained their interest for me independent of my enthusiasm for William Wyler in those days, I would certainly not have devoted so much space here to this director whom time has treated so rudely. I wrote this article at a time when Roger Leenhardt was shouting, "Down with Ford! Long live Wyler!" History did not echo that war cry, and wherever one places John Ford today, one must place Wyler below him. Both directors have their intrinsic artistic values, however, and it is from this point of view that one may continue to prefer the "writing in cinema" of some of Wyler's films to the spectacular cinema of John Ford.

CHAPTER 2

The Myth of Stalin in the Soviet Cinema

One of the original aspects of Soviet cinema is its daring in depicting contemporary historical personages, even living figures. This phenomenon is perfectly in line with the new Communist art, which extols a very recent history whose protagonists are still alive. Perhaps historical materialism came logically to treat men as facts, to give them in the representation of events the place they were generally denied in the West until an historical, critical distance could lift the psychological taboo. Two thousand years weren't even enough for Cecil B. DeMille to be so bold as to show more than Christ's feet in *Ben Hur.*[1] There is no way such artistic modesty could stand up against a Marxist critique; at any rate, it could not do so in the country where they erase from the records the names of comrades who have "betrayed" the cause, but where the body of Lenin is preserved. It seems to me, though, that the depiction of living historical personages on screen has taken on a central importance only with Stalin. If I'm not mistaken, the films about Lenin did not come out until after his death,[2] whereas Stalin appeared on screen as early as the war in historical films that did not consist of documentary footage. The actor Mikhail Gelovani, who incarnates Stalin, so to speak, in *The Vow* (1946; dir. Mikhail Chiaureli), is a specialist whom the Russians had already seen several times in this role starting in 1938, in particular in *Siberians* (1940; dir. Lev Kuleshov), *Valeri Chkalov* (1941; dir. Mikhail Kalatozov), and *The Defense of Tsaritsin* (1942; dir. Sergei Vasiliev and Georgi Vasiliev [they are unrelated]). It is no longer Gelovani, however, who plays Stalin's double in *The Battle of Stalingrad* (Part I, 1949, and Part II, 1950; dir. Vladimir Petrov), and still another actor plays him in *The Third Blow* (1948; dir. Igor

Savchenko).[3] Naturally, Stalin did not play himself in these historical re-creations. Incidentally, the original version of *The Vow*, which was cut for French distribution, showed, it seems, Georges Bonnet dancing the Lambeth Walk,[4] and the scenes in which Hitler appeared were much too long (the role of Hitler was played by a Czech railway worker whose resemblance to the Führer was striking). In *The Battle of Stalingrad* not only Hitler appeared, but also Churchill and Roosevelt. It is worth noting, moreover, that these latter two "creations" were far less convincing than Stalin's, and above all for these reasons: the actor portraying Roosevelt bore a distant (if finally acceptable) resemblance to the American president, while Churchill was an utter and intentional caricature.

To be sure, this device of depicting contemporary historical personages, even living ones, isn't totally original: one might go back in time to Méliès's *Dreyfus Affair* (1899) or to the comic fantasy by the same Méliès about a tunnel under the English Channel (in which film President Fallières and King George V are seen inaugurating construction on this tunnel)[5]; but back then, the newsreels had not yet created the demand for documentary realism. In the newsreels of the day, naval battles were reconstructed in washbasins, for example, even though the result was presented as if it had been recorded on the spot. From the point of view of texture, the look of the early newsreels was similar to that of what we know today as the front page in color, from its appearance in *Le Petit Journal*[6] to its ubiquitousness in modern photojournalism. Twenty years before Eisenstein, then, Georges Méliès could be said to have reconstructed the mutiny aboard the *Potemkin* in the manner of such early newsreels.[7] We have since learned how to distinguish the real thing from a reconstruction, so that we now prefer authentic footage that is incomplete and clumsy to a perfect imitation; or at least, we have learned how to treat the two as completely different cinematic genres. The Soviet cinema, with Dziga Vertov's famous theory of the "Kino-Eye,"[8] was one of the principal architects of this distinction. And the existence of this distinction is the reason why the modern viewer feels some uneasiness when he sees an actor playing the role of a famous historical figure, despite the fact that the figure has long been dead, as has, say, Napoleon or Saint Vincent de Paul. This uneasiness is perhaps compensated for by the near stupendousness of the spectacle and by admiration for the actor's performance. The compensation is far more in doubt, however, if the actor is portraying a contemporary historical figure such as Queen Victoria or

Clemenceau, and even more so if he is playing a living person. Imagine that the R.P.F.[9] has undertaken, for example, a propaganda film on the life of General de Gaulle in which all the historical events will be reconstructed and the role of the General will be played, let us say, by Louis Jouvet with a fake nose. Forget about it.

It is true that the lives of famous contemporaries have frequently inspired screenwriters, but what is remarkable is, first, that these contemporary figures are never politicians, and, second, that they had already become legends somehow while they were alive. Take, for instance, the lives of famous musicians or singers, which have been very much in vogue these last few years with Hollywood producers, or take, for a better example, the two films in which Marcel Cerdan played himself just before his death.[10] But, people will say, that was Cerdan in person; indeed it was, although there isn't that much difference between Cerdan playing Cerdan and an actor playing him. There is little difference between the two, in fact, and what difference there is serves only to illuminate the existence of this case as a phenomenon, as an extreme instance: what we have here, clearly, is the identification of Cerdan the man with his myth (from this point of view, the screenplay of *The Man with Clay Hands* is one of guileless transparency[11]). The cinema is here creating and consecrating a legend: it definitively transports the hero to the top of Mount Olympus. This operation can be successful only with figures who have already been deified in the minds of the public, that is, with stars, be they from the world of sports, theater, or film. To this group one should doubtless add science and philanthropy, be it secular or saintly—although, in the area of science and philanthropy, one must generally wait until after the death of the "beneficiaries" (Pasteur, Edison, and Dunant[12] come to mind) before depicting them on film. The reader will not fail to object, and with reason, to my putting Pasteur (for one example) and Cerdan on the same level. Let me distinguish, then, between the myth of a star and the illustrious and edifying legend that builds up around the memory of a scientist. The only trouble with such great men as Pasteur is that their lives are not considered edifying until they are dead! It is obvious that, in the West, the representation on film of living contemporary figures concerns itself solely with what we might call a para- or post-historical zone—where the hero belongs to a mythology of sports, theater, or film, or where the historical era of which he was a part is considered closed. (If a scientist, for example, were to be portrayed on film before his death, this would probably be because the scientific age to which he had brilliantly contributed was thought to be over, or in any event eclipsed.)

At first sight, the daring of Soviet cinema might be taken as a commendable application of the theory of historical materialism. Doesn't the taboo that I have mentioned in connection with Western cinema derive in the first place from a particular idealism, or at the very least from an outdated "personalism," and then from a chronic uncertainty in the face of History? In other words, paradoxically, we in the West attach too much importance to the individual at the same time as we feel constrained to confer on him a place in History only when his life is over. It is not very difficult for a Frenchman today to be proud of Napoleon. But for a Communist, a great man is one who takes part here and now in the making of History, the direction of which is infallibly determined by its dialectics and by the Party. This greatness of the hero is objective, i.e., it is connected to something outside itself: to the unfolding of History, of which the hero is at this very moment the driving force and the conscience. From the perspective of dialectical materialism, the hero must retain a human dimension, he must be categorizable only in a psycho-historical sense, and he must not possess the kind of transcendence that characterizes capitalistic mystification, the best example of which is to be found precisely in the mythology of the star.

From this point of view, the masterpiece of Soviet films with historic heroes is surely *Chapayev* (1934; dir. Sergei Vasiliev and Georgi Vasiliev).[13] If you have the opportunity to see it again at some film society, you will notice with what intelligence the failings of Chapayev, even in his manifestly most heroic acts, are suggested without diminishing him at all psychologically. It's the political commissar serving as Chapayev's adjunct who is the representative of historico-political objectivity in the film. Is this film, then, a glorification of Chapayev? Without question, but at the same time it is against him as it emphasizes the priority of a long-term political strategy over the deeds of an heroic and temporarily useful "gang leader." Although it deals with more distant history, *Peter the Great* (Part I, 1937, and Part II, 1939; dir. Vladimir Petrov) is as instructive and humane a work as *Chapayev*, rich with the same dialectic between Man and History. Peter's greatness derives first from the accuracy of his historical vision; for the rest, Peter is permitted to have his faults: he is portrayed as a drunkard and a whoremonger. His most faithful companion is essentially a rogue, but he shares in Peter's luster because, remaining faithful to him, he remains faithful to the truth of History. Conversely, in *Chapayev*, the White Guards and their leader are no less courageous than the small force headed by the Red commander, and, indeed, they have no faults—except one: they misinterpret the course of history.

Let me go a step farther. The general staff in *The Great Turning Point* (1946; dir. Friedrich Ermler) still evokes for me the true sense of man's responsibility in the face of History. The dialogue among these generals attempts less to convince me of their genius than of an historical conscience inexorably feeling its way through the character, the friendship, and the flaw of men in the service of History.

Let me now compare these examples with the example of Stalin in three recent Soviet films: *The Third Blow*, *The Battle of Stalingrad* (Part I), and *The Vow*. I'll put aside the quality of the directing, extremely uneven in all three films though better in the first two, which I am now going to examine. There is an evident unity of construction in these two war films: the opposition between the battlefield and the Kremlin, between the apocalyptic turmoil of military struggle and the studious silence of Stalin's office. In *The Battle of Stalingrad*, this office's thoughtful, almost retiring, serenity is in addition carefully contrasted with the hysterical atmosphere of Hitler's headquarters. Already in *The Great Turning Point* we had been struck by the radical division of labor between the soldier and his commander. We were far from the naive strategy of potato-throwing advocated and participated in, by Chapayev,[14] who had barely emerged from the era of medieval knights and brigands. Certainly one does not ask of these generals that they put their lives on the line, but that their strategy be correct. If one can shake free of jingoistic sentiment and romantic thinking, one will readily admit that formulating strategy is indeed the role of the general staff in modern warfare, and that we have seen lots of generals making mistakes without getting killed in the process. Let's nevertheless note that, even though this radical division of labor and of risk is in fact universal, one would be wrong to imagine our Western civilian and military leaders deriving any glory from it. Clemenceau regularly felt obliged to make a tour of the trenches in order to keep up his popularity. This immunity, I was going to say impunity, of the general staff in the West is not exactly its best claim to fame. That is why the chief of staff is usually shown in his car inspecting the front rather than behind his desk doing paper work. At the basis of this glorification of a deliberative and invulnerable general staff necessarily lies the individual soldier's exceptional confidence in his leaders. This confidence seems to be unshakable and considers the risks taken by the general in his underground shelter and those run by the soldier facing a flame thrower, to be exactly equivalent. But this confidence is, after all, logical in a truly socialist war. Thus, in *The Great Turning Point*, the battle of Stalingrad is barely shown despite the fact that it is the subject of the film. The sole interest of the screenwriter is the individual heroism of an ordinary soldier who, under heavy German fire, repairs a telephone line that is indispensable for the functioning of headquarters, of his army's nerve center: the soldier performs a neurological operation, as it were.

But in *The Battle of Stalingrad* and *The Third Blow*, this dichotomy between brains and brawn is so rigid that it obviously goes beyond the historico-materialist realism that I described earlier. For, in the end, even if we grant Marshal Stalin a hyper-Napoleonic military genius and most of the credit for the successful battle plan, it would be extraordinarily childish to think that events occurred inside the Kremlin as they are portrayed here: Stalin meditates alone for a long time in front of a map and, after taking a few puffs from his pipe, he alone decides what measures are to be taken. When I say alone, I'm well aware that Vassilievsky is still there, but he doesn't say a word and acts solely as a confidant,[15] doubtless to save Stalin from appearing ridiculous by talking to himself. This centralized and, one could even say, cerebral conception of war is confirmed by the depiction of the battle itself, which, unlike the same battle in *The Great Turning Point*, constitutes the major part of the film. Indeed, although the reconstruction of the battle achieves here a magnitude and an accuracy probably unequaled since Griffith's *Birth of a Nation* (1915), one might maintain that this reconstruction is analogous to the view Fabrice had of the battle of Waterloo.[16] Not in the physical sense, to be sure, for the film does not spare us the spectacle of war, but in the conceptual sense, because of our inability, owing to the position of the camera and the style of the editing, to place some order on the chaos of war. Similar in this way to live footage of a news event, the resulting picture of war is, so to speak, amorphous: it has no organizing elements, no visible evolution; it is a kind of human, mechanical cataclysm, which looks as chaotic as an anthill that has been stepped on. The camera and the cutting are careful not to make patterned choices from amidst this chaos, which we know, however, has its own secret organization; no details stand out, there is no artillery barrage with its own beginning, middle, and end, and there is no thread of important action or of individual heroism to follow.

The exceptions to this vision of war are rare, and they rather confirm the rule. In *The Battle of Stalingrad*, the military spectacle is framed by two circumscribed actions: at the beginning, the levying of a militia, and at the end, the defense of the post office building. But in between these two significant events, the former an example of collective enthusiasm, the latter an example of individual courage, lies the enormous mass of the battle. Just imagine that you are witnessing operations from an unassailable helicopter that gives you a view of the battlefield which is as large as possible, but which nevertheless does not reveal to you the outcome of the battle or even its unfolding and direction. Making sense of the war is thus exclusively reserved for the inserted exposition, for the animated maps, and above all for Stalin's voice-over commentary.

The effect of such a presentation of events is to suggest the following: at the base of a cone, there is the apocalyptic incoherence of the battle; at the apex, there is the singular, omniscient mind that directs this apparent chaos and resolves it by making an infallible decision. In between, there is nothing. There is no intermediate section in the cone of history, no meaningful reflection of the psychological and intellectual processes by which the fate of the men and the outcome of the battle are decided. It seems that there is a direct connection between the movement of a commander-in-chief's pencil and the sacrifice of a soldier, or at the very least that the intermediate mechanism is without real purpose, is a simple organ of transmission whose recommendations can consequently be ignored.

One might argue that there is some truth in this portrayal of events if what one wants is, not the facts, but a simplified, essential picture. Yet, one could question whether this way of thinking is truly Marxist, especially since it is incompatible with the concrete nature and the rigorous documentary presentation of *both* ends of the historical cone. Now we have been told that these films claim to be more than historical: they intend to be scientific, and we can easily see that every effort has been made to reconstruct the battle as exactly as possible. How could we doubt the objective precision of what we are being shown at the lower end of the chain of events? And when so much energy has been devoted to depicting the resistance at Stalingrad in all its human magnitude, how could we doubt the strict truth of the *Kremlin's* resistance?

One clearly perceives here that Stalin's traits of omniscience and infallibility can no longer be called psychological, but rather must be termed ontological. A quick glance at a map enables him, in detachment, to win the greatest battle in History, and a fast look at the engine of a tractor would enable him, equally in detachment, to see that its spark plugs were filled with soot.

I have read in *La Nouvelle Critique*[17] under the byline of Francis Cohen that Stalin was literally the greatest scholar of all time, since he was the receptacle of all the knowledge in the Communist world. I'll properly refrain from denying Stalin the personal and historical excellence that these films attribute to him. But what I am able to see after a moment's reflection is that I am being asked to accept as real an image of Stalin that rigorously conforms to what the myth of Stalin might be, or had better be!

No construct of the mind could better satisfy the demands of propaganda than this one. Either Stalin is a genuine superman, or we are being presented with a myth. It is not my purpose here to argue whether or not the idea of a superman is a Marxist one, but I will venture to say that myths function aesthetically in the same way for the Western bloc as for the Eastern, and that, from this point of view, the only difference between Stalin and Tarzan is that the films devoted to the latter do not claim to be rigorous documentaries.

All the great Soviet films used to be filled with an exemplary realistic humanism that was diametrically opposed to the starry-eyed mystifications of Western cinema. Recent Soviet cinema claims to be more realistic than ever, but this realism serves as an excuse for the introduction of a personal mythology foreign to all the great pre-war films, a mythology whose presence necessarily disrupts the aesthetic economy of these recent works. If Stalin, although still alive, can be the main character in a film, it's because he no longer has a human dimension and because he is endowed with the transcendence that characterizes living gods and dead heroes; in other words, his aesthetic physiology is not fundamentally different from that of the Western star. Both escape psychological definition. Thus presented, Stalin is not, cannot be, a particularly intelligent man, an inspired leader; on the contrary, he is a familiar god, a personified transcendence. That is why his representation on film, in spite of his existence in reality, is possible today. This representation is not the result of some director's exceptional effort at Marxist objectivity, or of an artistic application of historical materialism; it is made possible, again, by the fact that we are no longer dealing with a real man but with a social essence, a vehicle for transcendence—a myth.

If the reader doesn't accept this metaphysical vocabulary, I can substitute another one: the phenomenon might be explained as a journey to the end of History. To make Stalin the principal, determining force (even if he acts in conjunction with other people) in the re-creation of an actual historical event when he is still head of state implicitly establishes that he is henceforth immune to all human weakness, that the meaning of his life has been definitively ascertained, that he couldn't subsequently make a mistake or betray his country. The effect wouldn't be the same, let us keep in mind, if we were dealing with newsreels instead of historical re-creations. We possess footage of the Yalta Conference or of one or another appearance of Stalin on Red Square. Such documents can clearly be used to glorify a living politician, but, precisely because they record reality, they remain fundamentally ambiguous. It's the use that's made of them that gives them their glorifying value or, conversely, their vilifying one. They exist only as political rhetoric and only in connection with that rhetoric. For example, Leni Riefenstahl's *Triumph of the Will*, the official record of the Nazi party congress held at Nuremberg in 1934, appears to the democratic viewer to be an argument against Hitler, and these images could indeed be used in an anti-Nazi film. But Riefenstahl uses them to an entirely different end, of course.

It is astonishing enough that Stalin, played by an actor, appears periodically in historical re-creations the way the great Western or Soviet politicians do in the newsreels and documentaries that I am talking about. The fact that he is the dramatic force in these films implies even more: his life must literally be identified with History, it must become one with the imperious nature of History. Until now, only death could identify the hero or the martyr with his historical moment in this manner. And it was still possible to tarnish his memory, to discover in retrospect some breach of faith. But death remained a necessary, though not sufficient, condition. For Malraux, it is death that makes one's life one's destiny; for a Communist, only death can completely absorb the subjectivity of historical events (at least this was so until the example of Stalin presented itself). At the age of eighty, the "victor of Verdun" can become the "traitor of Montoire," and at the age of eighty-five, he can further become the "martyr of the Isle of Yeu,"[18] precisely because a man, whatever his genius or his special qualities may be, can only be judged in the light of History, when "eternity finally changes him into what he in fact was."

In this light, the astonishingly subjective nature of political trials in socialist states is worth explaining. From a strictly Marxist point of view, it would suffice to declare that Bukharin, Rajk, or Kostov embodies tendencies that the Party has decided to combat because they are contrary to History. The physical elimination of these men then wouldn't be any more necessary than that of our own ministers who are forced to resign. But as long as a man has taken part in History, as long as he has been involved in such and such an event, a part of his biography is irrevocably "historicized." An intolerable contradiction exists as a result between this decidedly objective part, which is frozen in the past, and the physical existence of a Bukharin, a Zinoviev, or a Rajk.[19] One cannot reduce man solely to History without in turn compromising this History through the subjectivity present in the individual. The living Communist leader is on the one hand a godlike figure who is sealed in History by his past acts, and on the hand a mortal figure whose present acts may place him in opposition to History.

The notion of "objective" treason, which at first seems to emerge so clearly from Marxism, did not in fact survive the test of political practice. From the perspective of Stalinist Soviet Communism, no one can "become" a traitor, because this would mean that he hasn't been one all along, that his betrayal had a beginning separate from the beginning of his life. It would also mean that the man who has become detrimental to the Party and to History had once been useful to both, had been good before he became evil. This is why it was not enough for the Party to decree that Rajk drop back down to the rank of simple activist and start again, or even for the Party to condemn him to death as if he were an enemy soldier. It had necessarily to proceed with a retroactive purge of History by showing that the accused had since his birth been a conscious and systematic traitor, all of whose actions up to now were consequently elements in a diabolically camouflaged plan of sabotage. To be sure, this procedure is too dangerous and too fraught with improbabilities to be used in all instances. That is why it can be replaced by a public *mea culpa* in the case of minor figures—artists, philosophers, and scientists, for example—whose historical influence is indirect. Such a somber and magnified *mea culpa* appears to be psychologically ineffective and intellectually superfluous only insofar as we fail to discern its exorcistic value. Just as confession is indispensable to divine absolution, so too is solemn recantation indispensable to the recovery of historical virginity. Here again, we are confronted with the scandal of subjectivity, with the implicit acknowledgment of subjectivity as the driving force of History—a force that is nonetheless said to be purely objective.

Thus, our Western, bourgeois conscience, which, paradoxically, is at once hypocritical and idealistic, accepts Pétain as both the "victor of Verdun" and the "traitor of Montoire," whereas the Soviet conscience must see to it that the old comrades are not only executed, but removed from the historical picture as well. So History, at least in its public manifestations, posits an exaggerated idealism in the latter case; it asserts a radical equivalence between subjectivity and social usefulness, an absolute Manichaeism where the anti-historical forces derive directly from the Devil and where treason results directly from diabolic possession.

One well understands that, from this perspective, the portrayal of Stalin on film cannot be underestimated. Such portrayal implies that identification has now positively been achieved between Stalin and History, and that the contradictions of subjectivity no longer apply to him. This phenomenon cannot be explained by the fact that Stalin has given sufficient proof of his devotion to the Party, and of his genius in addition; nor can it be explained by the fact that the possibility of treason on his part is so unlikely that there is little risk in treating him like a dead hero, even though he is still alive. In "The Little Statues of Boeotia,"[20] Jacques Prévert tells us of the misadventures of an admiral who becomes insane on the very day his statue is to be dedicated. Where a human life is concerned, one can never be sure of anything! The feeling of absolute security that emanates from a Soviet film depicting Stalin implies much more, however, than that one can be sure of constancy where Stalin's life is concerned. It also implies not simply the virtual death of Stalin, whose statue was erected while he was still living, but in addition the important reciprocal truth: the end of History or, at the very least, of its dialectical movement at the center of the socialist world.

The preservation of Lenin's body in his tomb and the obituary written by Stalin, entitled "Living Lenin," marked the beginning of this end. The actual mummification of Lenin thus becomes no less symbolic than the filmic mummification of Stalin. The latter signifies that the relationship between Stalin and Soviet politics is no longer conditional, no longer dependent; in short, it is no longer what one ordinarily calls "human." The idea that Man takes part in History only to have History then stand apart and judge him is henceforth out-of-date: Stalin is History incarnated, he is History become one with Man.

Thus it would be impossible to define him through his character, his psychology, or his personality (which categories still apply to the

Vasilievs' Chapayev and Petrov's Czar Peter), as we would any common mortal; these existential categories are no longer valid here. Instead, theological ones would be much more to the point. Throughout these films, Stalin is presented as a genuine symbol of History. As such, he is omniscient, infallible, and indomitable, and his destiny is irreversible. On the human level, his psychology is reduced to those qualities that best befit a symbol: level-headedness (as opposed to the hysteria of Hitler); reflectiveness or, rather, conscience; decisiveness; and goodness (this last quality, which is emphasized a great deal in *The Vow*, is obviously indispensable to making him the liaison between the people and History, a History that, from the Marxist point of view, is the expression of his will). It's as if any other trait would disturb this almost sacred image of Stalin's and precipitate his fall into human contingency.

At the beginning of *The Vow*, there is a highly significant scene that one might call "The Consecration of History." Lenin has just died and a meditative Stalin goes alone on a pilgrimage through the snow to the scene of their final conversations. There, near a bench where Lenin's shadow appears to be imprinted in the snow, the voice of the dead man speaks to the conscience of Stalin. But lest the allusion to the mystical coronation of Moses and to the mystical transmission of Mosaic law be missed, the director has Stalin look up *to heaven*. A beam of sunlight pierces through the branches of the fir trees and strikes the forehead of the new Moses. Everything is there, as one can see, even the flames of fire. The "flames" come from above in this case, in the form of the sun's rays, instead of from the burning bush. It is, of course, important that the sole beneficiary of this Marxist Pentecost (to switch the allusion from the Old Testament to the New) be Stalin and Stalin only, for there were twelve Apostles sent out by Christ to teach the Gospel. Next we see him, bending a little under the weight of all this grace, on the way back to his comrades, to the men from whom he has henceforth been set apart, not simply through his knowledge or his genius, but through the presence in him of the God of History.

There is another scene in *The Vow*, in a more down-to-earth vein, that is worth describing: the one that features the tractor. One morning on an almost deserted Red Square, the first agricultural tractor built in the U.S.S.R. arrives. As a Communist critic has said with contagious emotion, "This child is not very strong yet, but it is a child produced in our own country." All of a sudden, the sputtering, jerking machine breaks down. The operator desperately looks it over from top to bottom, checking first here, then there. A few passersby give him some advice and sympathetically assist him (these are precisely the dozen good people whom we encounter in the film wherever they are needed and whose biographies symbolize that of the Soviet people—Russia is big, but it's a small world!). But lo and behold, here comes Comrade Stalin, who happened to be in the neighborhood with some colleagues from the Supreme Soviet. He inquires about the trouble with avuncular kindliness and is told that the damned machine doesn't work. Bukharin remarks with a diabolical sneer that the farmers had better buy their tractors in America, to which the *vox populi* responds, in the person of the operator, that this is defeatism and that Russia will one day manage to manufacture her own fine tractors, even if there are some breakdowns along the way. Stalin is then seen approaching the tractor, feeling around inside the engine, and diagnosing to the admiring operator, "It's the spark plugs" (I'm depending on the subtitles). He proceeds to climb aboard and drive the tractor around Red Square three times. Zoom of Stalin behind the steering wheel: he is thinking, he sees the future; superimposition of thousands of tractors in a factory parking lot, of tractors everywhere, of tractors in the fields, pulling sophisticated plows . . . Let me stop here.

Unfortunately for our Communist critic, there are some points of reference for the admiring lyricism he directs at tractors. For example, we have the tractors of *The General Line* (1929; dir. Sergei Eisenstein), with the famous breakdown followed by the blundering rage of the driver, who is clad in brand-new leather and who little by little gets rid of his helmet, his glasses, his gloves, . . . to become again the peasant he was, as his laughing wife tears up her dress to make rags for his use in the repair process. In those days, Stalin wasn't yet playing the part of psychic mechanic; he was overseeing triumphant military processions, and he was envisioning the colossal epic of strange, steel insects scraping the earth, marking it with furrows as airplanes do the sky with the vapor from their exhausts. Apparently, Stalin was still envisioning this epic in 1946, when *The Vow* was filmed, albeit this time with Soviet-made tractors in the starring role![21]

As long as the glorification of Stalin was confined to the domain of language, or even of iconography, it could be described as a relative phenomenon, reducible to rhetoric or to propaganda and therefore reversible. But in the Soviet cinema, the supremacy of Stalin's genius is no longer advanced as propaganda or even as metaphor (i.e., Stalin is History): it is truly ontological. Not only because the reach and the persuasiveness of cinema are incomparably greater than those of any other form of propaganda, but also and above all because the nature of the film image is different: imposing itself on our minds as rigorously as it superimposes itself, in a manner of speaking, on reality, cinema is in essence irrefutable, like Nature and History. A portrait of Pétain, of de Gaulle, or of Stalin can be removed just as quickly as it was hung—basically, it doesn't mean a thing, even if it takes up one thousand square feet. By contrast, an historical re-creation on film of events concerning Stalin, above all an historical re-creation centering on Stalin himself, is enough to define irrevocably this man's place and importance in the world and to establish conclusively his essence.

POSTSCRIPT

Aside from a few stylistic corrections and some lightening of tone, I haven't seen the need to change anything in this article published in 1950 in the July-August issue of *Esprit* (17, no. 170, pp. 210–35).[22] No one will be surprised to hear that at the time it received the most violent reactions in *L'Humanité* and *Les Lettres Françaises*.[23] Since then, several events have occurred about which the least I could say is that they confirmed the thesis put forward in my article. The reader will judge for himself whether this confirmation has taken place or whether my thesis remains just that—a thesis.

Without going so far as to suggest that Mr. Khrushchev deliberately saved the issue of *Esprit* containing my article, I nevertheless can't resist the temptation of recalling some passages from his famous report.[24] Concerning Stalin's omniscience, which permitted him as well to determine the outcome of a battle with a single decision as to spot the worn spark plug that has caused a tractor to break down, Khrushchev notes, "Stalin believed that anything he said was true. After all, he was a genius, and a genius has only to take a quick look at a situation before penetrating immediately to its essence." Didn't Stalin himself write in his own *Abridged Biography*, "Stalin's military skill manifested itself both in defense and on the attack. The genius of Comrade Stalin enabled him to divine the enemy's plans and make them misfire"?[25]

But what is more remarkable than anything else is that Stalin had arrived at the point where he received information on Soviet life from the cinema of Stalinist mythology. Khrushchev is again the one who confirms this for us. Since Stalin hadn't set foot in a village since 1938, "it was through the films that he knew the countryside and the agricultural situation, and these films had very much embellished reality. Numerous films had painted life in the *kolkhozes* in such beautiful colors that one could picture tables collapsing under the weight of turkeys and geese. Evidently, Stalin believed that things were actually so."

Matters had come full circle. The mystifications of the cinema were now sealing Stalin off from reality—the very man who was responsible for these mystifications. It would scarcely be an exaggeration to say that Stalin came to convince himself of his own genius by means of viewing Stalinist films. Even Jarry couldn't have invented such a pump to reinflate the spirit of his Father Ubu.

NOTES TO CHAPTER 2

The Myth of Stalin in the Soviet Cinema

(All notes have been provided by the Editor.)

This essay was first published in French in *Esprit*, 17, no. 170 (July-Aug, 1950), pp. 210-235. Bazin wrote the postscript when he included "The Myth of Stalin in the Soviet Cinema" in vol. I ("Ontologie et Langage"), pp. 75-88, of his four-volume *Qu'est-ce que le cinéma?* (Paris: Éditions du Cerf, 1958-62). "The Myth of Stalin in the Soviet Cinema" was not included by Hugh Gray in his selected two-volume translation of Bazin's work entitled *What is Cinema?* (Berkeley: Univ. of California Press, 1967 and 1971).

1. *Ben Hur* (1925) was directed by Fred Niblo, not DeMille. Bazin may have the right film and the wrong director, or he may have the right director and the wrong film: he may be thinking of *The Ten Commandments* (1923), which DeMille did direct. I don't recall either film well enough to know which one shows no more than Christ's feet.

2. And they marked his death as well as his life. For example, *Leninist Film-Truth* (1925; dir. Dziga Vertov) and *October without Ilyich* (1925; dir. Dziga Vertov).

3. Alexei Diky portrayed Stalin in *The Battle of Stalingrad*. Bazin is apparently in error when he says that still another actor plays Stalin in *The Third Blow*. Yuri Vorontsov and Igor Rachuk list Alexei Diky in the role of Stalin in this film (*The Phenomenon of Soviet Cinema* [Moscow: Progress Publishers, 1980], p. 420). Other actors besides Diky and Gelovani *did* play Stalin, however: I. Goldstab portrayed him, most notably in *Lenin in October* (1937; dir. Mikhail Romm), before Mikhail Gelovani made a career out of the role; and A. Kobaladze played Stalin in *In the October Days* (1958; dir. Sergei Vasiliev). See Jay Leyda, *Kino: A History of the Russian and Soviet Film*, 3rd ed. (Princeton, New Jersey: Princeton University Press, 1983), pp. 352, 442, 459, et passim.

4. The Lambeth Walk was a jaunty ballroom dance combining a strutting march with figures resembling those of a square dance. From "Lambeth Walk" (1937), a song by Douglas Furber (d. 1961), British author, and Noel Gay (d. 1954), British musician; the song itself takes its name from Lambeth Walk, a street in London. See note 5, p. 192.

5. *Le Tunnel sous la Manche* (*Tunneling the English Channel*, 1907): a fantasy in thirty scenes in which King Edward VII—not King George V, as Bazin indicates—and

President Fallières of France dream jointly of an underwater tunnel between Dover and Calais.

6. Bazin is referring to *le Petit Journal*, which was published in Paris from 1863 to 1944. For a long time, of course, the color pictures on the front page of this newspaper were drawn or etched, not photographed. *Le Petit Journal* was especially known for its serialization of popular novels.

7. Bazin plays on the fact that Méliès was making (among other films) films depicting contemporary historical personages and events, even living figures and current events, in 1905, when the actual mutiny aboard the battleship *Potemkin* occurred at Odessa in the course of the revolution. Sergei Eisenstein made his *Battleship Potemkin* in 1925 as part of the twentieth-anniversary celebrations of the 1905 revolution.

8. Dziga Verov (1896–1954) is best known as the director of *The Man with a Movie Camera* (1929). In a 1922 magazine article he introduced his theory of *Kino-Glaz*, or *Kino-Oki* (Kino-Eye or Cine-Eye). "Life caught unawares" was Vertov's credo. What he meant by this was not that he would use the techniques of "candid camera"—in fact, his subjects were usually aware that they were being filmed—but that he would not stage or direct what the eye of his camera saw. The life in front of the camera was permitted to run its natural course; the filmmaker exerted creative control only through what and how he chose to shoot, and by the way in which he placed one shot in relation to another during the editing. From 1922 to 1925, Vertov produced *Kino-Pravda* (literally, film truth; cf., *cinéma vérité*), an irregularly released monthly "screen magazine" named after the Soviet daily newspaper *Pravda*. Each of the twenty-three editions was about one reel in length and consisted of two or three new episodes.

9. R.P.F. was the *Rassemblement du Peuple Français* (Assembly of the French People), the Gaullist political party of France, and a party of the right. It is known today as *Reassemblement Pour la République* (Assembly for the Republic; R.P.R.).

10. Marcel Cerdan (1916–1949) was the French-Algerian boxer who won the French middleweight title in February 1938 and the European middleweight crown in February 1947. On September 21, 1948, Cerdan took the world middleweight title from the American Tony Zale in Jersey City. But in June 1949, Cerdan lost his title on a technical knockout to the American Jake La Motta. En route to the United States for a return bout with La Motta, Cerdan was killed, along with his manager, Jo Longman, in an airplane crash over the Azores islands on October 28, 1949. For the last few years of his life, Cerdan had a much-publicized romance with the French chanteuse Edith Piaf.

11. *L'Homme aux mains d'argile* (*The Man with Clay Hands*), 1949, directed by Léon Mathot, screenplay by Marcel Rivet. This is a romantic biography of Cerdan; the boxer played himself, as Bazin notes, and professional actors took the other roles. Cerdan's second and last film was *Al diavolo la celebrita* (*Au Diable, la célébrité!*; *The Hell with Celebrity!*), made in Rome in 1949. At the end of this boxing film—boxing films almost formed their own genre in the 1940s, especially in the United States—Cerdan ominously dies in a car accident.

12. Jean Henri Dunant (1828–1910), Swiss philanthropist and founder of the Red Cross.

13. Vassily Ivanovich Chapayev (1887–1919), Russian Civil War (1918–1921) hero. The Civil War was an additional ordeal for a nation already racked by world war and revolution. The principal adversaries in this struggle were the Bolsheviks, known as the "Reds," on whose side Chapayev fought, and their opponents, the "Whites," who had had enough of Lenin's policies and were united in little else but their wish to over-

throw his Bolshevik regime. Chapayev was the commander of the 25th Division of the Red Army; his political commissar was Dmitri Furmanov, whose novel *Chapayev* was the source for the Vasilievs' film. In 1919, Admiral Kolchak's White armies launched a major offensive on the Eastern Front, which was valiantly defended and held by the Chapayev Division. In June 1920, the Whites began their last sally, into southern Russia from the Crimea, only to be beaten back, and by early 1921 the Bolsheviks were completely triumphant. Chapayev himself was killed at Lbishchensk, in the south of Russia, in 1919, in retreat from advancing Cossacks; his body disappeared in the Ural River.

14. This is an allusion to the fact that Chapayev's 24th Division was largely made up of peasant regiments. Chapayev himself fought alongside these peasants and thus become a people's hero, embodying in his common appearance the rawness of his comrades-in-arms and in his brave leadership their own heroism. Among Chapayev's failings, to which Bazin refers, were arbitrariness, hotheadedness, and lack of self-discipline.

15. Marshal A. M. Vassilievsky (1895–1977) was Stalin's new Chief of the General Staff at the time of the battle of Stalingrad. Vassilievsky had replaced Marshal G. K. Zhukov (1896–1974). In the previous sentence in the essay, Bazin writes that "it would be extraordinarily childish to think that events occurred inside the Kremlin as they are portrayed here," but he doesn't specify which film "here" refers to. He could mean either *The Battle of Stalingrad* or *The Third Blow*, but he's probably referring to *The Battle of Stalingrad*, which he specifically names later in this paragraph. Certainly stills from *The Battle of Stalingrad* show Vassilievsky acting as a confidant to Stalin. The structure of this film is similar to that of *The Third Blow*, as Bazin points out in the previous paragraph, and he seems to be putting forth his discussion of *The Battle of Stalingrad* as representative of both films.

16. Fabrice del Dongo is the hero of Stendhal's *The Charterhouse of Parma* (1839). At the start of this novel, the sixteen-year-old Fabrice journeys from Italy to France and joins Napoleon's armies; his many adventures culminate in the battle of Waterloo. So chaotic and haphazard is what he sees there, and so narrow the segment of the spectacle he can witness, that he must later ask himself if he was really present at a battle.

17. *La Nouvelle Critique: Revue du Marxisme Militant* (*New Criticism: Review of Militant Marxism*). First published in Paris in December 1948; ceased publication in February 1980.

18. Bazin is referring here to Henri Philippe Pétain (1856–1951), the French general and the premier of the collaborationist government at Vichy (1940–44). He was convicted of treason in 1945.

19. Gregory Zinoviev, a former chief of the Comintern, was publicly tried and executed with fifteen others in August 1936. Nicholas Bukharin, also a former chief of the Comintern, was publicly tried with twenty others in March 1938. Of this group, eighteen were executed, Bukharin among them. As Marxists, none of those tried could admit that the single person of Stalin, or any other individual, could be decisive in history. As members of Stalin's opposition, they were against his totalitarian rule.

The show trials, conducted under the direction of Procurator General Andrei Vyshinsky, amazed and puzzled the world. The defendants uniformly confessed to the crimes with which they were charged, which included plotting with the secret services of foreign powers to overthrow Stalin and the Communist Party, to "restore capitalism" in the U.S.S.R., and to cede territory to Germany and Japan. The Great Purge served its purpose: it was a warning to all opponents of Stalin past, present, or future that they were traitors and deserving of death.

In 1949, the Hungarian Lázló Rajk and the Bulgarian Traicho Kostov were executed for "nationalist deviations," that is, "Titoism." In Yugoslavia, Communism was more homemade than in any other country except Russia or China, and the attempt to bring it into line backfired. Tito's obvious desire to form a confederation of Balkan states under his own leadership worried Moscow, which sought to tie each "Communist" country directly to itself. Instead of submitting, Yugoslavia pursued a more than ever independent course, developing the Communist heresy of "Titoism." As a result, Yugoslavia for a time entered into moderately friendly relations with the West. Yugoslavia was protected by its mountainous terrain and by the fierceness of its nationalism, which had been steeled in its violent struggle against the Nazis. Lest its independence be imitated elsewhere, a number of leading Communists in the satellite states were purged in 1949, Rajk and Kostov among them.

20. Boeotia is a province of eastern central Greece, northwest of Attica; in ancient times, this region was dominated by the city of Thebes. The people of Boeotia were reputed to be dull and stupid, hence the figurative meaning of Boeotian, in English, is "a dull, stupid person." In French, the word enjoys the status of an adjective and an abstract noun as well: *béotien* (fem. *béotienne*), stupid; *le béotisme*, dullness, stupidity; *le Béotien, la Béotienne*, a dunce.

21. Stalin's First Five-Year Plan for the vitalization of the Soviet economy took place from 1928–32, during which time the (foreign-built) tractor was introduced to Russian farming. By 1946, the Fourth Five-Year Plan was in effect (1946–50).

22. *Esprit*, a journal of culture and politics, is the premier Christian socialist organ of France and Europe; its stance is socialist, even communist, but this stance is based on a liberal humanism opposed to the demagoguery of men like Stalin. *Esprit* began publication in Paris in October 1932, suspended publication between September 1941 and November 1944, and still appears today.

23. *L'Humanité: Organe Central du Parti Communiste Français* (*Humanity: Central Organ of the French Communist Party*). First published in Paris in 1904, still publishing.

   Les Lettres Françaises: Organe du Comité National des Écrivains Français (*French Letters: Organ of the National Committee of French Writers*). First published in Paris in September 1942; ceased publication in October 1972.

24. Bazin is referring to Khrushchev's four-hour-long "secret speech" delivered to the Twentieth Party Congress in Moscow in February 1956. Bazin doesn't make clear (and some may not remember in 1996 that Krushchev was speaking ironically in the quotation of the next sentence—he acknowledged the existence of the myth of Stalin, but his object was to *deflate* this myth. Khrushchev's speech marked the beginning of de-Stalinization in the Soviet Union. He talked of the imprisonment of thousands of blameless people; of the torture and execution of devoted, innocent Party leaders; of unjustifiable deportations; of Stalin's personal directives calling for terror, torture, and death; of grave, costly mistakes made during the war; and of other instances of malfeasance of office. See Nikita Sergeevich Khrushchev, *The Crimes of the Stalin Era (a.k.a. The Dethronement of Stalin): Special Report to the Twentieth Congress of the Communist Party of the Soviet Union* (New York: New Leader, 1962).

25. *Stalin, Kratkaya Biografya* (*Stalin, Abridged Biography*; Moscow, 1944). Stalin edited this official, abridged account of his own life written by the Marx-Engels-Lenin Institute.

CHAPTER 3

Adaptation, or the Cinema as Digest

The problem of digests and adaptations is usually posed within the framework of literature. Yet literature only partakes of a phenomenon whose amplitude is much larger. Take painting, for instance: one might even consider an art museum as a digest, for we find *collected* there a *selection* of paintings that were intended to exist in a completely different architectural and decorative context. Nonetheless, these works of art are still original. But now take the imaginary museum proposed by Malraux: it refracts the original painting into millions of facets thanks to photographic reproduction, and it substitutes for that original images of different dimensions and colors that are readily accessible to all. And by the way, photography for its part is only a modern substitute for engraving, which previously had been the only approximate "adaptation" available to connoisseurs.[1] One must not forget that the "adaptation" and "summary" of original works of art have become so customary and so frequent that it would be next to impossible to question their existence today. For the sake of argument, I'll take my examples from the cinema.

More than one writer, more than one critic, more than one filmmaker even, has challenged the aesthetic justification for the adaptation of novels to the screen; however, there are few examples of those who take actual exception to this practice, of artists who refuse to sell their books, to adapt other people's books, or to direct them when a producer comes along with the right blandishments. So their theoretical argument doesn't seem altogether justified. In general, they make claims about the specificity or distinctness of every authentic literary work. A novel is a unique synthesis whose molecular equilibrium is automatically affected when you tamper with its form. Essentially, no detail in the narrative can be considered as secondary; all syntactic characteristics, then, are in fact expressions of the psychological, moral, or metaphysical content of the work. André Gide's simple pasts[2] are in a way inseparable from the events of *The Pastoral Symphony* (1919), just as Camus's present perfects are inherent in the metaphysical drama of *The Stranger* (1942).

Even when it is posed in such complex terms, however, the problem of cinematic adaptation is not absolutely insolvable, and the history of the cinema already proves that this problem has often been solved in various ways. I'll take only incontestable examples here: Malraux's *Man's Hope* (*Espoir*; a.k.a. *Sierra de Teruel*; 1939), Jean Renoir's *A Day in the Country* (1936), after Maupassant, and the recent *Grapes of Wrath* (1940; dir. John Ford) from Steinbeck. I find it easy to defend even a qualified success such as *The Pastoral Symphony* (1949; dir. Jean Delannoy). It's true that everything in the film isn't a success, but this is certainly not due to what some consider to be the ineffable aspect of the original. I don't care much for Pierre Blanchar's acting, but I do think that Michèle Morgan's beautiful eyes—which are able to communicate the blind Gertrude's innermost thoughts—and the omnipresent motif of the ironically serene snow are acceptable substitutes for Gide's simple pasts. All it takes is for the filmmakers to have enough visual imagination to create the cinematic equivalent of the style of the original, and for the critic to have the eyes to see it.

To be sure, this theory of adaptation comes with the following warning: that one not confuse prose style with grammatical idiosyncrasies or, more generally still, with formal constants. Such confusion is widespread—and unfortunately, not merely among French teachers. "Form" is at most a sign, a visible manifestation, of style, which is absolutely inseparable from the narrative content, of which it is, in a manner of speaking and according to Sartre's use of the word, the metaphysics. Under these circumstances, faithfulness to a form, literary or otherwise, is illusory: what matters is the *equivalence in meaning of the forms*.[3] The *style* of Malraux's film is completely identical to that of his book, even though we are dealing here with two different artistic forms, cinema on the one hand and literature on the other. The case of *A Day in the Country* is subtler: it is faithful to the spirit of Maupassant's short story at the same time that it benefits from the full extent of Renoir's genius. This is the refraction of one work in another creator's consciousness. And there isn't a person who will deny the beauty of the result. It took somebody like Maupassant, but also someone like Renoir (both of them, Jean and Auguste), to achieve it.

The Pastoral Symphony (1949), dir. Jean Delannoy. Museum of Modern Art, New York.

The hard-liners will respond that the above-mentioned examples prove only that it is perhaps not metaphysically impossible to make a cinematic work inspired by a literary one, with sufficient faithfulness to the spirit of the original and with an aesthetic intelligence that permits us to consider the film the equal of the book; but they will also say that this is no longer the kind of "adaptation" I was talking about at the beginning of this piece. They'll say that *A Day in the Country* on screen is a different work, that's all, equal or superior to its model because Jean Renoir is, in his own right, an artist of the same rank as Maupassant, and because he has of course benefitted from the work of the writer, which is anterior to his own. They'll claim that, if we examine the countless American and European novels that are adapted to the screen every month, we will see that they are something completely different, that they are the condensed versions, summaries, film "digests" of which I spoke earlier. For instance, take aesthetically indefensible films such as *The Idiot* (1946; dir. Georges Lampin) and *For Whom the Bell Tolls* (1943; dir. Sam Wood), or those never-ending "adaptations" of Balzac, which seem to have more than amply demonstrated that the author of *The Human Comedy*[4] is the least "cinematic" of all novelists. To be sure, one must first know to what end the adaptation is designed: for the cinema or for its audience. One must also realize that most adaptors care far more about the latter than about the former.

The problem of adaptation for the audience is much more evident in the case of radio. Indeed, radio is not quite an art like the cinema: it is first and foremost a means of reproduction and transmission. The digest phenomenon resides not so much in the actual condensing or simplification of works as in the way they are consumed by the listening public. The cultural interest of radio—precisely the aspect of it that scares Georges Duhamel[5]— is that is allows modern man to live in an environment of sound comparable to the warm atmosphere created by central heating. As for me, although I've had a radio set for barely a year now, I feel the need to turn it on as soon as I get home; often I even write and work with the radio on as my companion. Right now, as I write this article, I'm listening to Jean Vittold's[6] excellent, daily morning broadcast on the great musicians. Earlier today, while I was shaving, Jean Rostand,[7] juggling with chromosomes, told me why only female cats (or was it male cats?) can be of three colors simultaneously, and I don't remember who explained to me while I was having breakfast how, through simple scraping with sand, the Aztecs carved extraordinary masks of polished quartz that one can see at the Musée de l'Homme.[8] Jules Romains's[9] appalling hoax on extraocular vision was itself seriously adapted for radio.

Radio has created an atmospheric culture that is as omnipresent as humidity in the air. For those who think that culture can only be achieved through hard work, the ease of physical access that radio allows to works of art is at least as antagonistic to the nature of these works as any tampering with their form. Even if it is well rendered or integrally performed on radio, the *Fifth Symphony* is no longer Beethoven's work when you listen to it while in your bathtub; music must be accompanied by the ritual of attending a concert, by the sacrament of contemplation. However, one can also see in radio the spreading of culture to everyone—the physical spread of culture, which is the first step toward its spiritual ascendance. Radio comfortably provides, like one more modern convenience, "culture for everyone."[10] It represents a gain of time and a reduction of effort, which is the very mark of our era. After all, even M. Duhamel will take a cab or the metro to get to the concert hall.

The clichéd bias according to which culture is inseparable from intellectual effort springs from a bourgeois, intellectualist reflex. It is the equivalent in a rationalistic society of the initiatory rites in primitive civilizations. Esoterism is obviously one of the grand cultural traditions, and I'm not pretending that we should completely banish it from ours. But we could simply put it back in its place, which should in no way be absolute. There is a definite pleasure in cracking or conquering the hermeticism of a work of art, which then refines our relationship to that work of art. So much the better. But mountain climbing has not yet replaced walking on level ground. In place of the classical modes of cultural communication, which are at once a defense of culture and a secreting of it behind high walls, modern technology and modern life now more and more offer up an extended culture reduced to the lowest common denominator of the masses. To the defensive, intellectual motto of "No culture without mental effort," which is in fact unconsciously elitist, the up-and-coming civilization now responds with, "Let's grab whatever we can." This is progress—that is, if there really is such a thing as progress.

A far as the cinema is concerned, my intention is not to defend the indefensible. Indeed, most of the films that are based on novels merely usurp their title, even though a good lawyer could probably prove that these movies have an indirect value, since it has been shown that the sale of a book always increases after it has been adapted to the screen. And the original work can only profit from such an exposure. Although *The Idiot*, for example, is very frustrating on the screen, it is undeniable that many potential readers of Dostoyevsky have found in the film's oversimplified psychology and action a kind of preliminary trimming that has given them easier access to an otherwise difficult novel. The process is somewhat similar to that of M. de Vogüe, the author of "abridged" classics for schools in the nineteenth century. These are despicable in the eyes of devotees of the Russian novel (but they have hardly anything to lose by this process, and neither does Dostoyevsky), yet extremely useful to those who are not yet familiar with the Russian novel and who thus can benefit from an introduction to it. In any event, I won't comment further on this, for it has more to do with pedagogy than with art. I'd much prefer to deal with a rather *modern* notion for which the critics are in large part responsible: that of the untouchability of the work of art.

The nineteenth century, more than any other, firmly established an idolatry of form, mainly literary, that is still with us and that has made us relegate what has in fact always been essential for narrative composition to the back of our critical consciousness: the invention of character and situation. I grant that the protagonists and events of a novel achieve their aesthetic existence only through the form that expresses them and that somehow brings them to life in our mind. But this precedence is as vain as that which is regularly conveyed to college students when they are asked to write an essay on the precedence of language over thought. It is interesting to note that the novelists who defend so fiercely the stylistic or formal integrity of their texts are also the ones who sooner or later overwhelm us with confessions about the tyrannical demands of their characters. According to these writers, their protagonists are *enfants terribles* who completely escape from their control once they have been conceived. The novelist is totally subjected to their whims, he is the instrument of their wills. I'm not doubting this for a minute, but then writers must recognize that the true aesthetic reality of a psychological or social novel lies in the characters or their environment rather than in what they call the "style." The style is in the service of the narrative: it is a reflection of it, so to speak, the body but not the soul. And it is not impossible for the artistic soul to manifest itself through another incarnation. This assumption, that the style is in the service of the narrative, appears vain and sacrilegious only if one refuses to see the many examples of it that the history of the arts gives to us, and if one therefore indulges in the biased condemnation of cinematic adaptation. With time, we do see the ghosts of famous characters rise far above the great novels from which they emanate. Don Quixote and Gargantua dwell in the consciousness of millions of people who have never had any direct or complete contact with the works of Cervantès and Rabelais. I would like to be sure that all those who conjure up the spirit of Fabrice and Madame Bovary have read (or reread, for good measure) Stendhal and Flaubert, but I'm not so sure. Insofar as the style of the original has managed to create a character and impose him on the public consciousness, that character acquires a greater autonomy, which might in certain cases lead as far as quasi-transcendence of the work. Novels, as we all know, are mythmakers.

The ferocious defense of literary works is, to a certain extent, aesthetically justified; but we must also be aware that it rests on a rather recent, individualistic conception of the "author" and of the "work," a conception that was far from being ethically rigorous in the seventeenth century and that started to become legally defined only at the end of the eighteenth. In the Middle Ages, there were only a few themes, and they were common to all the arts. That of Adam and Eve, for instance, is to be found in the mystery plays, painting, sculpture, and stained-glass windows, none of which were ever challenged for transferring this theme from one art form to another. And when the subject of the Rome Prize for Painting is "the love of Daphnis and Chloë,"[10] what else is it but an adaptation? Yet nobody is claiming that copyright has been violated. In justification of the artistic multiplication of Biblical and Christian themes during the Middle Ages, it would be wrong to say that they were part of a common fund, a kind of public domain of Christian civilization: the copiers or imitators had no more respect for the *chansons de gestes*, the Old French epic poems, than they did for religious literature. The reason is that the work of art was not an end in itself; the only important criteria were its content and the effectiveness of its message. But the balance between the public's needs and the requirements for creation was such in those days that all the conditions existed to guarantee the excellence of the arts. You may perhaps observe that those days are over and that it would be aesthetic nonsense to want to anachronistically reverse the evolution of the relationship among the creator, the public, and the work of art. To this I would respond that, on the contrary, it is possible that artists and critics remain blind to the birth of the new, aesthetic Middle Ages, whose origin is to be found in the accession of the masses to power (or at least their participation in it) and in the emergence of an artistic form to complement that accession: the cinema.

But even if this thesis is a rather risky one that would require additional arguments in its support, it remains true that the relatively new art of cinema is obliged to retrace the entire evolution of art on its own, at an extraordinarily quickened pace, just as a fetus somehow retraces the evolution of mankind in a few months. The only difference is that the paradoxical evolution of cinema is contemporaneous with the deep-seated decadence of literature, which today seems designed for an audience of individualist elites. The aesthetic Middle Ages of the cinema finds its fictions wherever it can: close at hand, in the literatures of the nineteenth and twentieth centuries. It can also create its own fictions, and has not failed to do so, particularly in comic films, from the first French ones to the American comedies of, say, Mack Sennett and above all Charlie Chaplin. The defenders of seriousnessness in the cinema will name instead examples like the Western epics and those of the Russian revolution, or such unforgettable pictures as *Broken Blossoms* (1919; dir. D. W. Griffith) and *Scarface* (1932; dir. Howard Hawks). But there's nothing that can be done to bring back the halcyon past. Youth is transient, and grandeur with it; another grandeur will take its place, if perhaps a bit more slowly. In the meantime, the cinema borrows from fiction a certain number of well-wrought , well-rounded, or well-developed characters, all of whom have been polished by twenty centuries of literary culture. It adopts them and brings them into play; according to the talents of the screenwriter and the director, the characters are integrated as much as possible into their new aesthetic context. If they are not so integrated, we naturally get these mediocre films that one is right to condemn, provided one doesn't confuse this mediocrity with the very principle of cinematic adaptation, whose aim is to simplify and condense a work from which it basically wishes to retain only the main characters and situations. If the novelist is not happy with the adaptation of his work, I, of course, grant him the right to defend the original (although he sold it, and thus is guilty of an act of prostitution that deprives him of many of his privileges as the creator of the work). I grant him this right only because no one has yet found anyone better than parents to defend the rights of children until they come of age. One should not identify this natural right with an a priori infallibility, however.

Instead of Kafka's *Trial*, which was adapted to the stage by André Gide (1947) from a translation by André Vialatte, I'll take the more appropriate example of *The Brothers Karamazov*, adapted by Jacques Copeau (*Les Frères Karamazov*, 1911), in my defense of the condensed adaptation. The only thing Copeau has done—but he did it more skillfully than M. Spaak[11] in *The Idiot*—is to extract the characters from Dostoyevsky's novel and condense the main events of their story into a few dramatic scenes. There's something slightly different about these theatrical examples, however: the fact that today's theater-going public is educated enough to have read the novel. But Copeau's work would remain artistically viable even if this were not the case.

To take another example, I suffered when I saw *Devil in the Flesh* (1947; dir. Claude Autant-Lara), because I know Raymond Radiguet's book; the spirit and "style" of that book had somehow been betrayed. But it remains true that this adaptation is the best one that could be made from the novel and that, artistically, it is absolutely justified. Jean Vigo would probably have been more faithful to the original, but it's reasonable to conclude that the resulting film would have been impossible to show to the public because the reality of the book would have ignited the screen. The work of the screenwriters Aurenche and Bost consisted, so to speak, in "transforming" (in the sense that an electric transformer does) the voltage of the novel. The aesthetic energy is almost all there, but it is distributed—or perhaps better, dissipated—differently according to the demands of the camera lens. And yet, although Aurenche and Bost have succeeded in transforming the absolute amoralism of the original into an almost too decipherable moral code, the public has been reluctant to accept the film.

In summary, adaptation is aesthetically justified, independent of its pedagogical and social value, because the adapted work to a certain extent exists apart from what is wrongly called its "style," in a confusion of this term with the word "form." Furthermore, the standard differentiation among the arts in the nineteenth century and the relatively recent, subjectivist notion of the author as identified with the work no longer fit in with an aesthetic sociology of the masses, in which the cinema runs a relay race with drama and the novel and doesn't eliminate them, but rather reinforces them. The true aesthetic differentiations, in fact, are not to be made among the arts but within genres themselves: between the psychological novel and the novel of manners, for example, rather than between the psychological novel and the film that one would have made from it. Of course, adaptation for the public is inseparable from adaptation for the cinema, insofar as the cinema is more "public" than the novel.

The very word "digest," which sounds at first contemptible, can have a positive meaning. "As the word indicates," Jean-Paul Sartre writes, "it is a literature that has been previously digested, a literary chyle."[11] But one could also understand it as a literature that has been made more accessible through cinematic adaptation, not so much because of the oversimplification that such adaptation entails (in *The Pastoral Symphony*, the narrative on screen is even more complex than the one in the novel), but rather because of the mode of expression itself, as if the aesthetic fat, differently emulsified, were better tolerated by the consumer's mind. As far as I'm concerned, the difficulty of audience assimilation is not an a priori criterion for cultural value.

All things considered, it's possible to imagine that we are moving toward a reign of the adaptation in which the notion of the unity of the work of art, if not the very notion of the author himself, will be destroyed. If the film that was made of Steinbeck's *Of Mice and Men* (1940; dir. Lewis Milestone) had been successful (it could have been so, and far more easily than the adaptation of the same author's *Grapes of Wrath*), the (literary?) critic of the year 2050 would find not a novel out of which a play and a film had been "made," but rather a single work reflected through three art forms, an artistic pyramid with three sides, all equal in the eyes of the critic. The "work" would then be only an ideal point at the top of this figure, which itself is an ideal construct. The chronological precedence of one part over another would not be an aesthetic criterion any more than the chronological precedence of one twin over the other is a genealogical one. Malraux made his film of *Man's Hope* before he wrote the novel of the same title, but he was carrying the work inside himself all along.

NOTES TO CHAPTER 3

Adaptation, or the Cinema as Digest

This essay was first published in French in *Esprit*, 16, no. 146 (July 1948), pp. 32–40.

1. Bazin's note: In a recent radio broadcast of *French Cancan*, during which Messieurs Pierre Benoit (1886–1962; French novelist, member of the Académie Française, author of *Koenigsmark* and *L'Atlantide*), Labarthe (obscure French literary figure of Bazin's time, co-author, with Marcel Brion, Jean Cocteau, Fred Bérence, Emmanuel Berl, Danielle Hunebelle, Robert Lebel, Jean-Lucas Dubreton, and Jean-Jaques Salomon, of a volume entitled *Léonard de Vinci* [1959]), and several others exchanged a great number of utter platitudes, we heard Curzio Malaparte (1898–1957; Italian novelist, the celebrated author of *Kaputt* and many other works, who contributed one film to Italian cinema, *Il Cristo Proibito* [*Forbidden Christ*, 1950], which he wrote, directed, and scored. The film was released in the United States in 1953) ask the speaker what he would think of a "condensed version" of the Parthenon, for example. In his mind, this was supposed to be the ultimate argument against the "digest." Nobody was there to respond that such a condensed version had been realized a long time ago in the casts that were made of the Parthenon's friezes, and above all in the photo albums of the Acropolis that anybody can buy at a reasonable price in a gift shop.

2. Editor's note: Bazin is here using the term "passé simple" in French. This tense does not exist in English. It is a form of the simple past, which itself is called "imparfait" in French. "Imparfait" tends to be used more often in everyday language, whereas "passé simple" is a more literary form of the same tense.

3. Bazin's note: There are types of stylistic transfer that are indeed reliable, however, such as those "simple pasts" of André Gide that unfortunately were not built into the actual cutting of *The Pastoral Symphony*, i.e., its filmic syntax, but did show up in the eyes of an actress and in the symbolism of the snow.

4. Editor's note: This was the title given by Honoré de Balzac to his collected stories and novels, thus casting his copious fictions as a single, secular reply to Dante's *Divine Comedy*. *La Comédie humaine* was published in 16 volumes by Furne, Paulin, Dubochet, and Hetzel between 1842 and 1846; a 17th supplementary volume appeared in 1847.

5. Editor's note: Georges Duhamel (1884–1966), now a largely forgotten figure, achieved fame before World War II, being elected to the Académie Française in 1935.

He is remembered for two cycles of novels: *Vie et aventures de Salavin* (1920–32) and the popular *Chronique des Pasquier* (1933–45). Writing with warmth and humor, Duhamel used the saga of the Pasquier family to attack materialism and defend the rights of the individual against the collective forces of society.

6. Editor's note: Vittold was a famous French musicologist.

7. Editor's note: Rostand was a well-known French biologist who did much to popularize the study of science.

8. Editor's note: Famous anthropological museum in Paris.

9. Editor's note: Jules Romains (pseud. of Louis Farigoule, 1885–1972) was a French novelist, dramatist, poet, and essayist, elected to the Académie Française in 1946. *La Vie unanime*, a collection of poems published in 1908, and much of his later verse and prose, were influenced by Unanimist theories of social groups and collective psychology. Before the outbreak of war in 1914 he published more collections of poetry, a verse play, *L'Armée dans la ville* (1911), and two novels, *Mort de quelqu'un* (1911) and the farcical *Les Copains* (1913).

   The farcical comedies *Knock, ou le Triomphe de la médecine* (1923), *M. Le Trouhadec saisi par la débauche* (1923), and *Le Mariage de M. Le Trouhadec* (1925) earned him much popularity after the war. Interesting collections of essays include *Hommes, médecins, machines* (1959) and *Lettre ouverte contre une vaste conspiration* (1966)—with its strictures on modern cultural attitudes and standards.

10. Editor's note: Daphnis and Chloë were two lovers in an old Greek pastoral romance of the same name, attributed to Longus (of the third century A.D. [?]). Daphnis himself is a Sicilian shepherd renowned in Greek myth as the inventor of pastoral poetry.

11. See note 3, p. 158.

CHAPTER 4

The Case of Marcel Pagnol

Together with La Fontaine,[1] Cocteau, and Jean-Paul Sartre, Marcel Pagnol completes the average American's ideal of the French Academy. But Pagnol owes his international popularity in the first place, paradoxically, to the regionalism of his work. In spite of all Mistral's efforts,[2] the rejuvenated Provençal culture remained a prisoner of its own language and folklore. Alphonse Daudet[3] and Bizet[4] did indeed win a national audience for this culture, but at the price of a stylization that robbed it of most of its authenticity. Later, Giono[5] came along and depicted a Provence that was austere, sensual, and dramatic. In between, the Midi[6] was hardly represented to its advantage by "Marseilles stories."[7] It is from these stories, joined together in *Marius*,[8] that Pagnol set out to constitute his southern humanism; then, under the influence of Giono, to leave Marseilles and go inland, where, in *Manon of the Springs*, with his inspiration finally at its peak, he gave Provence its universal epic.

Conversely, Pagnol has enjoyed calling into question his relationship with the cinema by proclaiming himself the champion of *filmed theater*. Looked as from this point of view, his work is indefensible. It constitutes in effect an example of what should not be done in the adaptation of theater to the screen. To film a play purely and simply by transporting the actors from the stage to a natural setting is the surest way to wrest from the dialogue its *raison d'être*, even its soul. Not that the transposition of a theatrical text to the screen is impossible; it can be done, but only at the cost of taking a whole series of subtle precautions whose fundamental aim is to *preserve* the play's theatricality, not minimize it. To substitute the Midi sun for footlights, as Pagnol seemed to do, would have been the surest way to kill a text by sunstroke. As for admiring *Marius* or *The Baker's Wife* (see note 8) by declaring that their only shortcoming is in "not being cinema," this matches the silliness of the critics who condemned Corneille for violating the rules of tragedy. "Cinema" is not an abstract idea, a distilled essence, but the sum of all that achieves, through an individual film's interpretation, the quality of art. For this reason, if only some of Pagnol's films are good, they can't be good and "not be cinema" at the same time. Rather, they're good because they have certain qualities that critics haven't been able to discern.

Manon of the Springs finally permits us to clear up this misunderstanding, for here is a script that could be performed in the theater only at the price of a tedious and garbled adaptation. In the best situation imaginable, *Manon of the Springs*, if brought to the stage, would be nothing but "theatricalized cinema." But, in a sense, has Pagnol ever done anything else except write texts for the screen that could also be adapted to the stage? Chronology has nothing to do with the matter: it's accidental. Even if *Marius* was a success at the Theater of Paris before Alexander Korda directed the screen version, it is clear that this work's basic form is, and will continue to be, cinematic. Any theatrical revival at this point could only be termed an adaptation for the stage.

What can we conclude from this, except that the preponderance of verbal expression over visual action is not sufficient to define theater in relation to cinema, because it doesn't account for the different way each medium uses language? An assertion of such magnitude cannot be properly supported within the limits of this article. Let's just say that the word in the theater is abstract, that, like all of theater, is itself a convention: in this case, of converting action into words. By contrast, the word in film is a concrete reality: at the least, if not at most, it exists by and for itself. It is the action in a film that prolongs the release of words and thereby almost consigns them to a lesser status. This is doubtless why the only play by Pagnol that has never really made the transition from stage to screen is *Topaze* (see note 8): its action, unlike that of his other plays which have been filmed, does not take place in Provence, and its characters therefore do not speak with the Provençal accent.

This accent is not just a picturesque addition to Pagnol's films; it's not there merely to inject a note of local color into the proceedings. It unites with the script, and thus with the characters, to create the essential nature of a Pagnol film. These characters have an accent the way others have black skin. The accent is the true substance of their language and is consequently at the heart of its realism. Pagnol's cinema is quite the contrary of theatrical, then: it immerses itself, through the intermediary of language, in the realistic specificity of film. It is hardly the authentic southern setting that is the filmic extension of a Pagnol play's theatrical boundaries; on the contrary, those boundaries are the reduction of the Provençal countryside, as it appears on film, to a bunch of wooden panels in the theater. Pagnol is not a dramatist who has been converted to cinema, but rather a screenwriter who can adapt to the stage. In short, he is one of the greatest authors of *talking* films.

Manon of the Springs is no more than a long, a very long narrative, not without action, but during which nothing ever happens unless it's brought about by the natural power of language. This is a wonderful and "fabulous" story about a wild girl who has become an orphan through a strange turn of events, and who becomes the enemy of the people in the village outside which she lives. Her father and brother are both dead and her mother has gone mad because the family does not know the secret of the water that once ran through their poor farm—a secret that everyone in the village does know. One day an old woman reveals to Manon the secret of the spring that supplies the village with water. A stone in the right spot will suffice to stop the flow of this spring and, just like that, condemn the village itself to thirst, desolation, and death. The calamity that follows makes the villagers conscious of their sin-by-omission: their silence is what caused the death of the two "strangers." Manon the goatherd and her mad mother are now the Furies of this large and ruthless family of villagers. In slyly roundabout ways and through guilty silences, the people of the village will slowly confess their sin. The man who had cemented off the flow of water to the farm will hang himself. The entire village will give propitiatory gifts to Manon, and the spring will begin flowing again, returning the community to a life of innocence. There is in this splendid tale the ancient grandeur of the Mediterranean, something at the same time both Biblical and Homeric. But there is also in it a familiar note: the mayor, the schoolteacher, the priest, the notary, and Manon herself are all country folk from contemporary Provence. And, unlike Aaron, they have no rod that can touch a rock and make water flow from it.

Let's consider now what, more that anything else, surprises the audience: the length of this film. We know that the original version ran some five or six hours. Pagnol reduced it to two films, each two hours long, which the distributor then edited down to a single film of three hours and fifteen minutes (with a ten-minute intermission). It is obvious that these cuts have disturbed the film's balance, that, paradoxically, they are responsible for all the longish moments. The commercial length of films is completely arbitrary or, rather, is determined by unique sociological and economic factors (such as amount of leisure time and how much of it will be devoted to moviegoing, and ticket prices) that don't have anything to do with the intrinsic requirements of art or even the psychology of the audience. The all too few experiments in this area prove that the public tolerates quite well presentations of more than four hours. To have demanded of Proust that he limit himself to 200 pages in writing *A Remembrance of Things Past* wouldn't have made any sense. For very different reasons, but no less imperative ones, Pagnol couldn't tell the story of *Manon of the Springs* in less that four or five hours, not because so much that happens is absolutely essential, but because it's ridiculous to stop the storyteller before he has fulfilled his vision. I'm not sure that it's a bore to watch *Manon of the Springs.* One must not mistake for boring certain moments of repose, those respites in the narrative, that are necessary for the maturation of the words. But if this film is boring, then the cuts are at fault.

If Pagnol is not the greatest *auteur* of sound film, he is in any case something like its genius. He is perhaps the only one who, since 1930, has dared a verbal plenitude comparable to the visual plenitude of Griffith or von Stroheim during the era of silent film. The only *auteur* who can be compared with him today is Chaplin, and for a specific reason: because Chaplin is, along with Pagnol, the only independent writer-director-producer.[9] The hundreds of millions of francs that Pagnol has earned making films he dares to spend, for his own pleasure, on cinematic oddities that organized and rational production could never even think of attempting. Certain of these, it is true, will not survive: they are tedious whimsies born of the copulation between rose-colored vision and Tino Rossi.[10] And this, alas, is what distinguishes Pagnol from Chaplin. *Limelight* is a phenomenally beautiful film as much because it is completely autonomous as for other reasons; it is the fruit of the meditations of an artist who is the sole judge of his means of execution, just as a painter or a writer is of his. But everything in Chaplin's art tends toward self-criticism and therefore creates a sense of necessity, economy, and rigor.

By contrast, everything in Pagnol's art tends toward self-indulgence and therefore creates, in his worst films, an incredible sense of superfluity, waste, and slackness. It is difficult to imagine an artist with less critical judgment than Pagnol, and his lack of judgment derives from the veritable pathology of artistic creation to which he subscribes. This Academy member doesn't really know whether he is Homer or Breffort.[11] Moreover, it isn't as a writer that he is at his worst, it's as a director. It would not have taken very much for *Manon of the Springs* to have been the epic of sound film, but it would have taken a director whose good artistic sense could overrule his screenwriter's flights of fancy. As silly as his critics, but with an opinion the opposite of theirs, Pagnol imagines that "cinema isn't of any importance." Incapable of drawing from his theatrical training the equivalent to what his genius has already given him of the purely cinematic, he keeps compromising both his genius and his training with filmed theater.

No doubt that, despite this contempt for cinema, there are some wonderfully right cinematic moments in *Manon of the Springs* (Hugolin's declarations of love, the public confession under the elm tree), but a talent founded on ignorance is subject to the gravest errors as well. The principal error here comes with the character of Manon (acted in the most artificially theatrical manner by Jacqueline Pagnol[12]). Manon, of all people, is precisely the one, and the only one, whose lines ring false from the beginning of the film to the end.

Perhaps all that Pagnol's cinematic genius needed was cinematic intelligence to make him the Chaplin of sound film.

NOTES TO CHAPTER 4

The Case of Marcel Pagnol

(All notes have been provided by the Editor.)

This article was originally published in French in Bazin's *Qu'est-ce que le cinéma?*, Vol. 2: "Le Cinéma et les autres arts" (Paris: Éditions du Cerf, 1959), pp. 119–25.

1. Jean de La Fontaine (1621–1695) was a French poet and writer of fables. His fame rests on his *Fables choisies, mises en vers*, the first six books of which were published in 1668, five further books in 1678–79, and the twelfth and last book in 1694. The fables are drawn from many sources, ancient (Aesop, Phaedrus, Horace, Bidpai) as well as modern, but the originals are only the skeleton that La Fontaine has filled out and vivified with details drawn from his own observation of nature and society. They are little pictures of life, universal in their quality, in which, often under the symbols of animals and by means of lively dialogues and sudden vicissitudes, men of all classes of society are depicted and their failings held up to gentle ridicule.

2. Frédéric Mistral (1830–1914) was a French Provençal poet. (Provence is a region and former province of Southeastern France, on the Mediterranean; Provençal is the ver-

nacular of the region, a Romance language comprising several dialects.) Mistral is perhaps best remembered as the leader, in association with Joseph Roumanille, of the mid-nineteenth-century movement ("le Félibrige") for the revival of the Provençal language and literature. He spent many years compiling *Le Trésor du Félibrige* (1878–86), a dictionary of Provençal words, proverbs, legends, etc.

3. Alphonse Daudet (1840–1914), French novelist and a fellow Provençal of Pagnol's. Today Daudet is remembered chiefly for *Lettres de mon moulin* (*Letters from My Windmill*), delicately sentimental, humorous sketches of Provençal life that appeared first in *Le Figaro* (1866) and then in book form in 1868. His novels, which made his fame in his lifetime, have been somewhat unjustly forgotten. For a time he was a leading *naturaliste*, writing with the care for documentation typical of the movement, but his work comes alive through his gift for vivid, impressionistic description and because his naturalism never excluded the warm, poetic, fantasy-loving side of his character. Pagnol directed *Les Lettres de mon moulin* in 1954 from his own screenplay based on Daudet's sketches.

4. Georges Bizet (1838–1875) was a French composer born in Paris. He composed operas and works for the piano. Works by which he is remembered include the music for *La jolie Fille de Perth* (1867), the opera based on Scott's novel; *L'Arlésienne* (1872), based on Daudet's play; and *Carmen* (1875), based on Mérimée's tale of Spanish gypsy life.

5. Jean Giono (1895–1970) was a novelist of partly Italian ancestry. He describes in his novels a pastoral life in the lower mountain slopes of Provence that is close to primitive nature and not only simple, but also beautiful and poetic. *Colline* (1929), *Un de Baumugnes* (1929), and *Regain* (1930) make up the early trilogy *Pan*. Giono is also the author of the novel *La Femme du boulanger* (*The Baker's Wife*, 1935; Pagnol directed *La Femme du boulanger* in 1938 from his own screenplay based on Giono's novel) and the pastoral play *Le Lanceur de graine* (1932).

6. The Midi is southern France.

7. Marseilles stories are long, drawn-out local anecdotes.

8. After gaining great prominence as a playwright in Paris in the 1920s with *Topaze* and *Marius*, Marcel Pagnol (1895–1974) decided to enter the new world of sound films. In addition to directing films from his own plays and screenplays, he wrote the script and dialogue for a number of screen adaptations of his plays that were directed by others. A selected filmography:

Marius (1930), script by Pagnol from his own play; directed by Alexander Korda.

Fanny (1932), script by Pagnol from his own play; directed by Marc Allégret.

Topaze (1932), script by Pagnol from his own play; directed by Louis Gasnier. (Pagnol himself directed two remakes of *Topaze*, in 1936 and 1951. *Topaze* was also produced in 1933, with a script by Benn W. Levy based on Pagnol's play; the producer was David O. Selznick, the director was Harry d'Abbabie d'Arrast, and the film starred John Barrymore and Myrna Loy.)

Direct au Coeur (1933), script by Pagnol from his own play; directed by Pagnol and Roger Lion.

César (1936), directed by Pagnol from a script based on his own play.

La Femme du Boulanger (*The Baker's Wife*, 1938), directed by Pagnol from his own screenplay based on Jean Giono's novel of the same title.

Manon des Sources (*Manon of the Springs*, 1952), directed by Pagnol from his own screenplay.

Les Lettres de mon moulin (*Letter from My Windmill*, 1954), directed by Pagnol from his own screenplay, which was based on Alphonse Daudet's sketches of Provençal life collected under the same title.

9. In the early 1930s, Pagnol established his own studio near Marseilles, Films Marcel Pagnol, which released through Gaumont.

10. Tino Rossi (1907–1983), popular tenor of French radio, operettas, music halls, and films.

11. Alexandre Breffort (1902–1971), French humorist and playwright. Author of, among other musical comedies, *Irma la Douce* (1956), with music by Marguerite Monnot; Billy Wilder based his film of the same name (1963) on this play. Breffort created the character of Grand-Père Zig, around whom he wrote two collections of humorous tales: *Les Contes du Grand-Père Zig* (1946) and *Nouveaux Contes du Grand-Père Zig* (1952).

12. Pagnol's third wife, the former Jacqueline Bouvier (b. 1926), who starred in several of his films.

CHAPTER 5

Cinema and Theology

The cinema has always been interested in God. The Gospel and The Acts of the Apostles were the first best sellers on the screen, and the Passions of Christ were hits in France as well as in America.[1] At the same time in Italy, the Rome of the first Christians provided filmmakers with subjects that required gigantic crowd scenes, which were later seized upon by Hollywood and are still present today in films like *Fabiola* (1948; dir. Alessandro Blasetti) and *Quo Vadis?* (1951; dir. Mervyn LeRoy).[2] This immense catechism-in-pictures was concerned above all with the most spectacular aspects of the history of Christianity. These films were simply amplified variations on the Stations of the Cross or on the Musée Grévin.[3]

The hagiographies appeared a little later. As the cinema is in itself already a kind of miracle, it was absolutely appropriate to show a rain of roses pouring down or springs gushing out of arid sands. Several films were made about Saint Thérèse of Lisieux (a.k.a. Saint Thérèse of the Child Jesus) and Bernadette Soubirous[4]; the latest of these films, an American one (*The Song of Bernadette*), is only a few years old. Here the cinema exploited above all the popular belief in miracles. This vein is not exhausted, and our children will probably one day see a *Golgotha* (1935; dir. Julien Duvivier) in 3-D after a color *Quo Vadis?*. We must note, however, that the hagiography has evolved considerably. *Monsieur Vincent* (1947; dir. Maurice Cloche) is a saint's picture without miracles,[5] and Rossellini seems not to have emphasized too much the stigmata and the enchantment of the birds in his *Flowers of St. Francis* (1950). Also made last year in Italy, *Heaven over the Marshes* (1949; dir. Augusto Genina) tells the story of little Maria Goretti, who was canonized soon after the

The Song of Bernadette (1943), dir. Henry King. Museum of Modern Art, New York.

Angels of the Streets (1943), dir. Robert Bresson. Museum of Modern Art, New York.

completion of this film. *Heaven over the Marshes*, which still has not been released in France despite its director's being awarded first prize at the Venice Film Festival, is the prototype of the accursed film that is likely to upset both Christians and non-believers alike. In it, sainthood isn't signified by anything extraordinary, either on the physical or the psychological level. Divine grace doesn't manifest itself in nature as the product of a tangible causality; at most, it reveals itself through some ambiguous signs that can all be explained in quite natural terms. Psychoanalysis or even her simple decency, heightened by a naive piety, could very well account for Maria Goretti's martyrdom, which, all things considered, is little more than a common news item: "Murdered by a Farmhand Whose Advances She Had Rejected!" From this point of view, I would consider *Heaven over the Marshes* the first theological film to assert, through the very nature of its characters, story, and events, the total transcendence of grace, which occurs at the expense of apologetics, of Christian propaganda that likes to suppose that sainthood is conferred a priori on saintly lives. Hence the embarassed reaction of Catholic circles to this film.

There is also a third category of religious movie, built upon a principle that perhaps represents an advance on Stations-of-the-Cross films and hagiographies. I'm talking here about the priest's or nun's story. I have to check this point, but I think we owe the international vulgarization of this type of film to America. The Catholic minority in Hollywood, whose influence is great, found in the cinema a remarkable tool of propaganda. The myth of the "cool" priest who loves sports and jazz easily overshadows the austere reality of the Protestant pastor with a large family. Bing Crosby in a cassock turned out to be irresistible (in *Going My Way* [1944; dir. Leo McCarey] and *The Bells of St. Mary's* [1945; dir. Leo McCarey]). I myself preferred Spencer Tracy in *Boys' Town* (1938; dir. Norman Taurog) and the ex-gangster priest (Pat O'Brien) in *Angels with Dirty Faces* (1938; dir. Michael Curtiz): Hollywood decadence! The same trend has not taken hold in France, where we have suppressed the typically Gallic tradition of the ribald monk and the red-nosed priest. Thank God, our cinema has remained relatively free of this new trend, and even if we have had to put up with *My Priest among the Rich* (1952; dir. Henri Diamant-Berger) and *Clochemerle* (a.k.a. *The Scandals of Clochemerle*, 1947; dir. Pierre Chenal), at least we have done so with an embarrassed smile. For its part, Tino Rossi's Sunday calling in *Fevers* (1941; dir. Jean Delannoy) must be considered a mere episode.[6] But let's get back to serious films.

The first one is relatively recent: *Angels of the Streets* (1943; dir. Robert Bresson), written by Robert Bresson, Jean Giraudoux, and Father Brückberger. In it, for the first time in the cinema, the problems of the spiritual life are described, if not in indisputable terms, then in any case in their intellectual, moral, and social ramifications. We are entitled to think that Robert Bresson's art in the forthcoming *Diary of a Country Priest* (1951) will be no less rigorous.[7] Here again, as in *Heaven over the Marshes*, there can be no question that what we are witnessing is greater sophistication in the treatment of religious themes. But in the three varieties of films that we have just examined, these themes are explicit and visible, since their protagonists are obviously martyrs, saints, priests, or monks. Although the artistic conscience of the filmmaker may have managed to interiorize the drama or lift it to an authentic religious level, it still rested on a glamorous myth, which is to say an extrinsic one for the most part: the wonder of sainthood or the mystery of priesthood. It's almost a filmmaker's trick: to give human dimensions—moral and psychological ones—to protagonists whose glamor in the eyes of the public derives precisely from their *difference* from common mortals.

Almost none of this holds for a film like *The Pastoral Symphony* (1946; dir. Jean Delannoy), in which the conflict is primarily moral and owes its intensity solely to the will of the protagonists. This is not to say that the movie has no religious significance, but only that this significance does not imply any a priori ideas, not even the idea of God; the only thing implied is *faith* in God. The protagonists are answerable to nobody but themselves; their damnation, like their salvation, is internal. Faith is the operative mechanism in the trap that the pastor sets for himself; it is the moral alibi for his sin. One may say that this complete interiorization of the religious problem was dictated by the Protestant nature of the subject, whose adaptors (Jean Aurenche and Pierre Bost, from the novella by André Gide) and director, incidentally, had the same (Catholic) education as Gide. And one can talk at length about a "Protestant cinema" in connection with Roger Leenhardt's *The Last Vacation* (1948). The term is appropriate, but it could very well be that the filmic Protestantism of Aurenche, Bost, and Delannoy was the best vehicle for a Catholic novelist in the cinema.

The history of religous themes on the screen sufficiently reveals the temptations one must resist in order to meet simultaneously the requirements of cinematic art and of truly religious experience. Everything that is exterior, ornamental, liturgical, sacramental, hagiographic, and miraculous in the everyday observance, doctrine, and practice of Catholicism does indeed show specific affinities with the cinema considered as a formidable iconography, but these affinities, which have made for the success of countless films, are also the source of the religious insignificance of most of them. Almost everything that is good in this domain was created not by the exploitation of these patent affinities, but rather by working against them: by the psychological and moral deepening of the religious factor as well as by the renunciation of the physical representation of the supernatural and of grace.[8] As for "mysteries," the cinema has been able to evoke only those of Paris and New York. We're still waiting for it to deal with those of the Middle Ages. To make a long story short, it seems that, although the Protestant sensibility is not indispensable to the making of a good Catholic film, it can nevertheless be a real advantage. And I see the evidence for this in the film based on Henri Queffélec's novel: *God Needs Men* (a.k.a. *Isle of Sinners, Island Priest,* 1950; dir. Jean Delannoy, wr. Jean Aurenche and Pierre Bost).

What was already present in Queffélec's novel, and was fully retained by the filmmakers, is first and foremost the absolutely *natural* character of events. This story is thus no less interesting to a non-believer than to a believer. It takes place century ago on the island of Sein, a rugged and barren tract off the Brittany coast upon which lives a small community of fishermen and pillagers of shipwrecks. Their way of life and their mentality are so primitive that they have caused the parish priest, a native of the mainland, to flee. But now that the priest is gone, this community, which the diocese considers a parish of savages and heathens, feels a strange emptiness; it can't go on without a priest, with an empty church. In the absence of a real priest, the former sacristan takes care of the candles, cleans the church, and makes the people say their prayers on Sunday morning. One day he even speaks to them, and to everybody's surprise, including his own, what he says is precisely what the parish priest had never been able to say. His moral authority begins to increase. Of course, he doesn't lose his head: he knows full well that he is not a priest, that he does not have the rights of a priest, except perhaps those that a layman may assume in order to save what he can of the souls of the parish. But little by little, the community pressures him to such an extent that he must identify with his function. He is not allowed to pardon sins, but should he refuse to hear the confession of a dying woman or of a murderer? He will hear

God Needs Men (1950), dir. Jean Delannoy. Museum of Modern Art, New York.

their confessions, if only to alleviate the suffering of such people or to save them from despair. And since he has heard them, since he is capable of keeping a secret that nobody will understand better than he, why should he refuse to give them absolution? The penitent would feel himself cleansed of his sin more by him than by the Pope in person. The false priest struggles with his scrupulous conscience; he does not disregard what ordination means, the powers it confers and without which he remains a poor devil. But he also feels that the confidence placed in him is like an almost irresistible calling, and that, wretched creature though he may be, he is nonetheless not unworthy. To live up to this confidence, he is forced to conform his life more and more to the model of the priesthood: he gives up his job, calls off his marriage, and moves into the rectory. This asceticism makes him resemble even more what the community wants him to be; it seems that nothing distinguishes him from a priest anymore, from a *good priest*, from the parish priest that the diocese is incapable of sending to the island. After numerous crises of conscience, he gives in and agrees to say mass.

Meanwhile, the diocese becomes concerned over the strange things happening on the island and finally sends a new priest. He's an old man who comes accompanied by his prejudices and the state police; he is at once frightened and frightening. What he sees scandalizes him, and the islanders for their part reject him; they prefer their false priest to this stranger in a cassock. Only one man could save the situation. But that man, who has relentlessly fought against the temptation of equating himself with a priest and who has given in only reluctantly—at least that's how he defends his actions—that man is overcome by dizziness at the sacrifice that the new priest is demanding of him. Was everything he did completely meaningless, was it all a sham? It isn't pride that is growing in him, just common sense, the sense of his usefulness, of the work he has accomplished. Does the real priest, who has the power of turning bread into the Body of Christ, also have the power of making men better than they are, as he has? Here the film cuts itself a bit short and definitely betrays the book in the process. After a spectacular manifestation of the false priest's independence (a "burial" at sea), the schism is avoided and all the islanders go to the real mass said by the real priest.

One can see in this theological happy ending a craftiness whose intent is not particularly pure. I fear that our Protestant filmmakers have let their own apologetics show through here: *in cauda venenum*, or the sting is in the tail. In the novel, the bishop gives in—twice: first, by allowing the sacristan to enter the seminary. But the stubbornness of the islander and his age prevent him from absorbing this delayed education, and he cannot be ordained. He goes back to the island, wishing only for peace and to be able to return to his normal occupation as a fisherman. Then, for the second time, the community pressures him to such a degree that he is forced to commit the same sacrileges. The schism would no doubt have manifested itself this time had not the bishop resigned himself at long last to consecrating this strange vocation and ordaining the priest of the island of Sein. This final reconciliation of the Catholic hierarchy and the priestly sacrament with the Christian community may very well be an historical accident, like the regularization of a free state, but it is nevertheless far more meaningful than the capitulation imagined by the filmmakers, a capitulation that guarantees the rebelling islanders the best role and the audience's sympathy. The spectacle of an ending substituted by the filmmakers, and made possible by the addition of the new, legitimate priest, guarantees the audience's laughter; it superficially resolves the crisis, but it doesn't solve anything.

Although this ending is likely to reassure the Catholic viewer, it leaves the Protestant one feeling secretly victorious, even exalted, over its evasion of the real issue. Of course, I don't reproach Aurenche and Bost for their veiled Protestantism here, but I do reproach them for no longer playing fairly, for cheating on both the dramatic and the religious levels. However, I will grant them extenuating circumstances. Film being what it is, I'm not certain that the ending of the novel would have been possible on screen. First, because of the simple necessity of dramatic concentration, a concentration that the novel does not require. Second, and above all, because the structure of the film narrative is completely different from what it was in the book, in that it is a *tragic* structure. According to the logic of the action (which is not the same thing as the psychology of the characters or the religious tendencies of the filmmakers), I would say that this conflict is irresolvable; the irreducible nature of the contradiction is evaded by the happy ending, which has about as much meaning as the classical Hollywood "they got married and lived happily ever after." The novel can escape this happy ending and satisfy us through a denouement that is at the same time credible and orthodox, because it can tolerate protractedness, which tragedy refuses to do. Just when the spectator is counting on the healing effects of time and patience, or on the good offices of the king, the curtain falls.

The truly religious meaning of the book isn't affected as much as one might fear by this tendentious denouement. The story as we see it unfold on the screen, doesn't aim for a moment at resolving the question, but rather it poses the question in terms of a tragic dialectic, and Delannoy couldn't have given it a more pressing form. The religious meaning achieves a maximum rigor and efficiency here because it simultaneously respects the sociopsychological reality and the transcendence of the sacred. It is, let us say, an apologetics set in relief. Although the sacerdotal reality transcends the natural order, it nonetheless springs from a social and historical milieu. As long as the priest remains part of the community, we are more aware of his shortcomings than of the community's need for him. Thus only after the islanders have chased away their parish priest does their need for a priest become obvious. These primitive beings, pillagers of shipwrecks as others are smugglers, discover that they can't live without a priest. The sacrament is part of their social economy; it is necessary for the elimination of sin. Deprived of its religious organ, society poisons itself, its blood becomes tainted. In front of the empty tabernacle, this community of murderers and thieves discovers that it is irremediably Christian. Since no priest is given to them, they decide to create one, and the one they create obviously deserves the office: out of his mouth come the words of Truth and Life that the parish priest hadn't been able to utter. However, as not only the calling but also a kind of grace gradually asserts itself in him, the absence of the priestly sacrament makes itself felt. All his sacrifices, all the good that he does for his brothers, can't change anything. What he incurably lacks is made even more poignant by the fact that we can't see what ordination would add to his natural capacities; it seems that it would not even add grace, which appears to inhabit him already as a result of the function he fulfills.

Two scenes are particularly significant in this regard. The first is the one in which the roof of the church is damaged by the storm, and the rain drips drop after drop into the holy-water basin. How could we not see in this a sign of the Lord's distinct approval? The other concerns the hosts, which are made with a flatiron by the women of the village so that the false priest can say mass, and which the new priest throws onto the ground. They are indeed only small pieces of bread. But even the most irreligious viewer will gasp at the horror of this gesture and will understand the grievous fear of the sacristan, who attempts to tiptoe softly on his clogs so as not to dirty what could be the Body of Christ. The sacramental reality is made palpable here by its absence, as in the geometric theorems that one can prove only *ab absurdo*.[9]

Although the film has modified the book somewhat, it has by no means done so in order to reduce its religious significance. On the contrary, since the novelist was less subject to dramatic requirements, and since he was able to count on the reader more than the filmmaker could count on the viewer, the novelist seems to have insisted less on the clash of religious forces, on the forging of religous significance: his book was above all a sociopsychological novel in which a casual reader could have interested himself for its human and historical picturesqueness. This is not for a moment to suggest that the film is better than the novel; on the contrary, I think that the book had a discreetly accomplished style that the film betrays in the process of moving the center of gravity of the subject from open-ended religious narrative to closed-off *theological tragedy*. Without turning away from the natural, historical, social, and psychological data provided by the book, the screenwriter has altered their dialectics. For once, the change of titles conforms to the spirit of the adaptation: from *The Parish Priest of the Island of Sein* to *God Needs Men*, one goes from the particular to the general, from the moral to the theological.

Are you aware that *The Pastoral Symphony* is the biggest box-office success since the Liberation? Although predictions in these matters are unwise and uncertain, if one could place bets on movie hits, I would wager a lot on *God Needs Men*. At first glance, one might have thought that, in order for the adaptors to bring a unique and relatively austere book to the public, they would have had to "humanize" the subject.[10] They could, for example, have made a love story out of it: the elements were there, since the false priest renounces marriage. It is to their credit that they managed to avoid doing this—but we expected no less from Aurenche and Bost. What is more astonishing is that they were allowed to make *this* film. For it means that a truly religious problem interests the general audience more than a sentimental drama. Thus the adaptors demonstrated that, in dealing with a religious subject, it is possible to renounce not only the facile and traditional conflict between love and duty, between *eros* and *agape*, not only the pomp and splendor of history and liturgy, but also the moral wonders of hagiography.

Given the exceptional value of this film and its wide success, the reservations one might have about it could only be concerned with details. These details are significant enough, however, to leave us with a certain dissatisfaction. The adaptation has at least one regrettable weakness: the character of the actual priest. Here again, Aurenche and Bost have not played fairly. The revolt of the islanders, and even more so of the false priest, is too easily explained by the stupidity of the new priest. Moreover, the casting of Jean Brochard, which was more appropriate in the comic *Clochemerle*, was itself an act of heavy-handed anticlericalism. The scandal loses its theological rigor and becomes almost accidental. The real choice is not between a false but appealing priest and an authentic but repugnant and stupid one. It is between the two halves of the priesthood, between consecration by the community and consecration by the sacrament. For, although it is true that the sacristan is worthy of being a priest in the eyes of his brothers, he can't give them what even the most unworthy of defrocked priests could. But the best of priests wouldn't do for these people, who wouldn't recognize themselves in him. The highest religous achievement of this work is in its reminding us of an eminent Christian truth that the last few centuries of Catholic history have dangerously shunted aside, but that the experience of the missionaries is bringing back to the forefront: namely, the communal origin of the priesthood. This "heathen" island, by defending its false priest, is perhaps not making any less Christian a statement than the Catholic hierarchy that becomes indignant at their sacrilege. The truth that the islanders are unconsciously promoting is, as it were, the complementary opposite of the truth to which the miserable priest of *The Power and the Glory* bears subjugated witness. Thus it is absurd that the viewer should be made to side with the sympathetic sacristan against the foolish priest: the tragedy lies precisely in the impossibility of choosing, in the inevitability of the scandal, which would be the same if the diocese had sent a "good" priest.

Moreover, the quality of the *mise en scène* is not quite sufficient to meet its objective. Material circumstances beyond Delannoy's control probably forced him to shoot most of the film in a studio; few scenes were shot in Brittany, and the physical landscape therefore plays only a secondary role. It would indeed be rather easy to adapt the film as it exists to the stage. This lack of a natural setting for the action could have been a major weakness, but Aurenche and Bost's adaptation makes us almost forget the artificiality of Delannoy's means. This moral and metaphysical drama barely needs the excuse of human geography to justify its existence. This is a bit of cleverness on the part of the screenwriters, but it is not a cinematic virtue, for, from a strictly cinematic point of view, it is better to make fatality tangible through things rather than through actors, and Delannoy succeeded remarkably in doing this with the snow in *The Pastoral Symphony*. The sea does not play nearly the same role here.

The acting—except for Brochard, who, as I have noted, is miscast—is astonishing in every respect. Pierre Fresnay, whom we admired so much in *Monsieur Vincent*, seems to me to be far superior here. The character of Vincent de Paul was relatively easy to play for such a skillful character actor. By contrast, the elemental protagonist of *God Needs Men*, who struggles against events that go beyond him but who nevertheless manages to cope, required a flawless mastery of simplicity. Almost by a miracle, Fresnay's aristocratic and slightly Southern accent becomes here a rugged tongue, a kind of barking of the soul.

NOTES TO CHAPTER 5

Cinema and Theology

This essay was first published in French in *Esprit*, 19 (Feb. 1951), pp. 237–45.

1. Editor's note: For example, in America: *The Passion Play* (1898; Edison Studios), *Ben Hur* (1907; dir. Sidney Olcott), *The Life of Moses* (1909; dir. J. Stuart Blackton), and *From the Manger to the Cross* (1912; dir. Sidney Olcott). In France: *Quo Vadis?* (1901; dir. Ferdinand Zecca), *La Passion* (1903; dir. Ferdinand Zecca and Lucien Nouguet),

La Vie du Christ (1906; dir. Alice Guy-Blaché), and *Mater Dolorosa* (1910; dir. Louis Feuillade).

2. Editor's note: For example, in Italy: *Quo Vadis?* (1913; dir. Enrico Guazzoni) and *Fabiola* (1917; dir. Enrico Guazzoni). In Hollywood: *The Ten Commandments* (1923; dir. Cecil B. DeMille), *Ben Hur* (1926; dir. Fred Niblo), *The King of Kings* (1927; dir. Cecil B. DeMille), and *The Sign of the Cross* (1932; dir. Cecil B. DeMille). In America subsequent to the publication of Bazin's essay: *Ben Hur* (1959; dir. William Wyler), *King of Kings* (1961; dir. Nicholas Ray), *The Greatest Story Ever Told* (1965; dir. George Stevens), and *The Last Temptation of Christ* (1988; dir. Martin Scorsese).

3. Editor's note: Famous museum of wax figures in Paris—the Parisian equivalent of the waxworks exhibitions of Madame Tussaud (1760–1850) in London.

4. Editor's note: Saint Thérèse of Lisieux was a French Carmelite nun (1873–1897), born Thérèse Martin, whose saint's day is October 3rd; she was canonized in 1925. Films: *Therese* (1916; dir. Victor Sjöström) and *Thérèse Martin* (1938; dir. de Canonge); recently: *Thérèse* (1986; dir. Alain Cavalier).

   Saint Bernadette Soubirous (1844–1879) was a peasant girl who had a vision of the Virgin Mary at what has become the shrine of Lourdes. Films: *The Song of Bernadette* (1943; dir. Henry King); more recently: *Bernadette of Lourdes* (*Il suffit d'aimer*; 1960; dir. Robert Darène) and *Bernadette* (1988; dir. Jean Delannoy). See note 4, p. 209.

5. Editor's note: Script co-written by Jean Anouilh. Saint Vincent de Paul was a French priest (1580?-1660) who founded charitable orders; his saint's day is July 19th.

6. Editor's note: Tino Rossi (1907–1983), popular (Corsican) tenor of French radio, operattas, music halls, and films.

7. Editor's note: See *"Le Journal d'un curé de campagne* and the Stylistics of Robert Bresson," pp. 125–43 in Hugh Gray, trans., *What Is Cinema?*, vol. 1, by André Bazin (Berkeley: Univ. of California Press, 1967).

8. Bazin's note: Except, of course, for films whose supernatural quality is both pervasive and authentically religious, like *The Green Pastures* (1936; dir. William Keighley and Marc Connelly) and *The Road to Heaven* (1942; dir. Alf Sjöberg).

9. Bazin's note: It is perhaps worthwhile to recall here that the same Aurenche, in a script of *Diary of a Country Priest* that its author, Georges Bernanos, vehemently rejected (in the end, Bresson directed the film from his own screenplay), had introduced precisely this theme of the desecrated host, which was not present in the novel. One would be tempted to see in this an obsession on the part of the screenwriter.

10. Bazin's note: We must, of course, take into account what part publicity plays in the choice of a title. John Ford's *The Fugitive* (1947), based on Graham Greene's *The Power and the Glory* (1940), was released in France under the title *God is Dead*. The change of titles had absolutely no intrinsic justification here, as it did in the case of *God Needs Men*, but at any rate it demonstrated that, in France, God is commercial. An interesting comparison could be made between Greene's *book* and Delannoy's film, which is, as it were, its negative instance.

CHAPTER 6

T he Life and Death of Superimposition

The opposition that some like to see between a cinema inclined toward the almost documentary representation of reality and a cinema inclined, through reliance on technique, toward escape from reality into fantasy and the world of dreams, is essentially forced. Méliès's *Trip to the Moon* (1902) did not negate Lumière's *Arrival of a Train at the Station* (1895). The one is inconceivable without the other. The cries of horror of the crowd at Lumière's genuine locomotive coming toward them prefigured the exclamations of wonder of the spectators at the Robert Houdin Theater.[1] The fantastic in the cinema is possible only because of the irresistible realism of the photographic image. It is the image that can bring us face to face with the unreal, that can introduce the unreal into the world of the visible.

It is easy enough to give the counter-proof of this proposition. To imagine, for example, *The Invisible Man* (1933; dir. James Whale) as an animated film is to understand immediately that it would lose all interest. What in fact appeals to the audience about the fantastic in the cinema is its realism—I mean, the contradiction between the irrefutable objectivity of the photographic image and the unbelievable nature of the events that it depicts. It is not by chance that the first to comprehend the artistic potential of film was Georges Méliès, a magician.

Three American films released in France right after the war reveal, however, the relativity of realism and the conditional believability of special effects. I'm referring to *Here Comes Mr. Jordan* (1941; dir. Alexander Hall), *Tom, Dick and Harry* (1941; dir. Garson Kanin), and *Our Town* (1940; dir. Sam Wood). None of these films presents us with spectacular special effects of the kind found in the classics of the science-fiction genre. It seems that Hollywood is giving up on traditional special effects in favor of creating the supernatural in a more purely psychological manner, as in *Here Comes Mr. Jordan*, where it is left almost entirely up to the audience to interpret the image on the basis of the action alone, as would be the case in the theater. For example, three characters are on the screen, one of whom is a ghost visible to only one of the other two. The viewer must keep his eye on the relations among these three characters—relations that never depend for their existence on the plasticity of the image.

From Méliès's *Les Hallucinations du Baron de Münchhausen* (1911) to Marcel L'Herbier's *La Nuit fantastique* (1942), the dream remains the epitome of the fantastic in film. Its recognized form has always included slow motion and superimposition (sometimes shots in negative, too). In *Tom, Dick and Harry*, Garson Kanin preferred to use accelerated motion to indicate when Ginger Rogers was daydreaming; he also distorts the appearance of certain characters by means of an optical effect that recalls the distorting mirrors of the Grévin Museum.[2] But above all, he built the drama of the dream sequences according to the tenets of modern psychology.

In reality, the devices that have been in use since Méliès to denote dreams are pure conventions. We take them for granted just as much as do the patrons of outdoor screenings at traveling fairs. Slow motion and superimposition have never existed in our nightmares, however. Superimposition on the screen signals: "Attention: unreal world, imaginary characters"; it doesn't portray in any way what hallucinations or dreams are really like, or, for that matter, how a ghost would look. As far as slow motion is concerned, what it may actually signify is the difficulty we often have achieving our ends in dreams. But Freud has entered the picture and the Americans, who are fond of him, know that a dream is characterized far less by the formal quality of its images than by their dynamic sequence, their inner logic, in which the psychoanalyst recognizes the expression of repressed desires. Thus when Ginger Rogers, in *Tom, Dick and Harry*, tries to please her mother-in-law to be by incongruously caressing her face, she is performing an act that social etiquette would have forbidden but that perfectly expresses her will. The comedy that fills Rogers' daydreams doesn't take away at all from the intelligence and the psychological realism of this film, which, in my opinion, outdistances by far many more pretentious films with their falsely aesthetic oneirism.

If a director wants all the same to employ special effects, he must use devices that are much more sophisticated and elaborate than the tricks handed down to us by Méliès. All he has to do, really, is find a technique that masks a small advance, but an advance that is nonetheless sufficient to render the usual special effects ineffective and therefore unacceptable.

Thus in *Our Town*, a young woman in a coma, dreaming she is dead, relives in her mind a number of moments from her life in which her ghost appears along with her. One scene takes place in the kitchen at breakfast between mother and daughter (the woman who is now "dead"); the latter, who is already supposed to be in the next world, tries in vain to reenter the event of which she used to be part but on which she can no longer have any influence. The ghost wears a white dress and appears in gauzy superimposition in the foreground of the set and the characters in the background. Up to this point, everything is normal. But when the ghost happens to walk around the table, we begin to feel strangely ill at ease: something abnormal is occurring and we can't quite figure it out. On closer inspection, we discover that our uneasiness resulted from the fact that this strange ghost was for the first time behaving like a real ghost, a ghost that is true to itself. This ghost is transparent to the objects and persons located behind it, but is apt to be hidden like you and me when there is something in front of it, and this ghost does not lose the power of walking in the most natural way through objects and people. Practice has shown that this little finishing touch to the properties of the occult makes traditional superimposition look like a very inadequate approximation of a ghost's appearance.

The Swedes made abundant use of superimposition in their heyday (the period of *The Phantom Carriage* [a.k.a. *Thy Soul Shall Bear Witness:*,1921; dir. Victor Sjöström]), when they were turning the fantastic into a national specialty. One might have thought that the process that had helped so many films to achieve the status of masterpiece, had once and for all gained its patent of nobility and credibility. In fact, though, we lacked points of comparison at the time for criticizing superimposition, and now America has rendered certain uses of it obsolete through the perfection of a process called "dunning."

Up until recently, it was easy enough just to superimpose two images, but they remained reciprocally transparent. Thanks to dunning, to certain improvements due in particular to the use of bipack film (two layers, one orthochromatic and one panchromatic, separated by a layer of red filter),[3] and to an important improvement in the synchronization of sound and image through the use of masking and counter-masking, it is now possible to obtain an opaque superimposition of the two images, or, as in *Our Town*, a one-way opacity for one of the two images, a device that is even more extraordinary. Thus the ghost in *Our Town* can be hidden by the objects in the foreground without ceasing to be transparent to the objects behind it.

If you think about it, such supernatural phenomena are essential to verisimilitude. There is no reason why a ghost should not occupy an exact place in space, nor why it should blend mindlessly into its surroundings. And the reciprocal transparency of superimposition doesn't permit us to say whether the ghost is behind or in front of the objects on which it is superimposed, or whether in fact the objects themselves become spectral to the degree that they share space with the ghost. This defiance of perspective and common sense becomes most annoying once we are aware of it. Superimposition can, in all logic, only suggest the fantastic in a conventional way; it lacks the ability actually to evoke the supernatural. The Swedish cinema probably couldn't get the same results from it today as twenty years ago. Its superimpositions wouldn't convince anybody anymore.

NOTES TO CHAPTER 6

The Life and Death of Superimposition

(All notes have been provided by the Editor.)

This essay first appeared in *Écran Français* in 1946, then was included in Volume 1 ("Ontologie et langage"), pp. 27–30, of *Qu'est-ce que le cinéma?* (Paris: Éditions du Cerf, 1958–62).

1. This was Méliès's own theater, named in honor of the renowned French magician, with whom he had been acquainted (and who also received a tribute from the American Erich Weiss, whose stage name became Houdini). Before he began making films and showing them at his tiny theater, Méliès used the space for fantastic sketches and magical acts, which he performed with the aid of trap doors, mirrors, invisible wires, and all the other trappings of stage illusion.

2. Famous museum of wax figures in Paris.

3. Bipack film is another name for integral tripack film, whose three-layer emulsion Bazin describes. Yet another name for this type of film is monopack—called this because the three layers of the emulsion are imposed on a single base material.

   The dunning process is a method for the combination of separately photographed foreground and background action. The foreground action is lighted with yellow light only in front of a uniform, strongly illuminated blue backing. Panchromatic negative film is used in the camera as the rear component of a bipack in which the front film is a positive yellow dye image of the background scene. This yellow dye image is exposed on the negative by the blue light from the backing areas, but the yellow light from the foreground passes through it and records an image of the foreground action at the same time.

CHAPTER 7

Will CinemaScope Save the Film Industry?

Everybody knows by now, even the average moviegoer, that Hollywood is trying to come to terms with one of the most severe economic crises in its history through the introduction of both 3-D, whose avant-garde stereoscopy has already been seen on French screens, and CinemaScope, whose big war machine, *The Robe* (1953; dir. Henry Koster), has already been shown in New York and is soon going to be exhibited in Europe.[1] Everybody knows, too, that Hollywood is forced to accept the risks of such an endeavor—which totally upsets the norms not only of production, but also of distribution—in view of the acute competition represented by television. At least everybody thinks he knows these things, for the details of the problem are not that simple. The aim of this article is precisely, then, to try to create some order out of all this.

Let's start with some interesting facts of a very general nature. First, we can observe that this time the crisis is not turning into chaos or panic. To be sure, great confusion still reigns, and one can see the "major companies" taking the most contradictory measures; each one has its own strategy—or claims it has, for it is very often the same strategy under a different name. While some big companies almost completely ceased production only a few months ago, one can see a minor company like Monogram double its annual schedule for the production of B-movies for normal screens. Clearly, the heyday of Hollywood is over. But, again, this confusion and decline have not become panic and hysteria, at least not yet. By investing totally in CinemaScope, Fox is not repeating Warner Brothers' gamble with the talkies. None of the American companies, in spite of a film-consumption crisis that has become worse and worse over the last five years, are yet on the verge of bankruptcy. They can probably all afford to indulge in a long period of Malthusianism[2] without being threatened with extinction. This means, of course, that the technical experiment[3] will be relatively controlled and that Hollywood will probably be able to draw some conclusions as soon as the moviegoing wind starts blowing one way or another.

The situation will probably be more serious for the unemployed technicians and actors. But it is not that alarming, and it won't get worse for at least a few months, because television needs a lot of small films that can be quickly made and in which there is work for many people. Some stars go over to television; others make the most of their forced holidays and come to Europe to act in a co-production over an eighteen-month period, thus avoiding the paying of income tax—which is well worth the corresponding loss of Hollywood salary. To cut a long story short, the situation could become very disquieting five or six months from now, but perhaps we will be able to see it more clearly then and work will resume, if at a different pace.

These remarks are not aimed at minimizing the importance of the crisis—on the contrary, since it would be impossible to do so in the face of the numerical figures that I'll give later—but only at defining its atmosphere and above all at underscoring that Hollywood is still in control. It is important to know this especially for those who naively believe in some huge crash, in Hollywood's sinking into an economic chaos from which Europeans could benefit. Hollywood won't cast its "three dice" like a desperate gambler. On the contrary, its operation will continue to be mounted with caution and firmness, and that operation will be massively supported by the various publicity departments. The reservations Hollywood has about responding to the challenge of television will be overcome thanks to the temporary financial advantages gained by the attractive transformation of movie screens, for example—thanks, that is, to all the assets of a powerful, conscious, and organized capitalism. Of course, this doesn't mean that all the obstacles—and we'll see that they are numerous—will be removed. But at least they will be dealt with, with maximum efficiency, in Europe as well as in America, and I don't really see how the American experiment could fail even if the old Continent resists the new developments. The film revolution will be universal or it won't take place at all. Whether we like it or not, Hollywood remains the magnetic pole of the film industry, at least as far as technical proficiency is concerned. We can particularly see it today: Cinerama, which is little more than Abel Gance's triple screen, and CinemaScope, which was invented twenty-five years ago by Professor Chrétien,[4] seem viable all of a sudden because of the interest that America has shown in them now that the moviemaking business is in decline.

Such a situation seems to lead to a pessimistic view of the notion of progress in film. I will no doubt have to clarify this aspect of the matter, but only after I've attempted to analyze its sociological and aesthetic aspects. Let's stick with the economic side of things for the moment, and let's briefly recall the causes and proportions of a crisis whose seriousness cannot be denied.

The immediate cause is the dramatic reduction of the number of moviegoers since the introduction of television. In the last five or six years, the American film industry has lost approximately half of its national audience; this has meant the closing down of five thousand movie theaters (all of France doesn't have that many) and will mean the bankruptcy in the near future of several thousand others. The simultaneity of the onset of the crisis and the rise of television naturally doesn't permit any doubt that television is indeed the principal factor in the crisis. Unfortunately, one cannot say that it is the only one. From various bits of evidence, one can conclude that the 20 million American TV sets have simply crystallized and accelerated a tendency in the moviegoing audience. Indeed, this tendency started to manifest itself even in areas where television had not yet been introduced, and it has continued to get worse and worse in the areas saturated with TV sets. Furthermore, we know that in various European countries, particularly France, where the number of television sets is still insignificant, a disturbing reduction in the number of moviegoers has been observed in the last few years. Everything, then, seems to indicate that a general, deep, and a priori weariness with the cinema on the part of the American public has found in television a visible means of manifesting itself. The viewer statistics are therefore all the more alarming, and they indicate that the hemorrhage cannot be checked through a mere cauterization—a CinemaScoping, as it were—of the wound made by television to the film industry.

By instinct—an instinct that is deep-rooted and that isn't without value, even from an aesthetic point of view, as we'll see later—Hollywood understood that the defense against television had to be of a *spectacular* nature. Let's not forget, at the same time, that the evolution of film (even in America) has been toward the interiorization of the *mise en scène* at the expense of spectacle. Moreover, the conditions of the market demanded such a reduction of spectacle as much as the laws of aesthetic evolution. The remaking of *The Birth of a Nation* (1915; dir. D. W. Griffith) with the latest cinematic technology would be unthinkable today because the film could no longer pay off (the success of *Gone with the Wind* [1939; dir. Victor Fleming] was miraculous, and the industry is careful not to try to repeat it). Today, Cecil B. DeMille's Biblical epics (e.g., *Samson and Delilah* [1949]) are made on ridiculously low budgets compared to his similar productions of thirty years ago (e.g., *The King of Kings* [1927]). Nowadays, we must go to Russia (and perhaps India) to find a film with an enormous crowd of walk-ons, or a movie that is produced regardless of cost. And yet . . . it is obvious that film owns a lasting superiority over television precisely because of its spectacular resources—indeed, only because of them. Lasting, because the television picture will in all probability remain limited in definition by the 625 scanning lines of the standard American set (just as the cinematographic film is limited by its 35 millimeters, a figure arbitrarily chosen by Edison). Whatever its other technical qualities (including color and 3-D, which will one day be available), the television picture will always retain its mediocre legibility. It will also remain a product essentially consumed in the family circle, and, as such, it will continue to be limited to a small screen. In any case, a big TV screen for collective viewing in movie theaters makes some sense only for live news programs; but the quality of the image of such "telecinema" would be very inferior to that of cinema itself. So it is logical that the counteroffensive of the film industry is being fought on its home turf, in the area of its only superiority: through a return to its potential for the spectacular.

To tell the truth, Hollywood has not chosen its strategy by deduction. Indeed, the impetus came from a New York film attraction (see note 4) whose success has taken on colossal and unforeseeable proportions: Cinerama. After two years of continuous running, seats still have to be booked six months in advance. You know what Cinerama is: the juxtaposition, on a huge, curved support, of three screens upon which three aspects of a single image are simultaneously projected. Abel Gance had done the same thing twenty-five years earlier in *Napoléon* (1927), and in addition had used every possible combination of images on the three screens in order to create sensational effects in the editing of space. This is also the principle behind panoramic photography. In any event, the effectiveness of the device is not to be measured in terms of its technical originality, for all those who have seen Cinerama agree that it is quite impressive.

But the increase in the use of Cinerama does not come without problems that are almost impossible to solve. This wide-screen process demands a theater of the appropriate size and shape, three projectors and three projection rooms, and last but not least a very delicate electronic synchronization of the three projectors. The result is not always perfect, even when all the conditions for Cinerama's use have otherwise been met. In the film industry, however, the fundamental question concerning technological developments remains the following: how are they going to complicate distribution? Thus a device such as Roux-color,[5] which is amazingly simple and cheap, does not stand a chance for the simple reason that it complicates the projection of the film. It will always be wiser and more profitable to invest millions of dollars in laboratories that perfect filmic processes than to provide the owners of movie theaters with flawed prints or prints that cannot be flawlessly projected.

Hence the enormous superiority of CinemaScope over Cinerama. Thanks to the anamorphosis of the image permitted by Professor Chrétien's lens, the triple picture of Cinerama finds itself laterally compressed to the dimensions of a standard film. A symmetrical lens then expands the image during projection. In fact, the image that is thus expanded is only about two and a half times the length of a conventional screen, but the experiment reveals that such a length—as opposed to that required for Cineramic projection—is absolutely sufficient for maximum effectiveness. Of course, CinemaScope is itself going to complicate rather seriously the issue of distribution. It is easy to comprehend that this wide-screen process demands an appropriate setting. The long and narrow movie theaters do not have a back wall that is wide enough for a CinemaScope screen. In France, for example, the number of theaters that *won't* have to be transformed is estimated only at 20 percent. Moreover, the CinemaScope equipment, temporarily monopolized by Fox, is rather expensive. Indeed, aside from the special projection lens, a special screen with high and uniform luminosity from all angles is necessary.

Consequently, these serious, if not insurmountable, difficulties have already become the pretext for the appearance of a surrogate CinemaScope, which crudely attempts to solve all problems. Today, for instance, one can see in Paris (and all the other capitals of Europe) a "panoramic screen," which is a rather strange kind of swindle. Its advantage is double: first, the size of the screen is variable within limits that make it adaptable to most normal movie theaters; second, and above all, it transforms any type of standard film into a "wide-screen" one. It is worth explaining through what wonderful geometrical sleight of hand the "panoramic screen" does this. It's a simple question of fractions: the conventional image is defined by its $4/3 \times 2$ proportions (I'm rounding off in order to simplify), i.e., $8/3$. But in every school, one learns that one can also multiply a fraction by dividing its denominator, which means that, instead of doubling the length of the image, I can *divide it into two lengthwise*: hence $8/3 = 4/1.5$. This half picture, projected with an appropriate lens, will cover an area of screen that is exactly identical with the area covered by CinemaScope, and the trick is done. I'm not joking: the very official, very serious, and oh-so-very wise "Technical Commission of the French Film Industry" recommends to all producers that from now on they make their films for potential projection on a panoramic screen, i.e., that they concentrate the "useful" part of the image in the central portion of the frame. The projector of the appropriately equipped movie theater will be fitted with a mask of the same proportions as the screen, and this mask will hide the "useless" part of the image. As things stand today, since not all films have been made to undergo this surgical operation, the framing is left to the initiative of the projectionist, who is supposed to choose between beheading the characters and cutting off their legs, according to his personal complexes. But already the most serious of filmmakers have come to compose their images in such a way that they can undergo, without too much damage, the removal of one sixth off the top and one sixth from the bottom. More stupid even than the catoblepas,[6] film is eating both its head and its tail, but only, of course, in order to grow larger.

What difference is there, then, between the wide screen and the standard, abbreviated one? Isn't the viewer's angle of vision the same? Perhaps, but here we must specify more what CinemaScope in fact is. The optics of cinema is defined not only by the proportions of the image, but also by what one can introduce into the frame. Unlike the eye, which has a single optical system, the camera has at its disposal a wide variety of lenses covering more or less unlimited angles. In the case of wide angles, the use of short focal lengths partly compensates for the narrowness of the screen. This system has its drawbacks, though, for the more one moves away from the physical properties of the eye, the more obvious are the distortions in perspective. The indisputable advantage of Professor Chrétien's Hypergonar[7] is its multiplication by two of the angle of its specially developed lens, without modifying the lens's other optical characteristics. What happens when the image is projected onto a wide screen, then, is not only that the viewer's angle of vision gets widened—an angle, moreover, that depends on where he is seated in the theater—but also that the depth of his perception of photographed reality is genuinely increased. By way of comparison, imagine that I have cut a flat rectangular window into a piece of cardboard, and that I have placed behind the frame thus defined a photograph that must come into contact with the cardboard. The angle formed by my eye and the sides of the picture varies with the distance at which I place the cardboard, but the image itself does not vary: it is still defined by the optical nature of this particular viewing. Let me now remove the photograph and consider as a "picture" what I see behind the "mask" of the cardboard. This time, whether I step back or get closer to the frame will indeed make a difference, for the true angle of vision really increases together with that of the triangle whose upper corner is my eye and whose base is the length of the "mask." It is this angle of view that matters first and foremost, before the one formed by the screen and my chair. In substituting for CinemaScope, the "panoramic screen" widens the latter angle only by making the picture shrink vertically. The true content of the image, then, is divided by two (relative to the conventional image as defined by its $4/3$ proportions) or by four, if we compare it with the CinemaScopic picture.

Thanks to this sad example of the "panoramic screen," one can see what purely commercial vicissitudes the evolution of film must undergo. This leads me to a meditation on what the notion of progress in film thereby becomes. Of course, in all the arts progress depends on the development of technique or technology. We know what the evolution of painting owes to the discovery of perspective, on the one hand, and to the invention of siccatives, on the other. However, one couldn't say that the history of harmony is totally dependent upon the history of musical instruments, and one well understands that, since the discovery of the grinding of powders in oil, the art of painting on an easel has evolved independently of any technical or technological innovation. Conversely, it is true that, at least roughly speaking, the evolution of architecture is determined almost completely by the materials used, or in any event by the hypothetical control one is able to achieve over them. Thus the

Romanesque and Gothic cathedrals are built with the same stones, but the architect of the latter has arranged them in a far more efficient way.

Must we therefore contrast the evolution of the so-called "abstract" arts, such as music or literature, with that of the so-called "concrete" arts, in which the materials are predominant? Probably not, for in both cases the aesthetician would discern a logic, a system of laws, inherent in each art form, and would define, at least a posteriori, the possible evolutions and involutions of that form. The quarrels among architects are not essentially different from those between traditionalist and twelve-tone musicians. In these fields, it is the mind that ultimately makes artistic decisions. Its decisions may later be altered or even misrepresented by the constraints of history, but the evolution of the art, even if it is thwarted, will still retain a theoretical integrity and a definable sense.

There are some who would say that this is not true for film as well. However, if we examine the history of cinema, we are permitted to doubt whether the artist's critical sensibility and will matter so little in its destiny. Certainly, film has had no shortage of creators, even creators of genius, who have contributed considerably to its progress: this is as irrefutable for the cinema as it is for the traditional arts. We need not be shocked by the fact that these filmic artists generally bowed to the demands of mass consumption. Such constraints also make for the greatness of film, and it has derived from them some excellent aesthetic benefits. Although these constraints are perhaps more numerous and heavy than anywhere else, essentially they still don't represent a condition peculiar to, and restrictive of, filmmaking. But normal aesthetic progress in the cinema is difficult, for this art form is at the mercy of technological disturbances that may interrupt its course for purely economic reasons. Thus silent film had reached an admirable point in its evolution when sound came along to challenge everything. It is obvious that not a single filmmaker had asked for this technological innovation, not even the ones whose personal style could only have benefited from it. The producers, and the producers alone, were responsible for the creation of this new attraction. In fact, talking pictures had already been possible for a number of years, and we would have had to wait several years more for the implementation of sound had the financial problems of Warner Brothers not prompted this studio to gamble everything on the new discovery. It is not at all absurd to imagine that, if the introduction of sound had been conducted in a slightly different way and had not been successful with the viewers, films would have remained silent. Indeed, it is always the initial response that determines the destiny of important changes in the processes of production and distribution. In 1927, Abel Gance made a film to be shown on a wide triple screen (*Napoléon*) and Claude Autant-Lara made another one with Chrétien's Hypergonar (*To Build a Fire*).[8] But the conditions under which these films were projected and the general industry context (attention was already focusing on the talkies) caused this potential revolution to fail at the time. The only difference today resides in the fact that a long and well-orchestrated publicity campaign, together with enormous financial reserves, may prime the commercial pump and determine the success of an endeavor that had failed twenty-five years earlier.

Conversely, a filmmaker couldn't possibly cause, through the sole power of his art, any kind of disturbance in the technological framework within which filmmaking is carried on. Of course, he can benefit tremendously from technological progress (the sensitivity of emulsions, the outfitting of the studios, etc.), but he never determines it. Let's go one step farther. Not only do the external or technological conditions of filmmaking exclude the filmmaker, but also the destiny of cinema as an art form does as well. No doubt, what fundamentally distinguishes the mechanical arts that have appeared since the nineteenth century from the traditional arts is the mortality of the former. The danger that television represents for the film industry is not at all like the threat that film has presented to the theater. Although, at the very worst, a reduction in the number of theatergoers might force the theater to switch either to more unusual or more modest dramatic forms, the disappearance of theater as an art form is unthinkable: it will necessarily and eternally be reborn in children's games, in social liturgies, or simply in the need that some people have to playact in front of their peers, be it only in the catacombs. The traditional arts were born at the same time as man and will disappear only if he does. In this respect, film is not an art form, it is not the fulfillment of an eternal need or a newly created one (are there any radically new needs?); rather, it is the result of the happy conjunction between a virtual need and the technological-economic state of civilization. In other words, film is not an *art* AND *an industry*, but instead an *industrial art* that is likely to vanish into thin air as soon as the industry's profits disappear. So if tomorrow television robs the film industry of the portion of its audience that was still making it a profitable enterprise, producers will invest their capital elsewhere and the cinema will vanish from the scene as quickly as it came onto the scene. And nothing will persuade me to believe, in the spirit of futuristic optimism, that television will take over from an aesthetic point of view, just as film has taken over (at least partially) from the novel and the theater. For, aside from the fact that television is an industrial form in whose evolution aesthetic logic plays only a very small part, the art of television is probably much narrower than that of film. It is superior to film only in the field of documentary reportage. For the rest, television is a means of communication and expression that is irremediably cruder than the cinema.

One must also understand that, from a materialistic point of view, film and television are not at all narrative or dramatic art forms; only within a given fragment of their evolution has their aesthetic destiny taken precedence over their materialistic or commercial one. Viewed objectively, at least in a capitalistic economy, film and television are two facets of the entertainment business. The latter may be substituted for the former, not because it is superior to it as an art form, but simply because it is easier to consume. In this respect, television contributes to the death of the cinema in much the same way as do sporting spectacles or even card games like bridge—places where people never dreamed of finding the dialectic extension of the novel, as they once did in the case of film.

So, unlike the traditional arts, which can merely decline or suffer, film in principle is mortal. And it's better to know from the start if one truly cares about its continued existence. I myself have underlined the danger to film's survival only to reaffirm my faith in its future. Up to now, the threat to the cinema has concerned only Hollywood, although, of course, no one would think of taking any pleasure from that. Even if we did, Hollywood remains, in all senses of the word, the capital of world cinema. I won't go so far as to say that filmmaking would be crippled without Hollywood, but it *would* lack an essential gland whose secretions influence all the other glands. Nonetheless, film would survive and would probably end up by compensating for the loss of its American capital. Certainly television is going to develop in Europe as it did in America, but nothing proves that French, English, or Italian viewers will so passively fall under its sway as the Americans have. One conceivable strategy for the cinema's survival would be a greater differentiation on the part of producers between the market for cheap B-movies and the market for *reasonably cheap* quality movies. The former would continue to be made for, say, 50 percent of today's filmgoers, while the latter would be aimed at precisely that international fringe of the audience capable of escaping the grip of television in order to go and see a good film. In fact, there is a certain audience that goes to the theater and the movies alike solely on the basis of the quality of the play or film presented. To be sure, this group of people is relatively small, but, on an international scale, it may be big enough to ensure the financial viability of the films that we like, such as those of Renoir, Rossellini, Bresson, and De Sica. One may also hope that television will later help the film industry by playing the role of a distribution network, for whose products customers will have to pay and which will be a source of additional income, beyond the profits made by the movie theaters themselves.

More still: not only does the death of the film industry seem improbable to me, but also the attempt to solve its economic crisis through spectacular developments seems to point in the direction of substantial and desirable evolutionary progress. It is significant that this industrial art form, which is dependent upon economic factors, should have had its aesthetic progress ensured exclusively by technological developments. That is, if one can really speak about progress in the arts, for, in a way, it will always be absurd to think of da Vinci's work as superior to the art of the caveman. From this point of view, progress never depends on material technique or technology, or, more accurately, each technique has its own evolution whose peak is as high as that of the technique, or the technology, which replaces it. There does tend to be agreement, however, that from murals to oil painting one can indeed see progress, as one can from the epic to the novel or from melody to counterpoint. My purpose is not to defend this thesis, which I think the reader will easily accept if only he considers the opposite one. Refusing the evolution of technique or technology amounts to condemning the life of civilization itself, to refusing to be *modern*—i.e., to refusing to exist. It remains true that not all technical-technological developments are *ipso facto* evidence of progress: they must in the end be brought into harmony with the internal laws of the art form, with its specific physiology. Thus, conversely, modern art strives to return (even if through some very sophisticated techniques or technology) to fundamental or primitive laws that have been buried under the brush of a false, or falsely prized, historical evolution: see Lurçat[9] and tapestry, for example, or Le Corbusier and architecture.

So I won't say that sound, by itself and through the mere fact that it added one element to the picture, has meant progress for film. If this is indeed so, it is because film is not at all in essence an art form of exclusively visual images. It is paradoxically true that its initial infirmity, by forcing filmmakers to create a silent language, contributed to the evolution of an art form that, as early as 1925, had already reached a kind of classical stage; it is equally true that speech challenged that language of silence and caused the temporary regression of cinema. But these accidents do nothing to controvert the fact that the essence of film from the very start (one might even say as early as its seed took root in the inventors' imagination) has been a quest for the realism of the image. One could say that this realism is implied by the automatic genesis of the cinematographic image, and that it aims at giving this image the greatest number of characteristics in common with natural perception. The abstraction that is necessary to art must paradoxically emerge here from what is most concrete in the image. Every convention that film retains from drawing, painting, and photography (black and white, the absence of a third dimension, framing itself) contributes to its abstraction, if only temporarily. The worst mistake we could make, however, is to think that these "genes," by their very existence, are exquisite and fecund. One must temper such a belief, which is too general to be true. It would be equally naive to think that the filmic image tends toward total identification with the universe that it copies, through the successive addition of supplementary properties from that universe. Perception, on the part of the artist as well as the audience of art, is a synthesis—an artificial process—each of whose elements acts on all the others. And, for example, it is not true that color, in the way that we are able to reproduce it—as an addition to the image framed by the narrow window of the screen—is an aspect of pure realism. On the contrary, color brings with it a whole set of new conventions that, all things considered, may make film look more like painting than reality. The same holds true for stereoscopic relief, which does indeed give the impression that objects exist in space, but in a ghastly or impalpable state. The internal contradiction of this relief is that it creates the impression of an unreal, unapproachable world far more than does the flatness of black-and-white film. This is why one shouldn't count on a victory for stereoscopic relief in the war among the 3-D processes. Even if we forget about the inconvenience caused by the Polaroid glasses, the unreality of this universe, which seems strangely spun out of a hole on the screen, would be enough to condemn it—except in the genres where the aim is precisely a certain union of fantasy and reality, especially horror films. It is nevertheless possible that, with the advent of the wide screen, one of the major disadvantages of stereoscopic relief will disappear, and certain films, detective stories and musicals in particular, will be shot with this photographic process.

In any event, the real revolutionary innovation will very probably be the CinemaScopic screen, and from now on we must take account of it. Let me say right away that the equation of this screen with stereoscopic relief is incorrect and the result of overzealous publicity. It must also be said that, after a few yards, binocular vision plays only a secondary role in the perception of depth, and that the location of objects in space is the result of a series of factors which could as well be taken in by a one-eyed viewer. The closer the conditions of filmic vision get to natural vision, then, the more the dimension of depth will appear; and in this respect, the CinemaScopic screen helps in that it gives us, instead of today's narrow window, a widened surface whose angle formed with the viewer's eye is closer to the normal angle of vision. But the impression of depth and perspective cannot be manufactured in all CinemaScopic shots and, even when it is created, it remains rather partial. The genuine contribution of CinemaScope lies elsehere: in the elongated format of its screen.

Up to now, the only things I have seen in CinemaScope (in Paris or in Venice) are spectaculars, of either a documentary or a dramatic nature (*The Robe*, for example), all of which employed this new method of framing. Its effect is undoubtedly sensational, especially when combined with stereophonic sound, which is required on account of the huge dimensions of the screen. We can well understand why Clouzot is furious that he made *The Wages of Fear* (1953) before the appearance of CinemaScope, since the film would have benefited 100 percent from it. CinemaScope has an affinity as well with genres like the Western, whose signature framing is the long shot showing the landscape stretching to the horizon. The cavalry marches, the stagecoach chases, and the Indian wars will at last find on the wide screen the space where they belong. But one can make some very serious arguments against CinemaScope, despite its partial advantages. What film is going to gain from it in the spectacular genres, isn't it going to lose in the area of psychological complexity and, more generally, in the power of its intellectual expression, precisely the qualities on which the more sophisticated genres depend? Furthermore, what's going to become of the sacrosanct close-up, the keystone of film editing, through this bay window that is being substituted for the old, narrow one?

That's the operative word here: *editing*. Ever since the filmic work of Abel Gance and Sergei Eisenstein, on the one hand, and a famous critical article by André Malraux, on the other hand, it has undoubtedly become the alpha of cinematic language, the omega being framing, which plastically organizes the contents of the image. Well, we must once and for all get rid of this critical prejudice, which in any case has been shown to be untrue by a number of silent masterpieces, such as those of von Stroheim and Chaplin, in which editing plays only a secondary role. It is not true that cutting into shots and augmenting those shots with a whole range of optical effects are the necessary and fundamental elements of filmic expression, however subtle that expression might otherwise be. On the contrary, one can see that the evolution of film in the last fifteen years has tended toward the elimination of editing. Already before the war, we had Jean Renoir's great lesson on this subject.[10] And we have had lessons since then from *Citizen Kane* (1941; dir. Orson Welles) and from *The Best Years of Our Lives* (1946; dir. William Wyler), in which most of the shots are exactly as long as the scenes taking place in them. It is true that the framing alone can often create within the image a kind of virtual editing. But isn't this fact of composition itself about to disappear in that it is a plastic artifice foreign to the essence of the *mise en scène?* Bresson's *Diary of a Country Priest* (1951) owes very little to photographic composition, and I can see in it few optical effects that are not translatable into CinemaScope. But I do see the additional meaning that the opposition, or rather the place, of the priest in the landscape in some shots would gain from filming in CinemaScope. A motion picture like *The River* (1951; dir. Jean Renoir), of whose innovative beauty I have sung the praises in *Esprit*, could also only profit from presentation on a wide screen. I'm still waiting for someone to give me the title of a single film—at least in recent years, and one whose import is not aesthetically reactionary—that couldn't have been shot in CinemaScope. And I won't accept *Othello* (1952; dir. Orson Welles), whose purpose seems to me to be the final exhaustion of montage in a flurry of artifice.

In contrast to Welles's Shakespearean film, the wide screen will only hasten the adoption of that most modern of tendencies beloved in fine filmmaking: the stripping away of everything extrinsic to the quintessential meaning of the image, of all the expressionism of time and space. Film will thus grow even more apart from the abstractions of music and painting, and will get even nearer to its profound vocation, which is to show before it expresses, or, more accurately, to express through the evidence of the real. Put yet another way: the cinema's ultimate aim should be not so much to mean as to reveal.

NOTES TO CHAPTER 7

Will CinemaScope Save the Film Industry?

(All notes have been provided by the Editor.)

This article first appeared in the October–November issue of *Esprit*, 21, no. 207–208 (1953), pp. 672–683.

1. *The Robe* was the first film shot in CinemaScope; it opened at New York's Roxy Theater in September of 1953.

2. A reference to Thomas R. Malthus (1766–1834), the English economist who theorized that population tends to increase at a faster rate than its means of subsistence and that unless it is checked by moral restraint or by disease, famine, war, or other disaster, widespread poverty and degradation inevitably result.

3. With 3-D films as well as with CinemaScope, Cinerama, Panavision, and other wide-screen Processes.

4. **Cinerama.** A wide-screen process originally utilizing three cameras and three projectors to record and project a single image. The three 35-mm cameras were set up to record three aspects of a single image simultaneously: one camera facing directly ahead and the other two slightly to the right and left. When projected on a special huge screen, curved to an angle of about 165 degrees, at 26 frames per second, the images blended together to produce an illusion of vastness and plasticity. Three electronically syncronized projectors were used, the middle one projecting straight ahead and the other two projecting to the right and left in a crisscross arrangement.

   Developed by Fred Waller of Paramounts' special-effects department, the system was first introduced at New York's 1939 World's Fair as Vitarama, and at that time the process involved eleven projectors. In 1952 the improved and simplified process described above made its sensational public bow in New York with *This Is Cinerama*, a thrill-filled travelogue type of film, which features a roller-coster ride, a plane flight over the Grand Canyon, and several other spectacular scenes. Other episodic Cinerama films followed until 1962, when the first story feature in the process, *How the West Was Won*, was released. Although commercially successful, Cinerama left much to be desired technically. The three images did not always match properly, causing an irritatingly jarring effect where the three images joined. As a result, the three-lens system was abandoned and a single-lens, 70–mm process, similar to other current wide-screen processes except for its curved screen, was adopted.

   Multiple camera-projector systems date back to 1896, when the French inventor Raoul Grimoin-Sanson used ten projectors to show a panoramic picture on a huge circular screen. He called the process Cinerama. Director Abel Gance used a triple-panel screen to project his 1927 *Napoléon*. He called his system Polyvision. Following the exploitation of Cinerama, other processes were attempted, including Cinemiracle, Thrillerama, Wonderama, Disney's Circarama, Quadravision, and the technically inferior Soviet system, Kinopanorama.

   CinemaScope. Trade name copyrighted by Twentieth Century Fox for a wide-screen process based on an Anamorphic system developed by Professor Henri Chrétien. The system involves special lenses that compress and distort images during filmmaking and spread them out undistorted during projection, over an area wider than the normal motion picture screen. In theory, the anamorphic effect has been known since the 1860s. Several anamorphic processes have been patented since 1898. The most successful of these was developed and demonstrated by Chrétien late in the '20s. French director Claude Autant-Lara experimented with Chrétien's invention on several short documentaries, but it seemed to have no commercial value and was soon shelved. In the frantic search by Hollywood studios early in the '50s for wide-screen systems to counter the threat of television, Twentieth Century Fox took an option on Chrétien's invention and named it CinemaScope. *The Robe*'s commercial success led to the adoption of the system by other major studios and to the rise of rival anamorphic systems, including WarnerScope, TechniScope, PanaScope, and the versatile SuperScope and Panavision. The CinemaScope image, photographed on normal 35-mm film, is about two and a half times as wide as it is high when it is projected, an aspect ratio of 2.35:1, as compared with the conventional screen aspect ratio of 1.33:1. The aspect ratio for 70-mm CinemaScope is 2.2:1.

5. Named after Lucien Roux (1894–1956), who with his brother Armand invented this color process in 1931. It can be seen at work in Marcel Pagnol's *La belle Meunière* (*The Lovely Mistress of the Mill*, 1948).

6. An unknown, perhaps mythical, African quadraped that has been identified with the gnu.

7. The original name for the anamorphic lens systems developed by Henri Chrétien and later developed into CinemaScope by Twentieth Century Fox.

8. In 1927, Autant-Lara tackled a wide-screen experiment with the short *Construire un feu*, an avant-garde adaptation of a Jack London story.

9. Jean Lurçat (1892–1966) was a French painter who greatly contributed to reviving the art of tapestry.

10. Bazin could be referring here either to *La Grande Illusion* (1937) or *The Rules of the Game* (1939).

CHAPTER 8

The Cybernetics of André Cayatte

The real value of independent criticism does not lie in its imperviousness to expedient compromise, as the cliché would have it, because it's been ages since critics received bribes under their napkins at restaurants, and the most favorable review these days wouldn't even get you the virtue of a starlet in return. No, in truth, the critic needs to make very few efforts to be honest. Temptation lies elsewhere: in judging works on the basis of the merit of their *intentions,* the nobility of their *ambition,* or the stupidity of their detractors, whereas in the final analysis we should judge them solely on the basis of the aesthetic principles that they bring into play. Although I don't at all like having serious reservations about a body of work that is worthy in many respects and that has been created by an intelligent and courageous filmmaker, I must nonetheless somehow disavow the films of André Cayatte.

The *auteur* of *Before the Deluge* (1954) has introduced into French cinema a new kind of social film, which has imposed itself with such force that it has inspired numerous imitations in more or less attenuated or exaggerated form, as the case may be. There is no denying that *Justice Is Done* (1950) and *We Are All Murderers* (1952) have changed the course of French cinematic production and that we find echoes of them, for instance, in *The Slave* (1953; dir. Yves Ciampi), *The Healer* (1954; dir. Yves Ciampi), and *The Rage to the Body* (1954; dir. Ralph Habib), to mention only the most worthy films they have influenced. In the meantime, what we would call the *Adorable Creatures* (1952; dir. Christian-Jaque) syndrome has been developing as well, and it has been gaining in popularity over the last three years.[1]

Justice is Done (1950), dir. André Cayatte. La Cinématèque Royale, Brussels.

I understand very well the easy paradox in placing on the same level the "social courage" of André Cayatte and the amiable cynicism of Christian-Jaque and company, with the screenwriter Charles Spaak pulling the strings for both men. I refuse to place these directors on the same level, not only for moral reasons and because experience has sufficiently proved on whose side the risks were, but also, and most sincerely, in the interest of film. There is a lot to say against the artistic principle behind Cayatte's films, and I won't refrain from saying it later, but only after I have acknowledged the qualities of his work, which could too easily be ignored if I gave an a priori, restrictive definition of the art of directing. Form and content, art and morality, are not as dissociable here as the genre of Cayatte's socially conscious films seems to indicate. Although *Before the Deluge* has provoked much hatred and indignation, although it is still the target of extremely cunning maneuvers by the pharisees, it would be wrong to think that it owes such a response only to its social, moral, or political implications as such. These elicited many objections only because of the exceptional efficiency of the film's *mise en scène*.

This film moves the viewer, it shakes him, putting him in a state of violent and strange uneasiness. Indifference to it is impossible. That Buñuel liked *Before the Deluge*, although nothing in the film appears to lend itself to the secret meandering of dreams, is not that surprising. I don't think I am espousing the vision of surrealist critics if I defend Cayatte from this point of view, for it seems to me that here lies his strongest alibi. I mean that I discern in *Before the Deluge*, just as in *We Are All Murderers*, I don't know what sort of logical atrocity, cruelty through abstraction, or terrorism in the linking or intellectual clarity of the facts, all of which give the work the traumatizing characteristics of a nightmare whose particulars we try to make fade away through the blinking of our eyes. Cayatte has transposed judicial rhetoric to filmic images under the guise of realism. But, as we shall see, facts, people, and events are not ideas. By presenting them as such, Cayatte distorts reality, substituting for it an exclusively logical universe peopled with beings made in our image, but who are also radically different from us because they are deprived of any ambiguity; this universe is irrefutable, however, because its physical evidence conceals a logical organization by which the viewer's mind is trapped without hope of escape.

In this respect, *Before the Deluge* is superior to *We Are All Murderers*. The latter film certainly was convincing; one left the movie theater horrified yet persuaded of the absurd monstrosity of the death penalty. And in its certainty, the viewer's shaken conscience ultimately found a kind of rest. But *Before the Deluge* doesn't even offer us this sort of refuge. Its logic is as open as the thread of an endless screw. If these adolescents are innocent, then their parents are guilty. Each of them embodies a different method of childrearing together with a maximum of paternal or maternal benevolence, which itself varies from social type to social type. It follows that their guilt is not only unconscious but also contradictory, because to be a parent means that one is always guilty. The force of this film, which is out to prove something, is that it doesn't prove anything at all. It ultimately abandons us in the hell of its logic, where we are terrified by the prospects it still leaves open.

My argument is perhaps a little paradoxical; I admit that I am pushing it a little too far. *Before the Deluge* is not a monument to logical delirium, but I think I'm right when I look for its true cinematic qualities in a certain representation of judicial rhetoric. This representation is artificial, and its indisputable efficiency derives from the uneasiness we are made to feel by the internal contradiction between the logic of its discourse and the illegitimacy of its concrete realization.

I guess that André Cayatte doesn't care much about being defended in such a way. I don't want him to think, however, that I'm making fun of him, or that I'm giving ground to the detractors of his film (I mean those who dismiss it for moral reasons), first because these detractors—representatives from the M.R.P.[2] or the mayor's office—wouldn't understand my reasoning in the least, but above all because I believe in the value of his films, even after what I have just said. The arguments of these films, like all arguments, are not indisputable, but their purely intellectual cogency is less important for my purposes than the efficiency of their cinematic form. Cayatte creates a shock in the narcotized mass of people whose sensitivity has otherwise been numbed by the popular cinema, a shock whose novelty alone would already deserve our consideration. In between the narrative (purely dramatic or novelistic) film and the propaganda film (in the good sense of the word, let's say in the style of *Potemkin* [1925; dir. Sergei Eisenstein]), which are both based on the identification of the viewer with the hero (in the two senses of the word)—that is to say, on the viewer's intellectual passivity—Cayatte introduces a rather new cinematic phenomenon. He justifies his movie on the grounds that it triggers the mechanisms of reasoning in the viewer. His are not simply films with ideas, or with a thesis (these wouldn't be new): they are instead a rather paradoxical endeavor in which the usual psychological mechanisms of film boomerang in a way, hurling themselves back toward the viewer only to set, little by little, his rational faculty in motion in synchronization with the script and the *mise en scène*.

Eisenstein used images and montage to provoke an emotional response, and he used emotion to make the viewer accept his ideas. After seeing his films, one is indeed enthusiastic and convinced, i.e., in a state completely different from the intellectual anxiety in which Cayatte leaves us. At the end of a traditional film, we feel vaguely inhabited for a more or less long time by the characters: the universe of the film is in us or we are in it; this is a state of mind and emotion that is at the same time passive and passionate. After seeing *Before the Deluge*, even the dumbest of viewers has become by force, if not more intelligent, then at least more logical. Once the film has launched in each of its viewers the ship of reason, however, the movement of its intellectual mass progressively subsides, although it continues for a while to chart its course in the waters of our mind. I don't see any reason why such a result cannot be considered one of the effects of art. To be sure, Cayatte's *mise en scène* has only a few of the qualities that we generally appreciate: it lacks feeling (how could it be otherwise?) and sometimes taste, and the actors are seldom well directed. But it must have qualities, among which I would number force and clarity—without them, how could the film achieve such an efficiency? One can also infer his films' qualities from the fact that Cayatte's imitators are always far less convincing than he is, even though they are sometimes more skillful.

And yet I must in a way expose this kind of filmmaking (at the same time I defend it against the majority of its enemies) because of the misconception it introduces into the filmic spectacle. Cayatte has invented a genre, but it is a false genre or, more accurately, an equivocal one that betrays at once the realism of cinema and its powers of abstraction, which are dialectically connected. I know what Cayatte is going to say in his own defense, and I'm not insensitive to the surprise and sadness he may feel when he sees that I'm not totally on his side. I'm surprised myself: in fact, I had for a while mistaken the heat of my indignation at the stupidity or the hypocrisy of his enemies for aesthetic approval of his film. On second thought, and after a second viewing of the film, I don't approve anymore. And I have to admit to André Cayatte that his arguments only confirm my reservations.

Let me refute his most immediate one first. In Cannes, Cayatte and Spaak did their best to refute a typical criticism, according to which *Before the Deluge* is a "film with a thesis" and "the work of a lawyer." "Of course," Cayatte said, "I used to be a lawyer, but more than anything else I used to be a journalist, and I was once even a locomotive engineer, so why wouldn't I also make locomotive engineer's films? But because *Justice Is Done* was about a trial, someone has determined once and for all that I am a maker of legalistic films, built like pleas and out to demonstrate a thesis." If you had your doubts whether Cayatte has remained a lawyer, it would be enough to listen to him defending his films to be convinced. But his plea has the same weakness as his film: its arguments are too convincing to be true. "I know," he said,

> where my mistake lies: I was wrong to seize on a trial as an excuse to tell a story. It was a convenient narrative device that enabled me to avoid repetition. Obsessed with my professional past, the critics have seen in it only another lawyer's plot. They have thought that my

intention was to acquit the children and to put the parents in front of an audience-as-jury. But I have removed the voice-over that came before the flashbacks and that could have suggested that I was putting somebody on trial, as a few people familiar with my work happened to think. Now there is simply a story a story that can't be identified in good faith with the trial that is used here only as a means to tell it.

I'm not the only one who saw the film in its new version and didn't think that these cuts were significant. But Cayatte believes, or pretends to believe, that his film looks like a trial only because of the trial it contains. Whether or not the movie explicitly accuses the parents is not the heart of the matter, however, for it is the taut nature or interlocking structure of the script at all moments of the action that is highly suspicious here. What characterizes *Before the Deluge*, as well as the two previous films (*Justice Is Done* and *We Are All Murderers*), despite the distinctions Cayatte wants to make, is that the characters and their actions are all completely driven by motivations that are individually clear as far as the movie's form goes, but socially determined where its content is concerned. People and their behavior are the product of a quadrilateral of forces whose longer side is the time period, the society, the environment, plus the historical circumstances, and whose shorter side is the kind of family upbringing they have had. So the parents themselves, who are the only physical embodiment of this upbringing, couldn't be anything other than the product of their era, their environment, and their own upbringing. And so on, *ad infinitum*, like the reproduction of identical images in a hall of mirrors. One is also reminded here of all those modern clocks with a glass case on the back as well as the front, so that the sight of the movement of the clock's components becomes even more important than the telling of the time. Despite Cayatte's subtle distinctions, the only difference I see among a "film with a thesis," like *Justice Is Done*, a "filmed thesis," like *We Are All Murderers*, and a "story," like *Before the Deluge*, is that somebody has removed the handles from the last clock. But the fact that it doesn't give us the time anymore does not change anything about the mechanism: its function is still to reduce reality to an intelligible and unmysterious organization, which is set in motion by the spring of logic and given a regular rhythm by the pendulum swinging back and forth between the pros and cons of the argument in question.

The argument that has puzzled me most in Cayatte's defense

(although he is ignoring it these days in his own defense of *Before the Deluge*) is that, since *We Are All Murderers* was a "filmed thesis," critics who advocate novelty and formal freedom of expression in film should be in favor of this movie's extension of traditional narrative methods. To be sure, in the past I accepted as my own Feyder's theory about the possibility of putting Descartes's *Discourse on Method* into filmic form. It is also true that Cayatte's films are absolutely Cartesian. But what's the point here? To reason in film? To come up with a series of abstract ideas based no longer on words but on the irrefutable replica of reality that we find in motion pictures? We know that this can be a legitimate and feasible goal, as it is the principle upon which numerous newsreels are based. I am not reproaching Cayatte for his ends in this regard, but rather for his deceptive means. By building a film like a story, he implicitly commits himself, in the viewer's behalf, to a respect for the laws of fictional reality. These characters exist and we must believe in them, just as we believe in our fellow man. Yet what distinguishes reality from abstraction, the event from the idea, the credible character from a mere psychological equation, is the portion of mystery and ambiguity therein that resists any attempt at analysis. The only true fiction hero is in a way more than what he is. But because of their intentions, Cayatte and Spaak need a very different reality, a reality "without rest" that is exactly divisible by its initial ideas, for which it is only the pretext. Once again, it is legitimate and even recommended to use realism on screen for the advancing of pure ideas, but only provided that one has first broken up reality and selected fragments therefrom. Take for instance a scene from the famous series *Why We Fight* showing newsreel footage of an Allied offensive moving from left to right—a scene that is joined to a voice-over text *signifying* a triumphant attack, whatever the real circumstance of the filming might have been.[3] The abstraction here lies in the editing and in the relationship between the pictures and the text. In other words, abstraction is legitimate in films only in the narrative modes that designate it as such. By claiming the innocence or guilelessness of his "story," Cayatte is condemning himself to an internal contradiction that is also, I must admit, the heart of his films' efficiency and, to a large extent, their paradoxical charm. In a time when critics love to make a criterion of filmic value out of the phenomenological description of objective, physical reality, André Cayatte gives us a judicial universe that is mechanical and peopled with automatons. We may now await the revolt of the robots.

The Cybernetics of André Cayatte

(All notes have been provided by the Editor.)

Bazin was writing in 1954 when he first published this article in *Cahiers de Cinéma*. It was later included in Volume 3 ("Cinéma et sociologie") of *Qu'est-ce que le cinéma?* (Paris: Éditions du Cerf, 1958–62), pp.169–76.

1. In *Adorable Creatures*, a Paris fashion executive remembers his past love affairs with four very lovely but very different women. This lightweight quartet of sex sketches, played with some class by Daniel Gélin, Danielle Darrieux, and several others, provided the naughtiness lacking in English and American products at the time. Yet Gélin still ends up with a "good" girl! The script was by Charles Spaak, who did the screenplays of Cayatte's *Justice is Done* and *We Are All Murderers*, in addition to writing films for Jacques Feyder, Jean Renoir, and Julien Duvivier.

2. A conservative political party at the time in France.

3. See Bazin's article on the *Why We Fight* series on pp. 187-192 of this volume.

PART TWO

BAZIN ON INDIVIDUAL FILMS

CHAPTER 9

Farrebique, or the Paradox of Realism

The extreme yet commendable bias of the supporters of *Farrebique* (1947), on the one hand, and the bad faith of Henri Janson and the few "anti-Farrebiquians" who took a polemical stance in the press, on the other, at bottom conceal a variety of intermediate opinions, which are far more measured for being expressed in private. Aside from two or three stupid judgments about the banality of *Farrebique*'s realism, everybody agrees on the exceptional quality of this film. People differ only in their estimation of the relative importance of some weaknesses in a work that is not absolutely perfect. One could reproach it, for instance, for partly betraying its documentary function, since it neglects the economic relations between the farm and the village. The "poetic" aspect of the film may also elicit diverse reactions. This aspect is to my thinking the most objectionable in the film, although certain of its elements, like the depiction of winter, work quite well. The same goes for the burial, which should undoubtedly be entered in the anthology of great screen burials. However, the directorial interpretations, the poetic transpositions that Georges Rouquier has made at several moments in the film, provoke my negative judgment—a judgment that the essential elements of the film escape. One must clearly distinguish in *Farrebique* between what pertains to the poet's personal sensibility (however more or less reliable his taste) and what pertains to the very essence of the work, to the initial and ultimate revelation of its profound originality. I hasten to add here that I consider Rouquier a poet and that the purely logical distinction that I'm making isn't aimed at minimizing everything that *Farrebique* owes to its creator's sensibility. I simply think it is important not to confuse arguably objectionable qualities with an objectively inarguable breakthrough from which the cinema can benefit in all its genres, not only the pastoral one.

One could almost say that the value of *Farrebique* is less aesthetic than moral. In order to bring this venture to a good conclusion, Rouquier needed more than the mere courage to undertake it: he had to use all his willpower in order to remain true to his initial intention. *Farrebique* is an ascetic enterprise whose purpose is to deprive reality of all that has nothing to do with it, especially the parasitism of art. More imagination and perseverance than one generally suspects were needed to discover the rules of the game and to stick to them without flinching. The risk was worthwhile, but some will say (or, alas, have already written!) that Rouquier really shouldn't have taken so much trouble if it was just to go back to the starting point. "For one-and-a-half hours I saw cows defecate, peasants eat, rain fall, mud stick to clogs...," M. Jean Fayard writes. According to M. Jean Fayard, events of so little significance are unworthy in themselves of appearing in a cinematic work. M. Jean Fayard thinks that it would be simpler just to go to the countryside or, generally speaking, that he needn't go to the movies to see things as they are.

Before responding to this criticism, I would like to observe that the cinema has never ceased to pretend that it shows us things as they are. "At the movies," says an old peasant woman in Jules Renard's *Diary* (*Journal,* 1887–1910),[1] "you always believe that what you see is real." Except for a few films in which the filmmakers have systematically tried to elude the realism of the scenery, the essence of the artistic efficacy of the cinema, even when set in a fantasy or fairy-tale world, has always been founded on material verisimilitude. The technical objectivity of photography finds its natural extension in the aesthetic objectivity of the cinema. It is for this reason that the history of set design, after the heresy of expressionism, has for the last thirty years been showing a consistent return to realism. Marcel Carné did not ask his designer, Alexander Trauner, to build a fantasy Barbès-Rochechouart subway station for *Gates of the Night* (1946); not one bar is missing from the gates of this metro. The role of the set designer in modern cinema is to imagine the set that would be the most credible within the framework of the screenplay. This set must of course contribute as much as possible to the drama, but above all it has to give maximum believability to the plot. Jean Gabin's bedroom in *Daybreak* (*Le Jour se lève,* 1939; dir. Marcel Carné) is thus the epitome of documentary precision in its representation of the dwelling of a working-class bachelor living in a suburb of Paris.

Farrebique (1947), dir. Georges Rouquier. La Cinémathèque
Royale, Brussels.

So let's not reproach *Farrebique* for its realism, or else we'd better address our reproaches to the entire film industry. If the "anti-Farrebiquians" now object that the realism of cinema in general achieves the status of art only insofar as it is artificial, calculated, constructed, and selected, not for itself but as one element of the work of art to which it contributes, then I would make another observation. Are my opponents so sure that this subordination to the aesthetic design (dramatic or otherwise) governing a work of art has not slowly altered our very sense of reality in the cinema? There is no lack of so- called realistic films about some insignificant event or other or some slice of life. There is no lack of peasant movies, either. Why is *Farrebique* labeled as the ugly duckling among them, then? In my opinion, this is due to Rouquier's genius, to his ability, if you will, to stand an egg on one end. He has understood that verisimilitude had slowly taken the place of truth, that reality had slowly dissolved into realism. So he painfully undertook to rediscover reality, to return it to the light of day, to retrieve it naked from the drowning pool of art.

Some people reproach *Farrebique* for its ugliness. The men and the women in it aren't very good-looking. This Rouergue[2] landscape is without grandeur. The houses are dirty and styleless. The village square, which we discover on a Sunday morning before and after mass, is depressingly commonplace. In France, we have plenty of villages whose historical and geographical picturesqueness would have provided an intrinsic beauty to justify the documentary interest in Rouquier's film. Henri Janson takes a moralistic and patriotic stance to deplore the image that *Farrebique* will give abroad of French peasant life: "They live like animals, without any hygiene. They express themselves in bad French." (Janson probably means dialect here.) But, clearly, Rouquier could not have brought his project to a successful end with material whose very beauty would have distorted in some way the chemical reaction of the camera. A beautiful landscape, a little Romanesque church, some entertaining folklore would have diverted us from nature, from the village itself, from the gathering of young men whose fun and games are limited to being half drunk on Sunday nights in some filthy barroom. Deprived of horror on the one hand and local color on the other, Rouquier's reality is situated in a neutral zone that minimally solicits our wonder or our pity. This reality is nothing but itself, the very kind of reality about which the artist has nothing to say. And yet, Rouquier has decided to focus his attention on it and it alone: his camera performs a mysterious and paradoxical photo-graphic operation at the end of which all we are left with is the con-sciousness of this reality.

At this point I must talk about the audience, which you'd think would be as bored with the film as M. Janson. I confess that, after two private screenings of *Farrebique*, I feared, despite all my admiration for the film, that the public would be bored. I even believe that Rouquier himself was not too sure that they wouldn't be bored. I had to see the film among viewers who were required to pay for their seats (and who were no mil-lionaires) to realize that, although it had no story and no star, this movie exhibited an almost demagogic charm, and that the audience was deeply attuned to the pleasure of simply *recognizing* things. We have seen the countryside a thousand times in the cinema, but in these instances it was used as a backdrop for the actors or as a pretext for displaying the skill of the cinematographer. The snow itself, when it wasn't made of boric acid, served exclusively as a pictorial or dramatic element (see *The Pastoral Symphony* [1946; dir. Jean Delannoy]), and the sheep wore around their necks the imaginary ribbons of the plot.[3] In *Farrebique*, by contrast, real-ity is never completely subordinate to the story or to art; indeed, it exists above all for itself. In the magnificent poem of winter, Rouquier's editing never elevates things to the level of abstract symbolism. (I have to say here that he is less successful in the spring sequence.) The frosted telegraph wires, the dog running in the snow, the ice in the rut cracked by the man's clog, are mere facts, no doubt trite and multiple, but not at all general: Rouquier preserves their total singularity.

Take for instance the fire in the hearth. There's no want of these in the cinema, and some have been better photographed than this one. In *It Happened at the Inn* (*Goupi-Mains-Rouges*, 1943; dir. Jacques Becker), the Emperor pokes the burning logs just like the grandfather in *Farrebique*. Only the grandfather's fire is a real fire, whose flames rise on their own and not on command from the special-effects man, which every one knows because the logs are still green and huff and puff as they bleed all their sap. Does anyone who sat around such fires in childhood dare deny that for the first time on screen he recognizes in this scene the peculiar and vast mystery of flames and wood? John Q. Public in any case is not to be fooled: he *recognizes* the mud puddle in the sunken lane that soils the shoes of the brother-in-law, who has come from the city on a little farm-holiday; he recognizes the aunt, the dealer in notions, the postal clerk in this little village in the center or southwest of France where his parents were born; he recognizes the fairground with its linden trees and its sparse, yellowish grass; he recognizes all the experiences he could have had if he had been born a peasant one or two generations earlier. He recognizes this slightly ridiculous and nostalgic world, which he vaguely feels he has somehow betrayed, the world of the land, of men and animals, which he dimly remembers from his childhood and from holidays past.

There is no story here, or very little, and there are no stars, no actors: only a reality that everyone, in the secrecy of his good or bad conscience, personally recognizes. "Look," shouted the first viewers of the Lumière cinematograph as they pointed at the leaves on the trees, "look, they're moving." The cinema has come a long way since the heroic days when crowds were satisfied with the rough rendition of a branch quivering in the wind! And yet, after fifty years of cinematic realism and tremendous technical advances, nothing less than a little bit of genius was needed to give back to the public the simple and elementary joy that the fictionalized and dramatized cinema was no longer providing: that of recognition.

This is why, in spite of its shortcomings, of a certain paradoxical aestheticism that is a little obsolete, a few slightly awkward moments in the narrative, and an uneven though undisputable poetic sense, I consider *Farrebique* a major achievement. It is one of the very few French films which, together with Malraux's *Man's Hope* (*Espoir*; 1939), has realized that the cinema is in bad need of a realistic revolution. This revolution just broke out in Italy, and the Italian filmmakers have done so much with it in less than two years that I fear their films may already constitute the classics of the neorealistic movement.

NOTES TO CHAPTER 9

Farrebique, *or the Paradox of Realism*

(All notes have been provided by the Editor.)

This article was first published in French in *Esprit*, 15, no.128 (1947), pp. 676–80.

1. Jules Renard (1864–1910) was a French writer of fiction and drama whose bitter, realistic attitude toward life found expression in terse, relentless studies of character and situation.

2. In the past, a country south of the Kingdom of France, annexed by King Henri IV in 1607; now the Département of Aveyron, with the capital city of Rodez.

3. This metaphor is an allusion to the seventeenth and eighteenth centuries when French aristocrats, especially the ladies, loved to "play peasant." They did so on miniature farms, where the animals were clean and the sheep wore ribbons.

CHAPTER 10

The Crisis of French Cinema, or *Scarface* and the Gangster Film

The films that have been released in the last two months are scarcely worth any attention. Since the question of quotas still has not been resolved,[1] American distributors simply content themselves with rereleasing old movies. Almost all new films are therefore French. Two years after the Liberation, the public paradoxically finds itself in a situation more or less similar to the one it experienced during the Occupation: a near cinematic monopoly. The partial elimination of the competition may have advantages—the quality of French production between 1940 and 1944 proves this—but only if it does not last too long and, even more important, if the film industry has the means to take advantage of this "intermission." Alas, our industry doesn't seem to have those means, since it can no longer do without either the importation of brand-new equipment or the exportation of its product, which is not financially viable when limited solely to its own national market. Your average twenty-million-franc film can no longer pay off on the French circuit. This explains why more and more films are being made under drastic money-saving conditions that are absolutely incompatible with minimum artistic standards; perhaps the few million that are thus being saved will help balance the producer's budget. The complexity and the seriousness of the problems that are today facing the French filmmaking industry require a specific and consistent policy that the proper authorities seem unable to conceive and implement. This is why the French cinema is slowly dying in studios that get their equipment from local flea markets, studios where some of the most qualified technicians in the world must hurry about playing the maddening role of Mr. Fix-it.

The delay that the publication rhythm of a journal imposes on me will perhaps explain why I won't talk this month about the half-dozen recently released films that could barely be called decent: I have little to add to what has already been written. Despite its dialogue, Henri Calef's *Jéricho* (1946) is doubtless the most respectable among the new crop. Georges Lacombe and his screenwriter Pierre Véry, for their part, have come close to success in *The Land without Stars* (1945), but in the end they have missed their mark. By contrast, the modesty of *Barbizon's Temptation* (1945; dir. Jean Stelli), its lack of pretentiousness, could serve as a sympathetic explanation for the pleasure it gives us. In any event, there's a good side to the re-release of American oldies: we get to see *The Green Pastures* (1936; dir. Marc Connelly and William Keighley) and *Scarface* (1932; dir. Howard Hawks) again. The latter has produced in me the only strong emotion of the last five or six weeks, so the reader will excuse me for elaborating on my rediscovery of this film. Its qualities emerge with extraordinary relief from a distance of fourteen years.

What's so remarkable about *Scarface* is that we realize today that it would be almost as superficial to consider it the epitome of gangster movies as to see in William Faulkner just another writer of gothic fiction. Everything that will later become the inevitable rhetoric of the genre is barely touched on by Howard Hawks in this film: it's all consciously rejected in favor of psychology and social realism. The siege of the gangster's hide-out and his capture by the police, for example, often provided the bravura finale of many a lesser film: in *Angels with Dirty Faces* (1938; dir. Michael Curtiz), the manhunt takes place in a skyscraper. In *Scarface*, everything begins as if an endless struggle with numerous reversals were going to take place, but the unfolding of the dramatic action almost immediately crosses over into the protagonist's psychology: the death of the gangster's sister makes him vulnerable and incapable of fighting. So he flees and, after knocking over a policeman, travels only three yards before being stopped by a hail of bullets from a submachine gun. Throughout the film, the authors systematically refuse to lean on the usual dramatic categories, preferring instead to trim the plot in order to concentrate all their attention on the characters. Scenes of violence are not slowly and suspensefully prepared for, nor are they ever lowered to the level of bloody set pieces; instead, they are simply inserted in the interstices left over between the sections of the narrative. Take, for instance, the execution of a rival gang in a garage: we are spared the details leading up to what became known as the St. Valentine's Day Massacre; the only thing that matters is the final episode in which the meaning of the action is encapsulated, and where the seven men are mowed down off-camera. This is why the film seems to be divided into brief scenes that are joined by purely emblematic links, as, for example, the tearing-off of calendar pages super-imposed upon the bursts of a submachine gun.

The kinship of such a technique with that of some American novels is obvious, as is the emphasis on the characters' psychology. I have already mentioned Faulkner, with whom comparison is impossible to avoid, even though it should not be exaggerated. George Raft's impassive blue eyes, his mannerisms, his boundless yet sickly strength, make him exist almost as intensely as the unforgettable Popeye in *Sanctuary*.[2] As for Paul Muni, he belongs to an aesthetic universe where the sympathy and antipathy required by melodrama no longer have any meaning. He is the way he is, fatally dangerous to himself, out of our judgment's reach. This is perhaps what makes *Scarface* so different from the traditional "gangster film," in which the action calls for the audience's reaction in favor or against the police, and which revives the old sociological motif of the captivating thief, whose most familiar attribute is the cunning that enables him to outfox the police.[3] The G-men in *Scarface* are only a technical element of the action: they are one of the forces with which Muni's frightening and naive will to power clashes. As in Faulkner, the impulses that drive such a puppet are at the same time totally perverse and absolutely irresistible. Money is seldom the root cause of this will to power, which more often than not is merely a childish vanity, an infantile and persistent longing (now that he has achieved the power he wants, Muni can at last change his shirt every day). It is an obsession that no force in the world could take away from him. Such a man is like the insect whose legs we must tear off if we want to remove him from the branch to which he is clinging.

If *Scarface* is the classic gangster film, there are two reasons why. First, because it sketched in the dramatic rhetoric of the genre, which other films have then developed. But this tradition of submachine gun bursts, bullet-riddled bodies, and screeching brakes is the one that's the least interesting, precisely because it had no trouble at all establishing itself and can now be found everywhere. Hawks himself, perhaps the most skilled craftsman in Hollywood, could have exploited this tradition much more fully had he wanted to. *Air Force* (1943; dir. Howard Hawks) showed us last year the extent of his cinematic eloquence when it comes to "action" scenes. But *Scarface* takes a different aesthetic direction, one that connects it with a particular vein in American fiction, the depths of which subsequent gang-ster films have hardly ever penetrated, even when they tried. Hence the second sense in which *Scarface* is the classic gangster film: it's practically one of a kind. The mobsters' violence and volatility are treated only as means to the end of establishing a special climate for the development of these human puppets with instinctive drives. Faulkner and Erskine Caldwell created a similar climate on their Southern plantations, and recently we have had the opportunity to see the same aesthetic design in Alfred Hitchcock's *Shadow of a Doubt* (1943). If the director hadn't in the end capitulated to the audience's moral sensitivity, this film would not have been unworthy of *Scarface*. One psychological theme in particular is developed in *Shadow of a Doubt*, as in *Scarface*, that of incest, with even the Faulknerian intensifying device in Hitchcock's film of giving the niece and her uncle the same first name. Psychoanalysis has truly become a Hollywood commonplace. *Blind Alley* (1939; dir. Charles Vidor), for instance, shows us a gangster who uses his submachine gun as a figurative means to kill his father. But this is nothing more than the cheap degeneration of a theme that American cinema has only seldom treated with the simultaneous daring and discretion found in *Scarface*.

One can see in its treatment of a theme like incest one of the limits the cinema imposes on itself, in contrast to the practice of the novel. What is astonishing is not that the American cinema so rarely enters the domain of modern fiction, but that it enters this domain at all. When one realizes the extent of censorship on the other side of the Atlantic, or even simply the extent of the public's self-censorship in the face of everything that disturbs its social and moral security, one really has to marvel when from time to time one encounters in the American cinema emotions of the kind and of the intensity we associate with American literature.

NOTES TO CHAPTER 10

The Crisis of French Cinema, or Scarface *and the Gangster Film*

(All notes have been provided by the Editor.)

This essay was first published in French in *Esprit*, 14, no.122 (1946), pp. 841–844.

1. A protectionist measure against new foreign movies imposed by the French government after World War II.

2. Raft played Guino Rinaldi, Tony (Scarface) Camonte's bodyguard and lifelong friend. Camonte was played by Paul Muni.

3. Bazin is referring here to Guignol, the winsome rogue of Punch-and-Judy shows who always manages to beat his nemesis, the *gendarme* (policeman), to a pulp.

CHAPTER 11

La Strada

The vitality of the Italian cinema is confirmed for us once again by this wonderful film of Federico Fellini's. And it is doubly comforting to declare that the rest of the critics have been nearly unanimous in singing the praises of *La Strada* (1954). Perhaps without this support, which hasn't hesitated to enlist snobbism on its side, the film would have had some difficulty in bringing itself to the attention of an inundated and undiscerning public.

Fellini has made one of those very rare films about which it can be said, one forgets that they are movies and accepts them simply as works of art. One remembers the discovery of *La Strada* as an aesthetic experience of great emotion, as an unanticipated encounter with the world of imagination. I mean that this is less a case of a film's having known how to attain a certain intellectual or moral level than of its having made a personal statement for which the cinema is most surely the necessary and natural form, but which statement nevertheless possesses a virtual artistic existence of its own. It is not a film that is called *La Strada*; it is *La Strada* that is called a film. In connection with this idea, Chaplin's last film also comes to mind, although in many ways it is quite different from *La Strada*. One could just as well say of *Limelight* (1952) that its only adequate embodiment was the cinema, that it was inconceivable through any other means of expression, and that, nonetheless, everything in it transcended the elements of a particular art form. Thus *La Strada* confirms in its own way the following critical premise: to wit, that the cinema has arrived at a stage in its evolution where the form itself no longer determines anything, where filmic language no longer calls attention to itself, but on the contrary suggests only as much as any stylistic device that an artist might employ. Doubtless it will be said that only the cinema could, for example, endow Zampanò's extraordinary motorcycle caravan with the significance of living myth that this simultaneously strange and commonplace object attains here. But one can just as clearly see that the film is in this case neither transforming nor interpreting anything for us. No lyricism of the image or of montage takes it upon itself to guide our perceptions; I will even say that the *mise en scène* does not attempt to do so— at least not the *mise en scène* from a technically cinematic point of view.[1] The screen restricts itself to showing us the caravan better and more objectively than could the painter or the novelist. I am not saying that the camera has photographed the caravan in a very plain manner—even the word "photographed" is too much here—but rather that the camera has simply *shown* the caravan to us, or even better, has enabled us to see it.

Surely it would be excessive to pretend that nothing can be created by virtue of cinematic language alone, of its abrasive intrusion on the real. Without even taking into account almost virgin territory such as color and the wide screen, one can say that the degree of relationship between technique and subject matter depends in part on the personality of the director. An Orson Welles, for instance, always creates by means of technique. But what one can say without question is that henceforth advances in the cinema will not necessarily be tied to the originality of the means of expression, to the formal composition of the image or of the images in relation to one another. More precisely, if there is a formal originality to *La Strada*, it consists in the film's always staying on this side of cinema. Nothing that Fellini shows us owes any supplementary meaning to the manner in which it is shown; nevertheless, what we see couldn't be seen anywhere but on the screen. It is in this way that the cinema achieves fruition as the art of the real. One knows, of course, that Fellini is a great director, but he is a great director who doesn't cheat on reality. If the camera doesn't *see* it, it isn't in his film. It wouldn't be in his film, in any case, if he hadn't first acknowledged the fullness of its being in the world.

In this sense *La Strada* doesn't depart at all from Italian neorealism. But there is a misunderstanding on this subject that requires clarification. *La Strada* has been received in Italy with some reservation by the critical guardians of neorealist orthodoxy. These critics are situated on the Left, which in France is called "Progressivist," although this term is misleading, since the Italian critics are both more Marxist and more independent than the French Progressivists. There are certainly Communist critics in

France as well, and some of them are cultivated, intelligent, and well-informed, but their point of reference seems to me to be only marginally that of Marxism. The tactics and the watchwords of the Party do play a clearer role in their writing, however, when the work of art in question draws its substance from the political arena, for then Party ideology takes over in spite of everything in the work that resists it. The criticism consequently does no more than render a good or bad judgment on the work according to whether its author's political views are "correct" or "incorrect." As for Progressivist criticism, it is either equivalent to the worst Communist criticism in slavishness and intellectual emptiness, or else it isn't Marxist and in that case has some scope.

In Italy, by contrast, it is Marxist criticism that occasionally gives evidence of a certain independence with regard to the interests of the Party, and without sacrificing the stringency of its aesthetic judgments. I am naturally thinking of the group around Chiarini and Aristarco at *Cinema Nuovo*.[2] In the last two years their criticism has, I dare say, rediscovered the concept of neorealism, which was held in so little regard at one time, and is attempting to define the term and give it an orientation. (Zavattini[3] is the figure whose work most conforms to neorealism's ideal, which conceives of a film, not as a fixed and tame reality, but as a work in progress, an inquiry that begins with certain givens and then proceeds in a particular direction.) I don't feel that I have the competence necessary to give a clear description of the evolution of neorealism as seen by these Marxist critics, but I also don't believe that I am distorting matters to call neorealism, as they define it, a substitute term for "socialist realism," the theoretical and practical sterility of which, unfortunately, no longer needs to be demonstrated. In fact, as far as one can trace it through the various tactical changes in the Party line on art that have occurred, socialist realism has never created anything very convincing in itself. In painting, where its influence is easy to determine because it stands in opposition to the whole course of modern art, we know that it hasn't produced any results. In literature and in cinema, the situation is confused, since we are dealing here with art forms from which realism has never been eliminated. But even if there are good films and good novels that don't contradict the precepts of socialist realism, it is still rather doubtful that these precepts had anything to do with the success of these works of art. On the other hand, one can well see the extent to which such precepts have eviscerated many other works.

The truth is that theories have never produced masterpieces and that creative outpourings have a deeper source in History and in men. Italy had the good fortune, like Russia around 1925, to find itself in a situation where cinematic genius began to flourish, and this genius was moving in the direction of social progress, of human liberation. It is natural and legitimate that the most conscientious among the creators and judges of this important movement are anxious today to keep it from falling apart; they would like neorealism to continue along the revolutionary path it set out on around 1945. And surely neorealism can, at least in the cinema, be a valuable substitute for socialist realism. The number of successful neorealist films and their oneness in diversity supply the Marxist aesthetician with food for productive thought, which is the way it should be. If the time comes, however, when such thought outstrips production itself, then neorealism will be in danger. Happily, we are not yet at that point. Nevertheless, I am worried about the intolerance that Marxist criticism is beginning to show toward those who dissent from, let us call it, socialist neorealism—namely, Rossellini and Fellini (who was Rossellini's assistant and in many ways remains his disciple).

"Italy is ever and adamantly the country of Catholicism: whoever is not on the side of Peppone must be in league with Don Camillo."[4] In response to this criticism from the Left, Italian Catholics run to the defense of those neorealist films whose ambiguity lends itself to Catholic coloration. The Congress of Varese, it could be said, is doing battle here with the Congress of Parma.[5] Needless to say, the results of this Catholic effort have been rather pitiful. But because of it, Rossellini and Fellini find themselves in a very difficult situation. It is true that their recent films could not be perceived as socially oriented. These films are not concerned at all with the transformation of social institutions; they aren't even genuine social documents. Their makers, as Italian citizens, don't flirt with Communism, but neither do they let themselves be taken in by the Christian Democrats. The result for Rossellini is that he is denounced by both sides. As for Fellini, his case is still under litigation, although the success of *La Strada* gives him the benefit of a favorable reception from both sides at the same time—a reception marred, however, by uneasiness and pronounced reservations on the part of the Marxists. Of course, political bias is just one part of a critic's makeup, with greater or lesser weight attached to it depending on his personality. It may even occur that a critic will set aside his political bias: we have seen Chiarini, for example, defend Rossellini's *Flowers of St. Francis* (1950), whereas *Cinema Nuovo* was divided over *Senso* (1954), which was directed by the Communist Visconti. But the precedent set by such instances certainly does not contribute to a softening of theoretical positions when these are synonymous with political distrust. Thus both the Marxists and the Christian Democrats threaten to evict Fellini from the neorealist pantheon as each defines it, and to hurl him out into the darkness already inhabited by Rossellini.

Obviously everything depends on the definition we give to neorealism from the start. Definition or no definition, however, it seems to me that *La Strada* doesn't contradict *Paisan* (1946) or *Open City* (1945) at all, any more than it does *Bicycle Thieves* (1948), for that matter. But it is true that Fellini has taken a route different from Zavattini's.[6] Together with Rossellini, Fellini has opted for a neorealism of the person. To be sure, Rossellini's early films, *Paisan* and *Open City* among them, identified moral choice with social consequence, because these two spheres had been equated during the Resistance. But his *Europe '51* (1952) to some degree retreated from social responsibility into the realm of spiritual destiny. What in this film and in *La Strada* nonetheless remains neorealist and can even be considered one of neorealism's genuine achievements, is the aesthetic that informs the action, an aesthetic that Abbé Amédée Ayfre has judiciously described as phenomenological.[7]

One can see very well, for example, that in *La Strada* nothing is ever revealed to us from inside the characters. Fellini's point of view is the exact opposite of the one that would be taken by psychological realism, which claims to analyze character and finally to uncover feelings. Yet anything can happen in the quasi-Shakespearean world of *La Strada*. Gelsomina and the Fool[8] have an air of the marvelous about them—which baffles and irritates Zampanò—but this quality is neither supernatural nor gratuitous, nor even "poetic"; instead, it comes across simply as another property of nature. Furthermore, to return to psychology, the very being of these characters is precisely in their not having any, or at least in their possessing such a malformed and primitive psychology that a description of it would have nothing more than pathological interest. But they do have a soul. And *La Strada* is nothing but their experience of their souls and the revelation of this before our eyes.

Gelsomina learns from the Fool that she has a place in the world. Gelsomina the idiot, homely and useless, discovers one day through this tightrope walker that she is something other than a reject, an outcast;

better, that she is irreplaceable and that she has a destiny, which is to be indispensable to Zampanò. The most powerful event in the film is, without question, Gelsomina's breakdown after Zampanò murders the Fool. From this point on, she is beset by an agony situated in that instant in which the Fool, who had virtually conferred her being onto her, ceased to exist. Little mouse-like cries escape uncontrollably from her lips at the sight of her dead friend: "The Fool is sick, the Fool is sick." The stupid, obstinate, and brutish Zampanò can't realize how much he needs Gelsomina, and above all he can't sense the eminently spiritual nature of the bond that unites the two of them. Terrified by the poor girl's suffering and at the end of his patience, he abandons her. But just as the death of the Fool had made life unbearable for Gelsomina, so too will Zampanò's abandonment of her and then her death make life unbearable for him. Little by little this mass of muscles is reduced to its spiritual core, and Zampanò ends up being crushed by the absence of Gelsomina from his life. He's not crushed by remorse over what he did, or even by his love for her, but rather by overwhelming and incomprehensible anguish, which can only be the response of his soul to being deprived of Gelsomina.

Thus one can look at *La Strada* as a phenomenology of the soul, perhaps even of the communion of saints,[9] and at the very least as a phenomenology of the reciprocal nature of salvation. Where these slow-witted individuals are concerned, it is impossible to confuse ultimate spiritual realities with those of intelligence, passion, pleasure, or beauty. The soul reveals itself here beyond psychological or aesthetic categories, and it reveals itself all the more, precisely because one can't bedeck it with the trappings of conscience. The salt of the tears that Zampanò sheds for the first time in his sorry life, on the beach that Gelsomina loved, is the same salt as that of the infinite sea, which will never again be able to relieve its own anguish at the sufferings of men.

NOTES TO CHAPTER 11

La Strada

(All notes have been provided by the Editor.)

First published in French in *Esprit*, 23, no. 226 (May 1955), pp. 847–51. Reprinted in Bazin's *Qu'est-ce que le cinéma?*, Vol. 4, "Une esthétique de la réalité: le néo-réalisme" (Paris: Éditions du Cerf, 1962), pp. 122–28.

  1. *Mise en scène* literally means "putting on the stage." In a French theater program, the credit for "directed by" would read, *"mise en scène de."* This term has been loosely

adapted for use with reference to the cinema, and covers such areas as visual style, movement of the camera and/or the actors, disposition of the actors in relation to decor, uses of lighting and color, etc. When Bazin speaks of "the *mise en scène* from a technically cinematic point of view," he is referring to camera position (e.g., close-up), angle (e.g., low-angle shot), and movement (e.g., swish pan) that call some attention to themselves.

2. Guido Aristarco has long been the editor of the Italian film journal *Cinema Nuovo* (*New Cinema*). Among his books are *The Art of Film* (1950), *History of Film Theory* (1951), *Myth and Reality in the Italian Cinema* (1961), and *Marx, the Cinema, and Film Criticism* (1965). Luigi Chiarini (1900–1975) founded the famous Italian film school Centro Sperimentale di Cinematografia in 1935 and, in addition to contributing to *Cinema Nuovo*, he founded his own journal, *Bianco e Nero* (*Black and White*), in 1937, remaining its editor until 1951. Among his books on film theory are *Five Chapters on Film* (1941), *Problems of Film Art* (1949), *The Battle of Ideas in Film* (1954), and *The Art and Technique of Film* (1962). In his day Chiarini was considered by many to be the dean of the Italian cinema.

3. Cesare Zavattini (1902–1989) emerged in the 1940s as a key figure of Italian neorealism with his theoretical writings and with his screenplays for some of the most important productions of the movement, notably the films of Vittorio De Sica (e.g., *Shoeshine* [1946], *Bicycle Thieves* [1948], *Miracle in Milan* [1950]).

4. Don Camillo, an eccentric Roman Catholic village priest, and Peppone, the village's militant Communist mayor, conduct a running war to gain the favor of the local populace in a series of novels by Giovannino Guareschi (1908–1968). The most famous of these novels, which satirize the politics of both the left and the right, was the first one: *The Little World of Don Camillo* (1948). This was made into a film in 1952 by the French director Julien Duvivier (1896–1967), with the French actor Fernandel (1903–1971) in the role of Peppone. Duvivier also directed *The Return of Don Camillo* (1953), the sequel to *The Little World of Don Camillo*. Several other films followed in what became the internationally popular "Don Camillo" series.

5. Bazin is referring to the various congresses held in the 1890s by the Catholics (in Varese, among other cities), on the one hand, and the Italian Socialist Party (in Parma, among other cities), on the other hand. The following is a description of Catholic politics of the period as it differs from Socialist politics:

> Leo XIII's famous encyclical of 1891, Rerum Novarum, not only condemned the existing liberal capitalist society, it ordered devout Catholics to transform it, and this seemed particularly apposite at a time of agricultural crisis, industrial depression, and high emigration. Employers should pay a "just wage," enough to permit the worker to save and acquire property. The State might legitimately intervene to safeguard workers' rights and prevent blatant exploitation, but essentially reforms should come by mutual agreement, through a series of "private" associations. Mutual-aid societies, cooperatives, and mixed "corporations" of workers and employers were the most favored kinds of association, but workers' trade unions were also permissible provided they did not engage in the class struggle. One of the purposes of this "Papal Socialism" was to combat the ever-present threat of Red Socialism. To the Catholics, Socialism would be a disastrous replacement for liberal capitalism, denying God, family life, and the right to property; under the mask of emancipation it would prepare an even more cruel and universal servitude. The remedy was "corporations"—i.e.,

guilds of employers and workers—profit-sharing in industry, small landowner-ship, share-cropping or long leases in the countryside, cooperatives to organize commerce, and banking to be run as a public utility. Catholics looked forward to a Christian democracy of the twentieth century, in which all classes would work together in social harmony. (Drawn from Martin Clark, *Modern Italy, 1871–1892* [London: Longman, 1984], p. 106.)

6. Fellini co-scripted *Paisan* and *Open City* for Rossellini; Zavattini wrote the screenplay for *Bicycle Thieves*, as I indicate in note 3 above.

7. Amédée Ayfre is a French ecclesiastic and critic. He is the author or co-editor of the following books: *God in the Cinema: Aesthetic Problems of Religious Film* (1953), *Truth and Cinema* (1969), *Cinema and Mystery* (1969), and *The Films of Robert Bresson* (1969).

   In describing neorealism as phenomenological, Ayfre means what Bazin says in the first sentence of the next paragraph: that "nothing is ever revealed to us from inside the characters" in the quintessential neorealist film. In philosophical terms, neoreal-ism limits itself to a description of characters' interactions with one another ("neoreal-ism of the person," according to Bazin) or with their environment ("socialist neoreal-ism," according to Bazin). What neorealism does not do is emphasize characters' par-ticular psychological problems or obsessions.

8. The Fool is an *artiste*—violinist, high-wire performer, clown—who is known only by his stage name in the film.

9. The communion of saints is, in the Roman Catholic Church, the union between the faithful on earth, the souls in Purgatory, and the saints in Heaven, by which all are members of the same mystical body under Christ, its head, and partakers in a commu-nity of spiritual works and gifts.

CHAPTER 12

G *ermany, Year Zero*

A child's face elicits from us conflicting responses. We marvel at it because of its already unique yet specifically childlike characteristics—hence Mickey Rooney's success and the proliferation of freckles on the faces of young American stars. The days of Shirley Temple, who unduly prolonged her own private theatrical, literary, and visual aesthetic, are now over; children in the cinema no longer look like china dolls or Renaissance representations of the infant Jesus. But mystery continues to frighten us, and we want to be reassured against it by the faces of children; we thoughtlessly ask of these faces that they reflect feelings we know very well because they are our own. We demand of them signs of complicity, and the audience quickly becomes enraptured and teary when children show feelings that are usually associated with grown-ups. We are thus seeking to contemplate ourselves in them: ourselves, plus the innocence, awkwardness, and naiveté we lost. This kind of cinema moves us, but aren't we in fact just feeling sorry for ourselves?

With very few exceptions (like Vigo's *Zero for Conduct* [1933], which is pervaded with irony), children's films fully play on the ambiguity of our interest in these miniature human beings. Come to think of it, these films treat childhood precisely as if it were open to our understanding and empathy; they are made in the name of anthropomorphism. *It Happened in Europe* (1947) is no exception to this rule. Quite the contrary: Géza Radványi, the Hungarian director, manipulates that anthropomorphism with diabolical skill. I won't reproach him for his demagogy to the extent that I accept the world he creates. But even though I get a tear in my eye like everybody else, I can't help seeing that the death of the ten-year-old boy, who is shot down while playing the "Marseillaise" on his harmonica,

Germany, Year Zero (1947), dir. Roberto Rossellini. The British Film Institute, London.

Germany, Year Zero (1947), dir. Roberto Rossellini. The British Film Institute, London.

is so moving only because it confirms our adult conception of heroism. By contrast, the atrocious strangling of the truck driver with a slipknot of iron wire contains, because of the pathetic reason behind it (to get a piece of bread and a strip of bacon for ten famished boys), something inexplicable and unforeseen that has its origin in the irreducible mystery of childhood. All in all, however, this film relies much more on our sympathy for children who manifest feelings that are comprehensible to us.

Roberto Rossellini's profound originality in *Germany, Year Zero* (1947) lies in his deliberate refusal to resort to any such sentimental sympathy, to make any concession to anthropomorphism. His kid is eleven or twelve years old, and it would be easy, even normal, most of the time for the script and the acting to introduce us into the innermost recesses of his conscience. If we do know some things about this boy's thoughts and feelings, however, it is never because of signs that can be read directly on his face, nor even because of his behavior, for we get to understand it only by inference and conjecture. Of course, the speech of the Nazi schoolmaster is the immediate source of the boy's murder of his sickly and "useless" father ("the weak must perish so that the strong may live"), but when he pours the poison into the cup of tea, we look in vain on his face for anything other than concentration and calculation. We cannot see on it any sign of indifference, or cruelty, or possible sorrow. A schoolmaster has pronounced some words in front of him, and these have made their way through to his mind and caused him to make this decision: but how, and at the cost of how much inner conflict? This is not the filmmaker's concern; it is only the child's. Rossellini could have given us an interpretation of the murder only through a piece of trickery, by projecting his own explanation onto the boy and having him reflect it for us.

Rossellini's aesthetic clearly triumphs in the final fifteen minutes of the film, during the boy's long quest for some sign of confirmation or approval, ending with his suicide in response to being betrayed by the world. First, the schoolmaster refuses to assume any responsibility for the incriminating gesture of his disciple. Driven into the street, the kid walks and walks, searching here and there among the ruins; but, one after the other, people and things abandon him. He finds his girlfriend playing with his pals, but they pick up their ball when he tries to approach them. The close-ups that punctuate this endless quest never show us anything other than a worried, pensive, perhaps frightened face, but frightened of what? Of making some transaction on the black market? Of swapping a knife for two cigarettes? Of the thrashing he's going to get when he returns home?

Only the final scene will give us a retrospective clue to the answer. The fact is, simply, that the signs of play and the signs of death may be the same on a child's face, at least for those of us who cannot penetrate its mystery.

The boy hops on one leg along the edge of a broken-up sidewalk. He picks up among the masses of stone and twisted steel a piece of rusty metal that he handles as if it were a gun. He aims through a hole in the ruins at an imaginary target: bang, bang, bang.... Then, with exactly the same playful spontaneity he puts the imaginary gun to his temple. Finally, the suicide: the kid climbs to the top floor of the bombed-out building facing his own house; he looks down and sees a hearse pick up a coffin and take it away, leaving the family behind; an iron beam sticks out sideways through the devastated floor, like a toboggan; he slides down it on his behind and leaps into the void. His little corpse lies on the ground now behind a pile of stones at the edge of the sidewalk. A woman puts down her shopping bag and kneels beside him. A streetcar passes by with a rattling noise. The woman leans back against the pile of stones, her arms hanging about her in the eternal pose of a Pietà.

One can clearly see how Rossellini was led to treat his main character in this way. Such psychological objectivity was within the logic of his style. Rossellini's "realism" has nothing in common with all that the cinema has given to us up to now in the name of realism (with the exception of Jean Renoir's films). His realism lies not in the subject matter but in the style. Rossellini is perhaps the only filmmaker in the world who knows how to get us interested in an action while leaving it in its objective context. Our emotion is thus rid of all sentimentality, for it has been filtered by force through our intelligence. We are moved not by the actor or the event, but by the meaning we are force to extract from the action. In this *mise en scène*, the moral or dramatic significance is never visible on the surface of reality; yet we can't fail to sense what that significance is if we pay attention. Isn't this, then, a sound definition of realism in art: to force the mind to draw its own conclusions about people and events, instead of manipulating it into accepting someone else's interpretation?

NOTES TO CHAPTER 12

Germany, Year Zero

This review was first published in French in *Esprit* (1949), then reprinted in Vol. 3 ("Le Cinéma et sociologie") of *Qu'est-ce que le cinéma?* (Paris: Éditions du Cerf, 1958–62), pp. 29–32.

CHAPTER 13

N *iagara*

Is it a coincidence or part of a plan, or simply my imagination at work in anticipation of the near future? Whatever the case, it seems as if the American cinema, before it dies in its present condition, wants to demonstrate by its choice of subjects and locales the superiority of CinemaScope. One can't help thinking this when one sees Henry Hathaway's *Niagara* (1952), in which the two protagonists are the famous falls and Marilyn Monroe. Indeed, it's much too obvious that at least one of the two would benefit enormously from an enlargement of our field of vision (the other would benefit from the use of 3-D, but that's another story).

It is so easy to treat with ironic contempt Hollywood endeavors such as *Niagara* that one is rather tempted to detect in them whatever positive things they have to offer. Besides, the contemptuous viewer could perchance be taken in by a film in which self-awareness and humor play a significant part. However, it is quite possible that Hathaway originally took this rather conventional script seriously, because he hoped he could renew interest in it through his employment of the *mise en scène*. The story concerns two newlywed couples. One of these couples has come to spend its honeymoon at Niagara Falls, where their bungalow neighbors are an oddly matched pair. He (Joseph Cotten) is closemouthed, short-tempered, and likes solitary walks. She (Marilyn Monroe) is an extraordinary type of perverse ingénue who seems to have no other concern than to provoke her husband's jealousy with her indecent attire and outlook. We soon understand that she wants people to think he is mad, so as to pass off as a suicide the murder she is planning with the complicity of her lover. But the Niagara does not return the body that she had hoped it would, and from then on she will have to deal with the fear of a vengeance against which she can't defend herself without admitting her crime. The falls will take care of the denouement and the moral.

Obviously, there is nothing original in this trite version of the *femme fatale* story, where the woman's sensuality provokes the man's destiny. There is one element, however—clearly indicated in the script but absolutely not developed in the film—that could have introduced a rather appealing secondary line of interest: in fact, *both* couples are oddly matched, for the newlywed young man is an oblivious fool, a champion salesman of cornflakes, whose pretty and intelligent wife (Jean Peters) would be far better matched with Joseph Cotten. Thus we would have had two protagonists made for each other but kept apart by their senseless love for someone who, for very different reasons in each case, does not deserve it. But the salesman embodies an ideal of American social morality that could be paired with Marilyn Monroe's lust only through a most audacious operation. And it is perhaps in the face of such an operation that the screenwriters retreated.

I think that the initial script was knocked off-center by the introduction of Marilyn Monroe as its star. This actress's personality, her promotional importance to Fox, necessarily made the film revolve around her. But it is obvious that this latest Hollywood sex bomb couldn't possibly pass herself off as a tragic figure. One could even question just how seriously her robust eroticism should be taken. The morphology of the vamp tends toward thinness: the kind you find in Marlene Dietrich, Greta Garbo (although not a vamp, she is in all respects a tragic figure), Joan Crawford....It was actually Mae West who originally created the figure of the comic vamp, by virtue of what I would call a sort of low-pressure pneumaticism. In any event, even if one hesitates to generalize in these matters, it at least remains obvious, in Marilyn Monroe's case, that at such a hyperbolic level vampishness has more in common with farce than with tragedy. Howard Hawks understood this perfectly in *Monkey Business* (1952), where, as rumor has it, he went as far as to add padding to the already obvious curves of Miss Monroe. We know that in America the characteristic feature of an actress who has a sufficiently marked sex appeal is nicely designated by a generic label. Thus Lauren Bacall is "the look," Jane Russell "the breath." A single word could characterize Marilyn Monroe, but it doesn't exist in English.[1] A long time ago, I wrote in a review of *The Outlaw* (1943; dir. Howard Hughes, with Jane Russell) that, since the war, eroticism in film had passed from the thighs to the breasts. Marilyn Monroe makes it fall somewhere in between the two.

Nevertheless, Hathaway has attempted to develop around his heroine a whole system of more complex erotic allusions and metaphors. First there is the motif of nudity. Marilyn Monroe always seems to be naked under something: a sheet, a nightgown, or her dress. It is around this film that Fox launched the following advertising campaign. Question: "Miss Monroe, what do you have on when you sleep?" Answer: "Chanel No. 5." But this is just another episode in the game of hide-and-seek that Hollywood has been playing for years with censorship, which the industry regards not as a restriction, but on the contrary as a stimulant to the imagination. More subtle and indirect is the motif of water, which the dialogue of the film reduces to the level of an elementary dramatic symbol (of the tumultuous fatality of passion). In reality, though, what matters here is not the dynamic force of the falling, rushing water, but the humidity that pervades the surrounding atmosphere. It is in this all-pervasive humidity that the protagonists are steeped and under which they suffer, and which even seems to be a quality inherent in the heroine's skin, as if it were something we could touch. As a matter of fact, a Canadian film magazine aptly described Marilyn Monroe's sex appeal as "humid eroticism."

NOTES TO CHAPTER 13

Niagara

This review was first published in French in *L'Observateur* (17 Sept. 1953), then reprinted in Volume 3 ("Cinéma et sociologie") of *Qu'est-ce que le cinéma?* (Paris: Éditions du Cerf, 1958–62), pp. 61–64.

1. Editor's note: It does exist in French, however, except not in one word: "chutes de reins," which means "small of the back" and suggests the curvaceousness of the areas surrounding this spot. The original title of Bazin's review was "Chutes de reins et autres Niagara," which is untranslatable because it plays on the words "chutes," which means "falls" (as in Niagara Falls), and "reins" ("kidneys," a euphemism for "bottom" or "back").

CHAPTER 14

F*orbidden Games*

Originally, *Forbidden Games* (1952) was supposed to be only a filmed short story, a movie well under feature length that would have been filled out by one or two other stories, as in *Le Plaisir* or *Three Women*.[1] But it soon appeared that the subject matter was rich enough to be extended to the length of a feature film. As it was, the crisis in the French cinema was putting the distributor in a difficult position, since the rest of a program containing an abbreviated *Forbidden Games* ran the risk of not being filled.[2] René Clément went through the same situation in the making of *Battle of the Rails* (1946), although for different reasons, and the result was not so bad. After all, it sometimes happens that novelists expand their short stories in order to publish them as novels.

Indeed, Clément's new film is taken from a "novel" by François Boyer that one might very well consider a short story: *Secret Games*. This book has a history. Its author had first conceived it as a film script. Then, for want of a producer, he fleshed out the script and published it as a novel. Appearing in 1947, *Secret Games* received almost no notice in France, but it was translated into English and became one of the year's best sellers in America. I don't know whether this unexpected success drew Clément to the book or whether it simply made it easier for him to gain approval for filming from a producer: in any event, the script had become a novel, and then was adapted back into a screenplay. Jean Aurenche and Pierre Bost were asked to write the adaptation. In fact, however, their work focused less on the novel than on Boyer's original script, which was already entirely in dialogue-form. This dialogue is largely retained in the film (as well as in the novel), and it would only be fair to point out that the credit for it should be given to Boyer, not to Aurenche and Bost, as most critics (myself included) had at first thought. I must say that the publicity for the film had led us to think that way.

Does this mean that the novel is as good as the film? I don't think so. On the contrary, François Boyer's novel has some strong features, which can almost all be found back in the film, but it also has some shortcomings. In my view, its success in America could be explained paradoxically enough by the influence of the American novel on its conception (an influence assimilated in a rather naive way). What's good in Boyer's book, beyond the technical aspect, has everything to do with authentic personal experience. Its weakness lies in its obvious and systematic intention of putting this personal experience into the objectivist mould of an Erskine Caldwell. This amoral tone with regard to the event and this disposition toward exteriority were in fact partly retained by Clément (so that the film owes even a little more than its scenario and dialogue to the book), but what was the weakness of the book becomes precisely the strength of the film. This reversal of values is not simply to be explained away as a question of stylistic measure, which Clément exercised and Boyer didn't, nor by any other capacity of the director, but first and fundamentally by the different point of view taken by the cinema. Whenever Boyer reduced some scenes of his novel to long exchanges of dialogue that contained only rudimentary information about the characters' behavior, one violently resented the absence of any psychological analysis as the affirmation of a kind of moral atomism. For when a novelist reduces a scene solely to the report of the dialogue, he deprives us of his characters. Frustration creeps in. In the cinema, the same dialogue is vivified before our eyes by the actors, so we necessarily have what was denied to us by the novelist: a total and unrestricted relationship with the characters. Of course, the director has at his disposal more than one device to re-create artificially some of the frustration felt by the reader, just as, conversely, the novelist's dialogue alone can evoke the characters, their demeanor and their psychology. Clearly, Faulkner's dialogue could not be filmed in the same way as Proust's; something of the two novelistic styles would have to be kept in their respective pictures, since each is so distinctly revelatory. But because of its technical objectivity, the cinema is less objective than the novel that aims at being objective, for we can do nothing against the writer who denies us the soul of his characters, whereas we always have the opportunity to penetrate the faces of the actors on-screen. Thus the excessive

Forbidden Games (1952), dir. René Clément. La Cinémathèque Royale, Brussels.

"Americanism," the tendency toward "behaviorism," in Boyer's novel naturally dissolves in Clément's film. What Clément has deliberately retained from the artistic strategies of the book, however, is not what is best in the film: I'm thinking here of the harsh treatment of the peasants.

Whatever the origins of the film—in Boyer's original script, his published novel, or both—if those origins certify the achievement of François Boyer, whose name might have appeared in the credits, they take nothing away from the achievement of René Clément: they even partly explain it. It was the intelligence of the director that made him want to keep the intimate structure of a novelistic story in his film. And he succeeded. I'll make myself better understood if I compare *Forbidden Games* with the "children's films" that have preceded it.

Comparison among children's films reveals that they have obvious similarities, despite differences in conception and style. The two archetypes come from the early days of talking pictures: *Road to Life* (1932, U.S.S.R.; dir. Nikolai Ekk) and *Emil and the Detectives* (1931, Germany;

dir. Gerhardt Lamprecht, from the children's novel by Erich Kastner).[3] The former set the trend for the numerous films of every nationality whose theme is unhappy or delinquent childhood and its purging: Jean-Paul Le Chanois's *Passion for Life* (a.k.a. *I Have a New Master*; 1949) is one of the most recent examples of this.[4] The latter set the trend for a whole series of police stories whose heroes are children. Among dozens of them one could cite *Portrait of Innocence* (1941, France; dir. Louis Daquin)[5] and *Hue and Cry* (1947, Great Britain; dir. Charles Crichton). Such thematic unity is not without equivalent in the cinema, but in this case it certainly reveals a unity of moral significance in addition. If we take all the films comparable to *Road to Life*, for instance, it is easy to detect in them beneath their alleged psychological and social realism a traditional ethical mythology. Fundamentally, they are all illustrations of a certain belief in the "original innocence" of children. Evil in a child's world (whether moral or physical, and especially when the child becomes a martyr to his misdeeds) is the supreme moral scandal. Hence there is no "guilty" or "bad" child, only a "delinquent," "misguided," or "unhappy" one. Laws and punishment, even justice with its fiery sword, have no place except outside this ethical paradise, in the universe of grown-ups. The criminal child is only a tainted soul contaminated by the society of man. Reform, seen as both punishment and enforced submission to moral law, is then opposed to a pedagogy of purgation through trust and love. This purgation is, in fact, a conversion; it has the instantaneousness of grace. When the teacher in *Road to Life* gives some money to the worst of his charges and tells him to go buy some groceries, he forces him to choose between two temptations: that of evil—to take the money and run—and that of good—to justify the grown-up's trust in him. By choosing good, the child is restored to his childhood and so to his original innocence. In *Los Olvidados* (a.k.a. *The Young and the Damned*; 1950), Buñuel cruelly plays with a similarly crucial moment in order to reverse its effect: the child does not voluntarily betray the adult's love; instead, the money that was given to him is stolen by another child. Since it is therefore impossible for him to go back and explain, he is confirmed in his "evil" by the very act that was supposed to save him.

If we now analyze films similar in type to *Emil and the Detectives*, we see that their resemblance extends to a moral mythology that is close to the one described above. The police story is nothing other than the dramatic incarnation of a Manichaeism in which the child represents the forces of good. The unparalleled success to this day of *Emil and the Detectives* in comparison with all its imitators can be attributed precisely to the skill with which Lamprecht managed to show, quite realistically, the diabolism of the grown-up who steals the young hero's money. The famous pursuit of the thief down the street takes on the epic grandeur of a celestial multitude's quest after evil itself.

This digression about films that *Forbidden Games* doesn't resemble was perhaps necessary in order to underline its originality. When one examines the thematic similarities among all children's films released up to the present day, one has to conclude that they could not be described as novelistic and psychological. Despite their realism and the reality to which these films seemingly refer, they are much closer to fairy tales or sacred parables than to contemporary novels. For instance, they are closer to *Beauty and the Beast* and to the *Parable of the Good Shepherd* than to Raymond Radiguet's *Devil in the Flesh* or to François Boyer's *Secret Games*. One might object here that *The Wanderer* is a novel, and it's about young people. Yes, but to begin with, Alain-Fournier's mythology is not moral, and the novelistic form permits him a subtlety that would be refused him by the epic simplifications of film. I don't want to say that *The Wanderer* by its very nature cannot be adapted to the screen: it can, but only if the film steers completely free of the aesthetic formula that produced *Road to Life* or even *Shoeshine* (1946, Italy; dir. Vittorio De Sica).[6] That is to say, if the film proposed to be the equivalent of a novel expressed through cinematic means.

That is precisely what *Forbidden Games* is. With *The Last Vacation* (1948, France),[7] Roger Leenhardt had given us one of the first film-novels on adolescence, in a less spectacular though more intelligent way than Claude Autant-Lara in *Devil in the Flesh* (1947, France). But Leenhardt still remained in a zone into which a grown-up could venture with only a minimum of reference points. To be sure, the adolescent is a future adult, and the adult himself retains some memory of his adolescence, but in the *The Last Vacation* he is unrelievedly constrained to stay on the outside of that adolescence, even though it is his own. Clément is doubtless the first director to give us an image of youth that does not limit itself to one of the mythologies that grown-ups routinely project upon youth in the belief that it is a mystery. His intention is not that of a moralist or a pedagogue, but of a novelist. He wants to have these two children occupy a place, in a story whose protagonists they happen to be, that is essentially identical to the one adult characters might have occupied. Their actions, their manner, what we can grasp of their thought, are not at all the reflection of an a priori idea about childhood. Michel and Paulette are neither good nor bad children: their behavior, which is by no means absurd, has to do only with psychology, and not in the slightest with morality. It is the adults, to whom the logic of Michel and Paulette's games is foreign, who project upon them a moral significance. Incidentally, the fact that the action takes place in a rustic setting is not an accident, for in its simplicity and lack of sophistication, this world is at once the closest to and the remotest from that of childhood.

When he discovers the theft of the crosses from the churchyard, Michel's father is scandalized not by the sacrilege of this act or its lack of respect for the dead, but by the offense it has supposedly caused the neighbors and by the material loss that its represents. By stealing all the crosses they can lay their hands on in order to build a cemetery for animals, Michel and Paulette totally appropriate a ritual from the grown-ups around them. That is to say, their appropriation reveals the ritualistic burial of dead human beings for the children's game that it is—the taming of death by means of harmless ceremony—despite the social seriousness it claims for itself. However, the confrontation between the children and the adults reveals that the seriousness is on the children's side, since the reasons they have for loving their game are in fact better. Paulette buries her dog, who died along with her parents at the hands of the Germans, because she doesn't want him to get wet in the rain. She then demands that Michel sacrifice an animal in order to give her dog some company, for he's bored. That is the origin of their cemetery, whose crosses are merely a nice decoration suggested by the crosses used in human cemeteries.

The so-called pessimism for which Clément has so often been reproached, and for which some people more or less condemn this film, is in reality nothing more than the director's refusal to insert his child characters into the moral framework by which we would like to define them. There is only one realism: the equal rejection of moral pessimism *and* optimism. If there is a moral in the film, it is only implicit, and it would at most postulate that the morality of childhood is first and foremost an amorality; this is the lesson of the book *Devil in the Flesh*. What is more, even if Clément acknowledges a psychology of childhood, he gives to it only a negative description (the only one that's possible). The hierarchy of feelings, wants, and acts is not the same for Paulette and

Michel as it is for the grown-ups. The grown-ups, however, have neither the time nor the intelligence to understand this. A burst of machine-gun fire kills Paulette's parents as well as her little dog, but since she hasn't ever experienced death before, the dead dog will command a far greater portion of the little girl's sorrow than the corpses of her parents, which she must leave behind at the side of the road.

If, on the other hand, we like to view childhood as if it were a mirror reflecting an image of us that is purged of all sin, cleansed of our adult stains, restored to innocence, then *Forbidden Games* refuses to play along—not out of cruelty or pessimism, but out of a desire to tell the truth. As such, it is the first example of its kind on the screen.

NOTES TO CHAPTER 14

Forbidden Games

(All notes have been provided by the Editor.)

This essay was first published in French in *Esprit* (1952), then reprinted in Volume 3 ("Cinéma et sociologie") of Bazin's *Qu'est-ce que le cinéma?* (Paris: Éditions du Cerf, 1958–62), pp. 15–21.

1. *Le Plaisir (House of Pleasure*; 1952, dir. Max Ophüls) is made up of three tales based on stories by Guy de Maupassant: "Le Masque," "La Maison Tellier," and "Le Modèle."

   Three Women (1924; dir. Ernst Lubitsch), based on the novel *The Lilie*, by Yolanthe Marees, tells the stories of three women, all of whom have been or are involved with the same man.

   Forbidden Games was originally intended as one episode in an anthology film to be entitled *Cross My Heart and Hope to Die*.

2. See Bazin's "The Crisis of French Cinema, or *Scarface* and the Gangster Film," translated in this volume.

3. Kastner's novel was filmed six times, twice by the Germans, once each by the British, the Japanese, the Brazilians, and the Americans (Walt Disney produced the most recent version of *Emil and the Detectives* in 1964).

4. French title of *Passion for Life: L'École buissonnière* ("Faire l'école buissonnière" means "to play hooky.")

5. French title of *Portrait of Innocence: Nous les gosses* (*Us Kids*).

6. *The Wanderer* (French title, *Le Grand Meaulnes*) was made into a film in 1967 by the French director Jean-Gabriel Albicocco. The following brief plot summary, together with critical comment, is taken from Ronald Bergan and Robyn Karney, *The Holt Foreign Film Guide* (New York: Henry Holt, 1988), pp. 603–604: "In the small town of Sainte-Agathe in the French region of Sologne, at the turn of the century, the young Augustin Meaulnes falls deeply in love with Yvonne De Galais, a beautiful and mysterious girl whom he meets at a strange house party. When she disappears, he searches for her and for his lost adolescence. Alain–Fournier's popular young people's classic waited 30 years...to be filmed...[but this] is a far too frenetic and flashy attempt to re-create the fairy-tale atmosphere of the novel in visual terms..."

CHAPTER 15

Europe '51

The year began with a misunderstood masterpiece (De Sica's *Umberto D.*), and it ended with an accursed masterpiece, Roberto Rossellini's *Europe '51* (a.k.a. *The Greatest Love*, 1952). Just as critics had reproached De Sica for making a social melodrama, they accused Rossellini of indulging in a confused, indeed reactionary, political ideology. They were once again wrong for the most part, for they were passing judgment on the subject without taking into consideration the style that gives it its meaning and its aesthetic value.

A young, rich, and frivolous woman loses her only son, who commits suicide one evening when his mother is so preoccupied with her social life that she sends him to bed rather than be forced to pay attention to him. The poor woman's moral shock is so violent that it plunges her into a crisis of conscience that she initially tries to resolve by dedicating herself to humanitarian causes, on the advice of a cousin of hers who is a Communist intellectual. But little by little she gets the feeling that this is only an intermediate stage beyond which she must go if she is to achieve a mystical charity all her own, one that transcends the boundaries of politics and even of social or religious morality. Accordingly, she looks after a sick prostitute until the latter dies, then aids in the escape of a young criminal from the police. This last initiative causes a scandal, and, with the complicity of an entire family alarmed by her behavior, the woman's husband, who understands her less and less, decides to have her committed to a sanitarium. If she had become a member of the Communist party or had entered a convent, bourgeois society would have had fewer objections to her actions, since the Europe of the early 1950s is a world of political parties and social organizations.

From this perspective, it is true that Rossellini's script is not devoid of naiveté, even of incoherence or at any rate pretentiousness. One sees the particulars that the author has borrowed from Simone Weil's life, without in fact being able to recapture the strength of her thinking. But these reservations don't hold up before the whole of a film that one must understand and judge on the basis of its *mise en scène*. What would Dostoyevsky's *The Idiot* be worth if it were to be reduced to a summary of its plot? Because Rossellini is a true director, the form of his film does not consist in the ornamentation of its script: the form is supplied by its very substance. The author of *Germany, Year Zero* (1947, in which a boy also kills himself)[1] is profoundly haunted in a personal way by the horror of the death of children, even more by the horror of their suicide, and it is around his heroine's authentic spiritual experience of such a suicide that the film is organized. The eminently modern theme of lay sainthood then naturally emerges; its more or less skillful development by the script matters very little: what matters is that each sequence is a kind of meditation or filmic song on this fundamental theme as revealed by the *mise en scéne*. The aim is not to demonstrate but to show. And how could we resist the moving spiritual presence of Ingrid Bergman, and, beyond the actress, how could we remain insensitive to the intensity of a *mise en scène* in which the universe seems to be organized along spiritual lines of force, to the point that it sets them off as manifestly as iron fillings in a magnetic field? Seldom has the presence of the spiritual in human beings and in the world been expressed with such dazzling clarity.

Granted, Rossellini's neorealism here seems very different from, even contradictory to, De Sica's. However, I think it wise to reconcile them as the two poles of the same aesthetic school. Whereas De Sica investigates reality with ever more expansive curiosity, Rossellini by contrast seems to strip it down further each time, to stylize it with a painful but nonetheless unrelenting rigor, in short to return to a classicism of dramatic expression in acting as well as in *mise en scène*. But, on closer examination, this classicism stems from a common neorealistic revolution. For Rossellini, as for De Sica, the aim is to reject the categories of acting and of dramatic expression in order to force reality to reveal its significance solely through appearances. Rossellini does not make his actors *act*, he doesn't make them express this or that feeling; he compels them only to be a certain way before the camera. In such a *mise en scène*, the respective places of the characters, their ways of walking, their movements on the set, and their gestures have much more importance than the feelings they show on their faces, or even than the words they say. Besides, what "feelings" could Ingrid Bergman "express"? Her drama lies far beyond any psychological nomenclature. Her face only outlines a certain property of suffering.

Europe '51 gives ample indication that such a *mise en scène* calls for the most sophisticated stylization possible. A film like this is the very opposite of a realistic one "drawn from life": it is the equivalent of austere and terse writing, which is so stripped of ornament that it sometimes verges on the ascetic. At this point, neorealism returns full circle to classical abstraction and its generalizing quality. Hence this apparent paradox: the best version of the film is not the dubbed Italian version, but the English one, which employs the greatest possible number of original voices. At the far reaches of this realism, the accuracy of exterior social reality becomes unimportant. The children in the streets of Rome can speak English without our even realizing the implausibility of such an occurrence. This is reality through style, and thus a reworking of the conventions of art.

NOTES TO CHAPTER 15

Europe '51

This review was written in 1953 but only published for the first time in French in Vol. 4 ("Une Esthétique de la réalité: le néoréalisme") of Bazin's four-volume *Qu'est-ce que le cinéma?* (Paris: Éditions du Cerf, 1958–62), pp. 97–99.

1. Editor's note: See Bazin's review of *Germany, Year Zero*, translated in this volume.

CHAPTER 16

The Last Vacation, or The Style Is the Man Himself

For several dozen people in Paris—novelists, poets, theater or film directors, actors, critics, painters, independent producers, most of whom used to meet in the vicinity of the Odéon, the Rue du Bac, and the Seine (long before the existentialist invasion, when the Deux Magots was still a literary center and people went to the Café de Flore to meet Jean Renoir, Paul Grimault,[1] or Jacques Prévert)—for a few dozen people in the Paris of Arts, Letters, and Friendship, then, there had been a Roger Leenhardt case ever since the war and even before it. This thin little man, slightly bent forward as if he were carrying the weight of God-knows-what ideal weariness on his shoulders, this little man occupied a discrete, unusual, and exquisite place at the border between French literature and film.

For some of these people, Roger Leenhardt deserves to be called one of the most brilliant critics and aestheticians of talking pictures, a man who has at least ten years' head start on everybody else. For others, Leenhardt is first and foremost a novelist who has never completely finished his novels; for still others, he is a curious mixture of poet and businessman who, after getting involved in the intensive growing of lemon trees (in Corsica) and going bankrupt, became a producer of shorts in order to satisfy the subtle complex of associations that tied him to film. I suspect that Roger Leenhardt is a producer in much the same way as he is a critic, i.e., just enough so that he can't be forced to admit he is a director. We have seen him prowl around film for ten years, pretend to forget about it, sometimes despise it, and then rejoin it with a single word during one of those wonderful and nonchalant conversations in which Leenhardt toys with ideas like a cat with a mouse. Some people were

The Last Vacation (1948), dir. Roger Leenhardt. La Cinémathèque Royale, Brussels.

wondering whether Leenhardt would ever be able to deal with a "big film," to tackle a major work, which the form of his intelligence has perhaps seemed doomed to do from the start. With Leenhardt, one could even be tempted to say that it would be a pity if this fount of lively ideas condescended to compromise itself by directing a film. In the end I suspect that Leenhardt convinced himself to accept the proposal of his friend, the producer Pierre Gérin, because he thought that making a film would be yet another way of putting an idea forward: the idea of creation, and in a way that is hardly less intellectual than his venture with the citrus plantation in the middle of the Mediterranean Sea.

If I pay so much attention to Roger Leenhardt's personality before I speak of *The Last Vacation* (1948), this is because it seems to me to be in a way more important than the film itself. The reason is that the essence of Leenhardt will forever be contained in his conversation and that his work, however significant it might be, will always be just a by-product of that conversation. Roger Leenhardt has perhaps given us his masterpieces in a minor key in the commentaries that accompany the shorts he has directed or produced. Do you remember, for instance, his documentary on the wind (*In Pursuit of the Wind*, 1943), in which the tall silhouette of Lanza del Vasto appeared on a sun-scorched and mistral-swept wasteland? I don't even want to talk about the text of his commentary, although the one for *The Birth of Film* (1946)[2] is wonderful; I'm thinking only of the diction, the tone and modulation of his voice that makes Leenhardt the best commentator in French film. The whole of Leenhardt comes out in that intelligent and incisive voice, which the mechanism of the microphone never manages to corrode to the extent that the voice ceases to imitate the movement of the mind itself. Leenhardt is first and foremost a man of the spoken word. Speech is mobile, flexible, and intimate enough to absorb and translate his dialectic without any appreciable waste of energy, and to preserve the vibration in his shadowless diction where light resounds with passion.

Even if he hadn't made any great films, Roger Leenhardt would be one of the most appealing and irreplaceable personalities in French cinema. He is a kind of "gray eminence" of the filmic thing, one of the few men who, after the generation of people like Louis Delluc and Germaine Dulac,[3] have given French film a conscience. It looked, however, as though Leenhardt's temperament would keep him from venturing too far into the no man's land between creativity and production, from crossing over from the semi-internationality of Saint-Germain-des-Près,[4] where everything is possible at the level of words, to the implacably stupid world of the Champs-Elysées, where everyone is subjected to the ruthless inquisition of success and money. I must also say the following because it is only proper: we have to give Pierre Gérin credit for offering Leenhardt the bridge of his trust and friendship, so that Leenhardt could cross from the left bank of the Seine to the right.[5]

I can admit it now: we were extremely afraid. First no doubt because his failure would have saddened us more as a result of our tenderness for the man than our esteem for him, but more importantly still because, like a few others before him, Leenhardt was going to bear witness to one of the most serious problems of filmic creation. Despite his intellectual familiarity with film, despite his experience as a producer and director of shorts, Leenhardt was entering the cinema without weapons, ignorant of studio techniques. He had practically never directed actors, yet now he was supposed to subdue at once all the monsters from which the union heads, if not the producers themselves, normally protect young, inexperienced directors. Leenhardt was virtually compelled to answer the following question: can an *auteur* in the film industry go straight to his style, that is, learn in a few days enough about technique so that he can subject it to his will and intention, then make a work that is both beautiful and commercial, without going through the rites of a long technical apprenticeship? We did not expect from Leenhardt a "well-made" film, but the work of an *auteur*, who in a major way would realize on screen something of the world that he carries inside himself. There are other examples of this kind of passage into film, but they are not numerous. Except for the wholly different case of Renoir, who, along with Georges Méliès and Louis Feuillade,[6] is probably the sole Mr. Cinema that France has ever had the privilege of knowing, only Jean Cocteau and André Malraux managed at once to subject cinematic technique to their artistic style. In Hollywood, the recent experience of Orson Welles further proves what technique may gain if it lets itself be violated by style. After this, how could it refuse to submit to one of the most intelligent men in French film?

Leenhardt was prudent enough to create the most difficult problems for himself; the safest way to proceed, under the circumstances, was through the field of greatest difficulty. So Leenhardt wrote his scenario and dialogue (with his brother-in-law, the late Roger Breuil, who was also his close friend) around a thin subject that was highly novelistic, and that presented almost insoluble problems for the actors. The initial idea was very simple and beautiful, and could have come from a novel by Jean Giraudoux. It often happens that, around the age of fifteen or sixteen, a girl has more psychological maturity than a boy; it will take him several years to catch up with her. The arrival of a young Parisian architect, who is in charge of selling the family estate, suddenly makes the sixteen-year-old Juliette aware of her destiny as a woman. She turns away for a while from her cousin of the same age, Jacques, who in his childish jealousy confusedly believes that Juliette is leaving him behind, that she is passing into adulthood and that he must also make his way toward the world of grown-ups, but more slowly and more painfully. This final summer vacation at the estate will teach him how to distinguish between the last slap in the face he got from his mother and the first slap in the face he will get from a woman. But Leenhardt has chosen to intimately link the theme of the end of childhood to the end of a family heritage and with it a certain kind of society: that of the Protestant bourgeoisie, which three generations of painstakingly amassed wealth and thus tremendous financial security have turned into a kind of aristocracy. Around 1930, in the aftermath of the First World War and at the start of the Great Depression, the decline of this bourgeoisie has already begun. The two adventures, that of the children and that of the parents, have a common ground: the estate, which has become too burdensome for its owners to manage and which they must sell to a hotel consortium.

This estate, where Jacques and Juliette will receive their first lesson in love, is also the product of a precise human geography, with its rock gardens, huge lawns, hayfields, bamboo alleys, flowering araucaria trees, blue cedars, grandiflora magnolias, and green oak trees, which identify the place as scrubland in the Cévennes of southern France. This estate is the outgrowth of bourgeois propriety as it can also be seen in twenty other French provinces. It is an enclosed space, an artificial paradise, something as old-fashioned and unusual in the middle of this sunburnt country, full of Roman ruins, as the guipure dresses and pearl settings of Aunt Nelly. It is the symbol of three or four bourgeois generations, whose charm and greatness consist in the fact that they created in three-quarters of a century both a lifestyle and a style for their estate. But this marvelous bourgeoisie has become even more anachronistic over the question of the parents' worries than the children's games.

One may wonder here why French film hasn't exploited more the theme of the "family estate," to which literature owes numerous masterly novels, from Eugène Fromentin's *Dominique* (1863) to Alain-Fournier's *Le Grand Meaulnes* (1913). What's even stranger: the bourgeoisie, whose life-style and decadence are the subjects of nine-tenths of the great novels from Balzac to Proust, has found little interest among filmmakers. Except for *The Italian Straw Hat* (1927; dir. René Clair), *Love Story* (1943; dir. Claude Autant-Lara), and *Devil in the Flesh* (1947; dir. Claude Autant-Lara), the eternal and wonderful *Rules of the Game* (1939; dir. Jean Renoir) is perhaps the only "bourgeois" film, if indeed it is that. And let's note, incidentally, how difficult Leenhardt has made his task by situating the action of the film between 1925 and 1930. Difficult, but distinctively so and therefore interesting, in that, in place of the classical prestige of dress around 1900, he had by contrast to substitute less-than-becoming costumes so close to our own that they could easily have become incongruous.

The problem of the acting was even more difficult to solve. Fifteen years old is a thankless age in film (whereas it is the age of choice for the novel), because you can no longer count on the animalistic charm of childhood to get you by, and because few older, professional actors can be sufficiently natural in the role. In *Devil in the Flesh* , Autant-Lara went to the limit—and succeeded—in asking the twenty-five-year-old Gérard Philippe to play a seventeen-year-old schoolboy. The script of *The Last Vacation* did not allow for such casting, however, and Leenhardt was rewarded for his daring: the young Odile Versois, who makes her screen debut, and Michel François, who wears his short pants quite naturally, are both almost perfect. In any event they are superior to the adult actors, who are largely responsible for the weaknesses of the film. Pierre Dux, in particular, is not at all the slightly weak yet good-natured *bon vivant* that the script required. Berthe Bovy lacks simplicity and Christiane Barry does not have enough talent or resources to play the role of the beautiful, divorced cousin. One can reproach Leenhardt as well for the change of tone that occurs at the end of the film. The first two-thirds, which are mostly devoted to the adventures of Jacques and Juliette, are admirably— I almost said "novelistically"—realized. The last third, by contrast, stresses the love affair between Dux and Barry and at times barely manages to avoid a farcical tone. Here perhaps the screenwriter ran out of energy and audacity.

However, no matter how interesting and for the most part new Leenhardt's script might be, it is the style of his *mise en scène* that should command our attention in my opinion. I'm sure that lots of experienced technicians will find the film's *mise en scène* poor, if not downright clumsy. The audience will see the austerity of the film's technical effects, which it will perhaps also consider, more or less consciously, a defect. The reason is that people no longer know, or don't know quite yet, what style in film is. In fact, for every one-hundred films, at least 98 have the exact same editing technique, despite some illusory "stylistic" devices. A film by Christian-Jacque or even by Julien Duvivier cannot be recognized by its style, but only by the more or less frequent use it makes of certain effects that are perfectly classical and on which these directors have simply worked some improvements of their own. Conversely, Renoir's films, in which the cutting often goes against all logic and is done without any regard for cinematic grammar, are style itself. Leenhardt is not the sort of man who despises form or even rules, and I do not mean to say that there isn't a certain awkwardness discernible in the solution he has found to this or that problem of editing. A little more experience would probably have

Man's Hope (1939), dir. André Malraux. La Cinémathèque Royale, Brussels.

enabled him to solve such problems better, but for the most part he has discovered the style and technique appropriate to his themes. His filmic sentence has a syntax and a rhythm that are uniquely personal, but his originality by no means signifies a lack of clarity. And although he has a wonderful feel for the concrete continuity of a scene, Leenhardt knows how to play up the significance of the distinctive parts that form its whole.

As a novelist, Leenhardt would have been a moralist. The writing here in a way, and through its own means, recovers the syntax of lucidity that characterizes the whole of French novelistic classicism, from Mme de la Fayette's *Princess of Clèves* (1678) to Camus's *The Stranger* (1942). Considered as description or as a documentary, the screenplay of *The Last Vacation* would indeed seem primitive. But above all the film depicts a way of thinking, the movement of a mind, in which the most striking contradictions of Leenhardt's personality find their exact aesthetic solution. If one had to look for plastic instead of literary reference points, I would compare the best scenes of *The Last Vacation* with those engravings where the careful observation of detail derives its meaning and value precisely from the linear clarity of the overall design. Although partly influenced by Renoir (his camera, like Renoir's, manages never to kill a scene as if it were a vivisectionist's scalpel), Leenhardt differs from him in that he never completely gives up on trying to understand an event and to judge it. This *auteur*'s hereditary Protestantism is discernible not only in the subject matter of his script and in the Cévennes landscape where the action takes place, but it also informs the movement and cutting of the camera, imposing a morality that we do not find in Renoir (which, after all, is why we find Renoir so charming).

I fear that this novel work, in which neither the script nor the *mise en scène* resorts to spectacular effects and artificial devices, and which was made with little money, won't get the attention it deserves. In any event, that's what we're forced to conclude after the persistent coldness with which the selection committees have omitted *The Last Vacation* from all the international competitions of 1947. The reason is that its aesthetic nature is essentially novelistic. Leenhardt has made into a film the novel that he could have written. However paradoxical it might seem, the opinion of the public and even of the critics would have been much more favorable if *The Last Vacation* had been an adaptation. Since the movie could then be easily integrated into a literary tradition, almost without our realizing it, we would no longer notice how extraordinary and profoundly original its filmic essence is. André Malraux makes us feel the same ambivalence about a filmic work that could also be literary. But make no mistake: *Man's Hope* (a.k.a. *Days of Hope*, 1939; dir. Malraux)[7] is the very opposite of an adaptation, despite the fact that it is based on Malraux's own, radically different kind of novel. The film and the book are the refraction in two different artistic mediums of the same creative impulse, which places them on the same aesthetic level. Even if Malraux had not written *Man's Hope* (which actually was completed after the film), we would nevertheless have felt that what we were seeing could have been a novel. *The Last Vacation* gives us the exact same feeling.

Everything that has really counted in the last ten years of movie production throughout the world, from *The Rules of the Game* to *Citizen Kane* to *Paisan* (1946; dir. Roberto Rossellini), has, in fact, been a novel (or short story) that chose instead to become a film. And doesn't the language of film owe its greatest progress during the same period precisely to these aesthetic mutations (which, I repeat, are not adaptations or transpositions)?

The Last Vacation, *or The Style Is the Man Himself*

(All notes have been provided by the Editor.)

This article was first published in French in *Revue du Cinéma* (July, 1948), then reprinted in Volume 3 ("Cinéma et Sociologie") of Bazin's *Qu'est-ce que le cinéma?* (Paris: Èditions du Cerf, 1958–1962), pp. 33–41.

1. Paul Grimault (b. 1905) began by making entertainment cartoons for the screen, at first short and later also feature-length. His work is traditional in style but stands out for its intelligence and delicate lyricism. His *Le Petit Soldat* won first prize at Venice in 1948. Grimault's influence on the development of French animation has been considerable.

2. Released in English as two films: *Animated Cartoons* and *Biography of the Motion Picture Camera.*

3. Louis Delluc (1890–1924) was one of the key figures in the renewal of French cinema after the collapse of the industry's world dominance in the years before World War I. Though in no sense the leader of a unified movement or faction, Delluc has considerable importance as both critic and filmmaker. His impact was crucial during the years after 1919, though he died in 1924 before the full flowering of the French film renaissance to which he had made such a great contribution.

   Filmmaking was only one phase of the career of Germaine Dulac (1882–1942); she was also predominant as a theorist and promoter of avant-garde film, and as an organizer of the French film unions and the ciné-club movement. Her role in French film history has been compared to that of Maya Deren in the United States, three decades later.

4. All the places Bazin mentions in the first paragraph are located in Saint-Germain-des-Près, supposedly the artists' neighborhood of Paris.

5. Saint-Germain-des-Près is on the left bank of the Seine, and the Champs-Elysées is on the right bank of the river.

6. Louis Feuillade (1873–1925) was one of the most solid and dependable talents in French cinema during the teens. He succeeded Alice Guy as head of production at Gaumont in 1906 and worked virtually without a break—aside from a period of war service—until his death in 1925, producing some eight hundred films of every conceivable kind: comedies and contemporary melodramas, biblical epics and historical dramas, sketches and series with numerous episodes adding up to many hours of running time. It was the supreme lack of logic, the disregard of hallowed bourgeois values—so appropriate at a time when the old social order of Europe was crumbling under the impact of World War I—that led Surrealists such as André Breton and Louis Aragon to hail the crime-melodrama series *Fantômas* (1913–14) and *Les Vampires* (1915–16). Most of Feuillade's subsequent advocates have similarly celebrated the films' anarchistic poetry.

7. The only feature directed by the esteemed French writer Malraux, based on his novel *L'Espoir* (this is also the title of the film in French; alternate French title: *Sierra de Teruel*). In it a small group of ill-equipped Republican fighters in the Spanish Civil War attempts to blow up a bridge to prevent arms and supplies from reaching Franco's troops.

CHAPTER 17

Cruel Naples (*Gold of Naples*)

As strange as it might seem on first consideration, Vittorio De Sica is an accursed filmmaker. I may sound paradoxical, or I may seem to be looking for an argument, because my statement increases in ambiguity when you simultaneously consider the popularity of De Sica the actor and the critical importance assigned to *Bicycle Thieves* (1948). However, all we have to do is to reflect a little to realize that *Miracle in Milan* (1952) has enjoyed critical but not popular success and that *Umberto D.* (1952) hasn't enjoyed any success at all. The conditions under which the latter film was released in Paris, moreover, amounted to a guarantee of failure. The festival prize lists are also quite significant in this regard. The year *Umberto D.* was shown in Cannes (at a matinee screening), the jury preferred to honor *Cops and Robbers* (1951; dir. Mario Monicelli). In 1953, the jury underlined the Hollywood-style immorality of De Sica's *Stazione Termini* (a.k.a. *Indiscretion* or *Indiscretion of an American Wife*, 1953) by deciding to ignore it; this year again, the audience and the jury have coldly received *Gold of Naples* (1954), and De Sica wasn't even awarded a tiny tin palm. In the end the film is going to be released in Paris only at the cost of cutting two of its six original episodes, including the best one, or at least the most significant. In the meantime, however, De Sica's popularity as an actor continues to grow thanks to films like *Bread, Love, and Jealousy* (1954; dir. Luigi Comencini).[1]

It is fashionable among young critics to drag De Sica's name through the mud, and I grant that he occasionally deserves some serious condemnation. But before condemning him, one should at least try to understand why the festival juries, half the traditional critics, and the public in general ignore or despise not so much his most ambitious films, like *Umberto D.*, as his compromised projects such as *Stazione Termini* and *Gold of Naples*. For it is indeed quite strange that, even when De Sica resigns himself, for reasons far too obvious, to making a film with stars and vignettes and built around clever tricks and purple passages, everything turns out as though he had again been far too ambitious for a festival audience. The criticisms I have heard people make of his work at Cannes are not at all justified. Granted, *Gold of Naples* is a prostituted film, but it is still so classy that it seems prudish and boring to those who admire our own *Adorable Creatures* (1952; dir. Christian-Jacque) or bourgeois psychological dramas tailor-made by good French craftsmen.

Everything, then, depends on your point of reference. Absolutely speaking, or compared with his own work and with what we like of other Italian films, De Sica has not hesitated in *Gold of Naples* to make deplorable concessions. But compared with what the public and often even the critics know—or don't know—of Italian cinema, his film remains a monument to austerity. One must nonetheless reproach De Sica first with betraying neorealism here by pretending to serve it. In fact, *Gold of Naples* is an essentially theatrical film, through the twists of its plot as well as through the decisive importance it accords to acting. Certainly, the movie's episodes can be considered "short stories" or "novelettes," but their skillful and rigorous construction deprives them of the dramatic indeterminacy that constitutes neorealism. The incidents and the characters proceed from the action in *Gold of Naples*, they don't precede it. De Sica has succeeded in regenerating the structure of conventional drama or the dramatic novel through certain elements borrowed from neorealism. By multiplying the picturesque and unexpected touches, he wraps his dramatic construction in a coral-like cover of small facts that deceive us as to the make-up of the rock underneath. Neorealism being in essence a denial of dramatic categories, De Sica substitutes for them a micro-dramaturgy that suggests the absence of action. In the process, however, he evidences only a superior theatrical cunning.

This is why the episode I prefer is perhaps the one that people generally deem the most offensive: I mean the card game, because it is also the sketch whose scenic resources are the least camouflaged. This story of a monomaniacal baron whom the baroness forbids to gamble yet who ends up gambling away his jacket and glasses with the concierge's son, is a farce conceived for acting effects. There are limits to the ambition of this genre but these limits are acceptable, especially when you consider that what De Sica adds to the genre considerably increases its aesthetic

Gold of Naples (1955) ["The Rocketeer"], dir.Vittorio De Sica.
La Cinémathèque Royale, Brussels.

value. It is always better to give more than you had promised rather than
to fail to live up to the promises you have made.

Conversely, I much admire—without liking it very much—the sketch
that the filmmakers undoubtedly prefer: I refer to the burial of a child
(unfortunately cut by the French distributor). De Sica and Zavattini
wanted to give a guarantee of neorealism here; unlike other episodes,
which are artfully constructed, this one appears to be a reconstituted
scene from a news bulletin. De Sica limits himself to following the funer-
al procession of the dead child. The mother's behavior, the wretched
exhibition she displays all along the way in order to give her child's last
voyage a solemnity that is both tragic and joyous—this never crystallizes
into "action," yet manages to hold our interest from beginning to end.
Such an astonishing bravura passage in principle belongs to the same aesthetic family as the maid's wake-up scene in *Umberto D*. Why do I feel
embarrassed by it, then? Probably because of the moral contradiction
between the subject matter and the almost unseemly cleverness-by-
understatement with which the sequence is handled. Such control over the
means and ends, when the situation of the characters calls for sympathy

and even pity, is somewhat irritating. Think by comparison of the simple, efficient, and sincere lyricism of Jules Dassin in *Rififi* (1955) during the return of the Stéphanois[2] with the kid.

As you can see, my reservations are not small. They won't prevent me, however, from acknowledging the merits of *Gold of Naples* from a relative point of view. If the film was not successful at Cannes, that must be because it nonetheless contains something good and worthy. We must explain the paradox of its failure not by the shortcomings that I have just mentioned and that on the contrary should have contributed to its success, but by the upholding at its very core of a union of form and content, which justifies a certain admiration.

First and foremost, craft is craft, and one had better realize this before criticizing its use. I apologize to our Hitchcocko-Hawksians, whom I am going to shock, but it is Hitchcock whom I can't help thinking of here. Of course, De Sica's skill does not bring itself to bear on the same elements of the *mise en scène* as Hitchcock's. The structuring of the image plays only a secondary role (although there is an unforgettable find in *Gold of Naples*: the elevator in the baron's house). The *mise en scène* is practically identified here with the directing of the actors, but you have to consider that the result is the same in that nothing in the picture seems likely to escape from the filmmaker's control. Although there are fifty kids scattered like a flight of birds in the frame, each of them seems to be making at every instance exactly the gesture that needs to be made, paradoxically even when that gesture must be unexpected. It *is* in fact unexpected, and that is the amazing part. De Sica relies on a certain margin of freedom and spontaneity that his walk-ons give him, but this man and his power are such that not a single discordant or approximate note is struck in the crowd. God and the Devil submit to that power. This director's self-assurance verges on obscenity during the scene of the baron's card game. Before De Sica, filmmakers had managed to make children play-act, but even the most gifted child is capable after all of only two or three expressions, which the director then strives to justify. For the first time, one can see here a ten- or eleven-year-old kid express in ten minutes a gamut of feelings whose variety equals that of his grown-up partner, in this case De Sica himself.

As for the professional actors, it would be an understatement to say that De Sica brings out the best in them: he reconstitutes them entirely. Not through the facile device of giving the professional a role that is different from the part he usually plays, but by somehow revealing in him another actor, a richer one who is more imbued with the character he is playing. Take, for instance, the extraordinary acting of Silvana Mangano, but take also the acting of Totò in the story of the racketeer. When you consider that it has become a commonplace of French criticism to maintain that our own Fernandel is a dramatic actor who too seldom finds work as one, all you can do is burst out laughing. Fernandel at his best looks like nothing more than an industrious clown alongside the simplicity and intelligence evidenced here by his Italian rival. God knows, however, that their usual antics are pretty much alike. But everything happens in this film as though De Sica had the power of endowing his nonprofessional actors with the skill of experienced performers and his established stars with the spontaneity of common people. Of course, I'm not saying that this is my personal ideal, but it is, at least implicitly, the one which almost all filmmakers would strive to attain if it were in their power to get close to it. De Sica achieves it so perfectly that the audience, which is used to approximations of the ideal, perhaps feels more ill at ease than pleased in front of it.

I don't think, either, that in general the qualities of the script have been properly appreciated. Whatever one may think of the choice of subjects, it goes without saying that each of these could have been treated in a different way. Yet, the construction of all the episodes, and particularly of their denouements, is amazingly intelligent. As a general rule, each story calls for an ending in, say, the style of Marcel Pagnol, i.e., a false and moving one. Naturally, the average French filmmaker would substitute for such an ending one in Charles Spaak's[3] style, i.e., a true-to-life and pessimistic conclusion. The ambitious filmmaker would reject both the "good" and the "bad" endings and, in an act of supreme daring, would not end the story at all. De Sica and Zavattini manage to go them all one better. The story seems at first to be moving toward a happy ending. We expect a surprise, and it comes with an unexpected development in the action, which makes us believe that in fact there will be no ending. Then, in the last few seconds, the script uncovers the most unexpected yet most necessary ending, which is the dialectical synthesis of all the endings that it had rejected. This is not due to the cleverness of an inventive screenwriter who seeks to surprise us at all costs, but rather to a constructive determination that throws a far more illuminating light on the whole action. The device presupposes such a dramatic strictness that it sometimes goes unnoticed even by the most attentive viewers, who cannot even imagine that the filmmaker might have aimed so high.

The ending of the episode entitled "Theresa," for example, was incorrectly interpreted by almost everyone. This is the nearly Dostoyevskian story of a young and rich Neapolitan bourgeois who decides to marry a prostitute to punish himself for having let a young woman die of love for him. This marriage, which must necessarily, and according to his own wishes, destroy his happiness, endanger his wealth, and ruin his reputation, takes place without the poor girl's understanding the game that she is being made to play (this is almost the plot of *The Ladies of the Bois de Boulogne*[4] in reverse). When she discovers that she is present only to remind her husband of his sin, her despair is immense. In his masochistic madness, the man hadn't even considered any of the most humanly plausible propositions: first, that his prostitute could make a nice and sweet wife, if only out of her gratitude to him, or second, that she could summon up enough female dignity to reject such a hateful game. Projecting onto the whole world his desire for castigation, he can see the woman he has chosen as true only to the a priori moral ideal of the prostitute, that is, as a diabolical and wicked being.

This summary clearly indicates the two possible endings: (1) the man, longing for unhappiness, finds happiness in spite of himself with a good girl (the Pagnol ending); (2) the prostitute, her female pride injured, prefers going back to the street in spite of her dreams of bourgeois respectability, comfort, and fidelity (the Spaak ending). Well, after her awful wedding night, the girl does run away; then, in the street, she thinks the situation over and goes back. I have heard people account for this third ending with psychological explanations that vary more or less according to the following: after she has run away out of wounded pride, the poor woman finds herself alone on the street in the rain and realizes all that she is going to lose; resigned, she silences her dignity and returns to bourgeois society, which is the ideal of every "self-respecting" prostitute. This explanation, however, suggests that the viewer has not carefully watched the last two shots. Primarily because Silvana Mangano's face, carefully lit by a street lamp, expresses a whole range of feelings, the final one of which is neither resignation nor envy but rather hatred, which is moreover confirmed by the way she knocks on the door to ask her husband for admittance. The only plausible explanation, then, is that she had left on account of the blow to her pride, and that she comes back for the same reason, after some deep reflection. She has understood that flight is a doubly absurd solution, since it will deprive her of the material advantages of marriage as well as the consolations of revenge. Her return is therefore neither resigned nor submissive; it is an even higher manifestation of her femininity than flight, for it proves she thought that even a prostitute had the right to be loved. And now she's going to prove something even greater: that she is capable of avenging herself.

Thus matters finally get settled according to the man's will, but for moral reasons that are exactly the opposite of those he imagines. The girl is going to take her expected place in the unbelievable scheme of things; toward her husband she's now going to behave according to the conventional idea of a prostitute, because she will have ceased to be one passively. She will thus affirm her womanhood through hatred. Fulfilling the man's wish, she will then bring him to his doom, not because prostitutes will be prostitutes but out of deliberate choice, as a free woman of the world. You will recognize that this ending is not only unexpected and brilliant (provided that you at least see it), but also and above all that it retroactively raises the action from the primitive level of psychosociology to the higher plane of morality and even metaphysics.

Gold of Naples seems to me to contain still other important lessons. To the extent that the filmmaker's intention is perhaps more or less deliberately impure, some aspects of the Zavattini–De Sica collaboration come out more clearly. I will first underline the fact that *Gold of Naples* is a film of cruelty—a cruelty that has undoubtedly contributed to disconcerting the festival audience, which is used to associating good humor with southern European verve. Naples in this sense is nothing but a super-Marseilles. I myself have made rather naive statements in the past about De Sica's kindheartedness. And it is true that sentimentalism drips profusely from his films. But much will be forgiven him here for the authenticity of his cruelty. Granted, goodness in art can quickly become revolting. Chaplin's tramp may indeed look so good to those who don't discern the ambiguity in his heart. Goodness in itself does not signify anything, but its close and almost inevitable association with cruelty has a moral and aesthetic meaning that psychology alone cannot account for. Am I wrong? It seems to me that such kind cruelty, or cruel kindness, is far more than simply the invention of De Sica and Zavattini.

In any case, what seems very clear to me is that the director's talent essentially proceeds from his talent as an actor, and that this talent is not neorealistic by nature. If the collaboration between Zavattini and De Sica has been so successful, this is perhaps due to the attraction of opposites. In this marriage, the writer has brought the realistic temperament and the director the knowledge of theatrical exploitation. But these two artists were too intelligent or too gifted just to add the latter to the former: they subtly combined the two or, if I may be permitted such an image, they emulsified them. Theatricality and realism are so subtly mixed in their work that their aesthetic suspension gives the illusion of a new body, which would then be neorealism. But its stability is uncertain, and we can very well see in *Gold of Naples* how a great deal of the theatricality precipitates to the bottom—or is it the foundation?—of the *mise en scène*.

NOTES TO CHAPTER 17

Cruel Naples (Gold of Naples)

(All notes have been provided by the Editor.)

This review was first published in French in *Cahiers du Cinéma*, no. 48 (June 1955), then reprinted in Vol. 4 ("Une Esthétique de la réalité: le néoréalisme") of Bazin's four-volume *Qu'est-ce que le cinéma?* (Paris: Éditions du Cerf, 1958–62), pp. 104–111.

1. In *Bread, Love, and Jealousy*, De Sica plays the police sergeant of a mountain village whose engagement to the local midwife is endangered by gossiping neighbors. This film was the sequel to the comedy *Bread, Love, and Dreams* (1953), also directed by Comencini and starring De Sica.

2. An inhabitant of the French city of Saint-Etienne.

3. Belgian screenwriter whose credits include *Carnival in Flanders* (1935), *La Grande Illusion* (1937), *Justice Is Done* (1950), and *Adorable Creatures* (1952).

4. *Les Dames du Bois de Boulogne*, 1946 (scenario by Robert Bresson, after an extract from Diderot's *Jacques le Fataliste*; dialogue by Jean Cocteau).

CHAPTER 18

S*enso*

The action of *Senso* (1954) takes place in 1866 at the time of the "Risorgimento."[1] Venice is under Austrian occupation. The performance of a Verdi opera (*Il Trovatore*) at the Phoenix Theater is the occasion for a patriotic demonstration during which Marquis Ussoni, one of the leaders of the "Resistance," provokes a young Austrian officer, Franz Mahler. Ussoni is arrested upon his exit from the theater. To save him, his cousin, Countess Livia Serpieti, seeks to make the acquaintance of the handsome Austrian lieutenant, who easily takes advantage of the situation in order to try out on the imprudent countess his abilities as a skillful and cynical seducer. The result is that he becomes her lover. Such a limited summary hardly permits me to analyze the at once subtle and elemental dealings that unite for the worst this weak yet lucid young man and this beautiful older woman, who will sacrifice all honor and decency for him and ultimately betray the cause of her friends in the "Resistance," whom she had served as an advisor.

According to impeccable logic, Visconti develops the action on two levels: the historical and the individual. The love relationship of the two protagonists begins and evolves in an irreversibly downward direction, whereas all the values (moral as well as political) that attach to the historical context are progressive and bracing. But this moral-political Manichaeism is not the product of a clever screenwriter's or director's trick: it is inherent in the story from the start, and subsequent events simply conspire to bring it out. To be sure, there are villains (Count Serpieri, for example, who is the typical "collaborator"), but the protagonists are doomed without them, and Franz Mahler, in his refined and clear-eyed ignominy, knows it. Marquis Ussoni, however, is there as proof of the fact that history does not dispose of anyone a priori. On the contrary: he digs deep into his family's heritage to find the courage and determination with which to go on. And if she hadn't been blinded by love, Livia herself would perhaps have continued to participate in the triumph of History. But as soon as she is blindfolded, she can but fight in vain against the current as she is dragged down along with her social class to the bottom of the abyss, where she will have only the fatal consolation of joining her lover.

What should be transparent even from my poor summary of the action are both the film's transposition of time from the "Risorgimento" to the Occupation and Resistance of World War II (this transposition is carried very far in its details, especially where the relations between the underground "Resistance" and the official national army are concerned), and its Marxist analysis of a romantic entanglement. From these two points of view, *Senso* would certainly deserve a fuller discussion than I am able to give here. But I must at least point out that the appeal of this ideological perspective is in its never appearing to have been slavishly applied from outside the aesthetic logic of the narrative; on the contrary: the ideological component comes across as an added dimension that naturally attends the revelation of the romantic truth. Nevertheless, I don't think that this breaks any absolutely new ground. In this respect, *Senso* is probably simply adhering to the novelistic aesthetic that originated with Flaubert and that was particularly affirmed by naturalism. The film thus allies itself with a literature that is simultaneously descriptive and critical. Still, and for reasons completely contingent on their source, good examples of Marxist inspiration are so rare that it would be difficult to remain insensitive to this one.

But let's try to define the style adopted by Visconti in this film. I don't think that, stylistically, *Senso* is essentially different from *Ossessione* (1942) or *La Terra Trema* (1948), as some of Visconti's own comments might suggest. I recognize, on the contrary, the same fundamental preoccupations in this latest work. Of *La Terra Trema*, for instance, I would not hesitate to say that Visconti had indulged in the "theatricalization" of doubly realistic material: realistic, in the normal sense, since the film was about a real village and the authentic life of its authentic inhabitants, but also in the restrictive, "miserabilistic" sense. There's nothing less "beautiful," less noble, less spectacular than this poor society of fishermen. Naturally, I don't intend the term "theatrical" in its pejorative sense. I use it instead to suggest the nobility and extraordinary dignity that Visconti's *mise en scène* injected into this reality. These fishermen were not dressed in rags, they were draped in them like tragic princes. Not because Visconti was trying to distort or simply interpret their existence, but because he was revealing its immanent dignity.

Of *Senso* I would conversely say that it reveals the realism of theater. Not only because Visconti gives us this motif from the start with the opera whose action, as it were, leaves the stage for the house, but also because the historical aspect, despite all its ramifications—especially in matters aristocratic and military—is experienced first on the level of decor and spectacle. This is true for all "period films," of course, especially those in color. But starting from this point, Visconti continuously seeks to impose upon this magnificent, beautifully composed, almost picturesque setting the rigor and, most importantly, the unobtrusiveness of a documentary.

Let me give only one example among a hundred. A few moments before battle, the Italian soldiers, who had been hiding behind haystacks, come out and fall in for the attack. The folded-up flag is brought to the commanding officer; brand-new in its protective covering, it must be taken out before it can be unfurled. This detail is barely visible in an extreme long shot in which every element is given the same, strict weight. Now imagine a similar scene shot by Duvivier or Christian-Jaque: the flag would be used as a dramatic symbol or as an integral part of the *mise en scène*. For Visconti, what matters is that the flag is *new* (as new as the Italian army); he calls attention to it, however, not through the framing, but only, where possible, through heightened realism.

Visconti claims that in *Senso* he wanted to show the "melodrama" (read: the opera) of life. If this was his intention, his film is a complete success. *La Terra Trema* had the magnitude and the nobility of opera; *Senso* has the density and the import of reality. It is possible that Visconti's film satisfies another kind of dialectic. It would hardly take away from the film's achievement if it didn't exclusively satisfy the one described here.

Senso

This review was first published in French in *France-Observateur* (Feb. 1956), then reprinted in Vol. 4 ("Une Esthétique de la réalité: le néoréalism") of Bazin's four-volume *Qu'est-ce que le cinéma?* (Paris: Éditions du Cerf, 1958–62), pp. 117–021.

1. Editor's note: Italian for "resurrection": the nineteenth-century movement for the liberation and unification of Italy.

CHAPTER 19

T he Style Is the Genre (*Les Diaboliques*)

Les Diaboliques (1954) will probably rank among the minor creations of Henri-Georges Clouzot, as a mere entertainment. But at the same time it is without question his only perfect film. That its perfection comes at the expense of an ambitious subject is not necessarily a shortcoming, if it is true that aesthetic pleasure derives from the exact appropriateness of means to ends. Compared with *Les Diaboliques*, *The Wages of Fear* (1953) was a monumental work, but one in which Clouzot could be faulted for not having fulfilled the epic dimension implicit in the story from the start. An irritating lack of dramatic necessity presided, if not over the choice of episodes, then at least over their length, and the ending, which was supposed to be tragic, obeyed the dictates of conventional storytelling. With *Les Diaboliques*, however, Clouzot seems eager to prove that he can build a solid narrative if he wants to.

You already know that this is a classic murder story—I mean, one whose essential interest is in the police investigation: the depiction of character and milieu is subordinated to the functioning of the plot. So *Les Diaboliques* is neither Clouzot's *The Raven* (1943) nor his *Quai des Orfèvres* (*Jenny Lamour*, 1947), although the background for the action is a private school not far from Paris. Clouzot has a weakness for such cloistered settings, but here the realistic elements are sketchy. What detail there is, is intended to trick the viewer, to be the bait that lures him onto the investigatory trail. The prospective viewer will eventually thank me for not revealing anything that might help him to solve the puzzle; for my part, I started to figure it out only thirty seconds before the end. The mystery is essential here. Allow me all the same to supply at least the givens of the situation. The headmaster of a private school that is at once middle-class and seedy terrorizes his wife and his mistress. These two end up becoming co-conspirators. The mistress, who is the more aggressive one, persuades the wife to set them both free by murdering their torturer. The crime will be camouflaged as the perfect accident. Everything seems to happen according to plan... but I realize that by going any further I would already by depriving you of several nice surprises, so let's stop here.

What is certain is that Clouzot has achieved 100 percent of his goal and that the viewer cannot help but experience all the emotions the director has prepared for him, as if along a scenic highway. Of course, we all know that Clouzot is a master at playing with our nerves. You leave the movie theater broken, quartered, and battered, but also relieved and happy—evidence of the film's success. The catharsis is total because the art with which the film is invested neither outstrips its subject nor falls short of it. The genre is realized to perfection, and it is this perfection, the complete absence of any dramatic residue, that mollifies the soul after having shaken it so violently. A short time after seeing *Les Diaboliques*, I saw Feydeau's *How to Get Rid of Your Mistress* (1955; dir. Guy Lefranc), with Noël-Noël,[1] and these two films that are so different left me in fact in the same state of inner jubilation, because both execute the precise unwinding of an impeccable dramatic mechanism. Some might say that the Feydeau film is immoral, but this would be as silly as saying that the Clouzot film is pernicious: the content of these works is completely transfigure by their form. The famous Aristotelian conception is not true only for tragedy. Each genre, even the most humble, such as the crime film or farce, has its nobility and produces catharsis as long as it is a true genre, i.e., as long as it has its own style and as long as this style is properly fulfilled.

From all that is admirable in *Les Diaboliques*, I'll pick out only two examples. The first pertains to the film's dramatic construction. The solution that is given to us in the last few seconds of the film could very well have been a little twist whose faulty logic or feeble psychology would quickly be covered over by the detective's comments and by the words "The End." This is often the case in crime films, where the director tries to fool the viewer right to the finish before hastily tying things up. At that point, the viewer is no longer very demanding. In Clouzot's film, by contrast, one can marvel at the simplicity and retroactive soundness of the solution to the criminal puzzle. I mean that Clouzot doesn't limit himself to unraveling the mystery: he gives it a new meaning in addition; it is as if another film grows out of this one's resolution.

I have suggested that it is useless to look for a psychological drama or a social portrait in *Les Diaboliques*. The characters here are as deliberately typed as if they were pieces on a chessboard. But naturally Clouzot has not deprived himself of all realistic support; if his characters are conventional, they are so within a convention grounded in this director's particular world. There is in the film, however, one quite remarkable character whose creation seems to me to deserve praise: that of the police inspector, played by Charles Vanel. It was hardly an easy matter to revitalize this role. Since I won't give away the conclusion to *Les Diaboliques*, the viewer will have to see for himself how Clouzot had managed to carry to the next factor, at it were, the traditional figure of the inspector as well as his dramatic function, or perhaps more accurately, and in keeping with the algebraic metaphor, how the director has given this character the minus sign in the police equation: Maigret[2] multiplied by -1 equals the solution to the film's puzzle.

NOTES TO CHAPTER 19

The Style Is the Genre (Les Diaboliques)

(All notes have been provided by the Editor.)

This review was first published in French in *Cahiers du Cinéma*, 8, no. 43 (January 1955), pp. 42–43.

1. Georges Feydeau (1862–1921) was a French writer of over sixty stage farces, a number of which have been filmed. Regarded in his lifetime as nothing more than an adroit purveyor of light entertainment, Feydeau has come to be regarded as an outstanding writer of classic farce.

    Noël-Noël was born Lucien Noël in Paris on August 9, 1897, and died in 1989. A leading comic and character actor of French films, he is best known for his characterization of the befuddled soldier Ademaï in films of the 1930s and for his portrayal of petit bourgeois types in the 1940s and 1950s. Noël-Noël wrote many of his own screenplays, including the one for *How to Get Rid of Your Mistress*, and directed one film, *La Vie chantée* (1951).

2. Georges Simenon (1902–1989), prolific novelist of Belgian birth who wrote in French, created the imperturbable Commissaire Maigret, who relies on psychological intuition rather that scientific methods in his detective work. Simenon's output ranges from straight detective fiction to purely psychological novels, which depend for plot and interest on the workings of the characters' minds and their reaction to the outside world. For the most part his characters belong to a violent, corrupt underworld, seldom described but evoked with a remarkable sense of sinister atmosphere.

CHAPTER 20

M. *Ripois*, with or without Nemesis[1]

I consider *M. Ripois* (1954) a very important film (even the most important of all René Clément's films). It is wonderful in many respects, but it
is not the masterpiece that some people would like to see in it. My major
criticism is that it is too intellectual and calculated a creation and therefore insufficiently suffused with sensibility. I mean by that the filmmaker's
sensibility, that of the protagonist being a completely different matter
which will also command my attention.

M. Ripois is perhaps more important than even its most enthusiastic
supporters have argued, first and foremost because of the able and original solution it found for the problem of fictional adaptation. If this problem has dominated the aesthetic evolution of postwar cinema, *M. Ripois*
advances its solution in a decisive manner. Films like *The Pastoral Symphony*
(1946; dir. Jean Delannoy) and *Devil in the Flesh* (1947; dir. Claude Autant-
Lara), which had seemed courageous and admirable in their day, today
look like labored and timid enterprises. One sees very well how Aurenche
and Bost's talent strove above all, albeit with an intelligence and taste that
were still unusual for the screen, to transpose the plot and the characters
from the linguistic universe of the novel to the dramatic universe of the
screen. We must give the screenwriters Aurenche and Bost credit for being
primarily concerned with remaining faithful to their source material. With
them the literary work ceased to be only the pretext for a script and the
provider of the prestige of a title, which is the role to which previous adaptations had unmistakably reduced literature. Whatever the modifications
made to the organization of the original, or even to the characters and the
plot, Aurenche and Bost considered everything there to be necessary.

M. Ripois (1954), dir. René Clément. Museum of Modern Art, New York.

Their sincere purpose was to give us a film that, in following its model, would remain worthy of it.

The history of cinema must give them credit for having reversed the trend of previous adaptations by promulgating the idea—through their belief in faithfulness to the source, even loosely defined faithfulness—that film could compete with the novel on its own grounds. But, unknowingly perhaps, they still retained in their work a reactionary and pernicious postulate: that of the irreducible difference between the novel's literary reality and "the screen's visual element." They remained convinced that any precise translation was impossible and that the mission of the adaptor-screenwriter consisted in transposing the essence—not the whole—of a book from one system of signification to the other. We won't blame them for using this working hypothesis as a pretext for introducing their own inventions and thus in a way claiming co-authorship of the novelist's work. The fact that their fidelity is limited to the subject matter and characters of a book is not particularly important. But we see very well today how in thinking they were engineering the true filmic reconstitution of the novel,

Aurenche and Bost were behaving like Viollet-le-Duc,[2] who was less an archaeologist than a Romantic. Yet he was nevertheless the precursor of modern archaeology, which prefers to leave the old freestone in its raw state rather than copy anew its carvings with great accuracy.

We'll give Robert Bresson credit for having destroyed this bias; his respect for literature is equal only to his total faith in film. He has given us, with *Diary of a Country Priest* (1950), an example of complete fidelity, not only to the plot and characters, but also to all that in the novel may seem to derive its very existence from language. This faithfulness is imaginative, however (so much more so than that of Jean Delannoy or Claude Autant-Lara!), because it is based not on the adaptation of literature to film, but on the reaction of one to the other and on the relationship between word and image. Objectively, and if we forget momentarily the existence of Bernanos' book, one sees very well that the film "also," not "first," has literary value, and that the essence of Bresson's profound filmic originality perhaps derives from this fact.

In *Diary of a Country Priest*, Bresson almost made the *ab absurdo* demonstration of the novelistic potentialities of film. I'm thinking in particular of the blank screen at the end, where the image, at the peak of its dramatic intensity, fades out behind the word, the writer's pure language, which derives additional solemnity and spiritual effectiveness from this blinding of the senses. But although it is good for an art to renounce its powers in order to get a better feel for their existence and importance, it would be foolish for it to reject systematically the employment of these powers. Moreover, the case of Bernanos' book was rather peculiar, if only because of its author's death and the exceptional importance of verbal style in the expression of its meaning. Beyond this extreme case, quasi-literalness ceases to be the supreme ideal of adaptation. More important than such faithfulness is knowing whether the film can integrate the powers of the novel (let's be cautious: at least the novel of the classical kind) and whether it can, beyond the spectacle, interest us less through the representation of events than through our comprehension of them.

So I won't reproach René Clément for what liberties he has taken with Louis Hémon's novel; I will simply discuss them later. Whatever the results of the comparison between the novel and the film, however, the director must be given credit for his dazzling inventiveness and remarkable intelligence, which knows exactly how to make the conditions of spectacle accord with those of novelistic acuity. Take for instance one of the most brilliant scenes, that of the French lesson that convinces M. Ripois to seduce his future wife. Although the action is supposed to take place in the past, the narrative is seemingly always related in the present and the camera purports to show us the event objectively. But the cuts here integrate the psychological or subjective commentary. The "dramatic" or objective action, if I may call it that, as defined by the protagonists' behavior and their words, indeed takes place on the screen before our very eyes,. However, the cuts (i.e., the shifting of the frame and the movement of the camera) are built not on this apparent reality, but rather on the thoughts of Ripois, who notices first the legs of his beautiful visitor, then more than anything else her marvelous cigarette case made of solid gold, and little by little decides to attempt the conquest of one or the other. To be sure, Clément's intention here might not be very original, and one could find examples of it even in silent film. His innovation lies in the fact that the duality of points of view, the objective and the subjective, is always simultaneously expressed through the *mise en scène*, without really resorting to such telling effects of editing as close-ups and superimposition. The secret meaning of the scene, the one it has in the characters' minds, is no longer given by the way it is "described," but by the way it is "written." The very image that simply shows the action at the same time analyzes and comments upon it.

Furthermore, Clément does not refrain from resorting to voice-over commentary or from combining it, in an act of extreme virtuosity, with actual dialogue and direct sound. One must force oneself to be extremely attentive if one is to notice the moment when the scene becomes silent and commented upon, for the soundtrack continuously intermingles the two literary or verbal levels—to which we must even add that of music, which is itself always critical. Of course, Raymond Queneau's commentary and dialogue are not "written" exactly like those of *Diary of a Country Priest*, but their literary nature is evident despite the fact that one could be fooled by their realism, although not more than one would be by the realism in any other novel by the same author.

The intelligence of the stylization perhaps finds its most original expression in the combination of brute reality with the *mise en scène*. Clément radically revives in *M. Ripois* the "neorealistic" device of placing the camera in the street. I put "neorealistic" between quotation marks to indicate that I personally do not define neorealism by this technique, however successfully the Italian directors have employed it. In fact, the hidden camera on location is quite an old idea and was used very often, but never, it seems to me, as Clément has used it. Dziga Vertov in *Man with a Movie Camera* (1929) or Jean Vigo in *À propos de Nice* (1930) filmed passers-by without their knowing it. The result could be funny or monstrous, but very often it revealed a human reality to which in everyday life we unconsciously adapt our eye or, more often still, which adapts itself to our eye. The implacably objective eye hidden in a hatbox shatters the belief that all our public actions are other-directed or "business as usual," perhaps just as much as the exposed camera shapes the behavior of the person who knows he is being watched. In the case of the Italians, it is actually different, for in general (except, incidentally, in *The Italians Turn Themselves Around* [1953; dir. Alberto Lattuada as part of the anthology film *Love in the City*]) they don't try to reveal the humanity of the street through a voyeur's objectivity. Conversely, they try to blend their characters with the street so that we can no longer even think of making a distinction between the action of the film and the reality we experience every day of our lives. In order to achieve this effect, the neorealist directors don't hide their camera; rather, the passers-by more or less become unsalaried walk-ons, but always consciously. The theatrical genius of the Italian people does the rest, since the Italian street is a theater where everyone continuously improvises his own *commedia dell'arte* whether a camera is present or not. In all probability, the camera concealed in a hatbox would not record anything essentially different.

It's not the same in London, and I can't resist noting here that Jean Vigo, in *À propos de Nice*, closely observed the "Promenade des Anglais"[3] because he had come to a similar conclusion. It would be interesting, although it would take too long, to explain how Clément managed to film his actors in the street, unnoticed by the passers-by, who continue to come and go "as if nothing were happening." Portable cameras camouflaged in newspapers and mounted on a delivery truck, a whole crew of assistants mounting guard, and above all a battle plan that was prepared like a bombing mission and that took into account all kinds of foreseeable incidents, such as the times at which buses passed, allowed Clément to show us Gérard Philippe and Joan Greenwood in the London crowd, playing their roles in the middle of a multitude of daily activity, on the same level as the reality they were invading. Some scenes shot there are even more significant than they are juicy: take, for instance, that of the passer-by who is both scandalized and delighted to see two lovers kissing in the street (Gérard

Philippe and a fellow actress), or that of the young girl who recognized the French actor and stopped to ask him for his autograph. Without losing his composure, Gérard Philippe gestured to her as if he were giving directions. I don't know whether Clément has thought about putting all these incidents together in a montage of a film distinct from the real one, but it would be a "Diary of *M. Ripois*" that would not be without interest. Anyway, these intrusions of brute reality on the world of the film perfectly illustrate Clément's intention and success. For the first time, I think, a director has managed to insert, indeed to blend, social reality into his movie as he was shooting it, while preserving that reality's quality of absolute objectivity yet always submitting it to the demands of the narrative action.

For clarity's sake, I'll borrow the following comparison from film technique. Frequently, when a love scene has to be shot in the street, directors use a special effect called "rear projection." It consists in filming first the street, then the scene in a studio in front of an immense screen of translucent glass upon which the film of the street is being projected. One easily understands why the protagonists are always forced to stay "in front of" things and people. To the expert eye, other details betray the special effect: the heterogeneousness of the lighting, the slight shaking of the background, its coarser grain. Even if these slight imperfections were eliminated and the street scene were filmed without the knowledge of the passers-by, one sees very well that the device would still rest, because of its very principle, on the impossibility of mingling the two universes. The "acted" action floats upon rather than mingles with brute reality, like a cork on the ocean.

Clément makes the former penetrate the latter, while managing to avoid both the dissolving of his novelistic creation into reality and its rejection by its opposite number. Social reality as such is kept intact; it is revealed objectively in its brute state, but it is nevertheless subjected to the narrative and used as a kind of reaction to it. Another example of this type of scene, filmed "on the sly," will express my point even better. It has the eloquent power of a fable: M. Ripois has lost his job; he hasn't a penny left, hence no place to stay and soon nothing left to eat. He wanders the streets, unshaved, hungry, and worn out. He looks through the windows of the shops and above all through those of the fast-food restaurants, where hurried people eat along a counter facing the street. For those who watch him go by or for those he watches as they eat on the other side of the window, Philippe is what he looks like: a bum-to-be, a famished man; they don't so much as even look at him. Apparently fallen into misery, the star has also fallen into the loneliness of a man abandoned by society. One sees here the force that such a situation could derive from a *mise en scène* that reconstituted it with walk-ons "taken from the street," but walks-ons whom one would have told to "look" indifferent. Yet under such conditions the action would be no more than invented and represented. Through the insertion of the fictional element of the actor into a reality that ignores him, the action seems virtually real. The moral loneliness of a poor man in the city is no longer the believable creation of the writer or scenarist: its representation coincides with our experience of it. To record it is to devise it.

If, on almost all important points, Clément has deliberately departed from Hémon's book, he has nonetheless done better than be faithful to it. The filmic rendition of London in *M. Ripois*, for example, is in no way inferior to its depiction in the novel, where it plays a crucial role. One could cite, in connection with the above-mentioned scene, Hémon's marvelous passage about hunger, which Clément manages to surpass by putting the food into the mouths of the passers-by—the restaurant customers—who *don't* stop eating when they see the famished Philippe on the street: "M. Ripois bought two portions of pudding for a penny and ate them while walking along a dark street, taking from his pocket big chunks that he greedily ingested from the wrapping paper, slowly chewing but suddenly ceasing to chew, his jaws frozen, each time he met another passer-by." You don't always have to swallow your pride: sometimes you must chew on it, too!

We should also credit the film with other successes— secondary ones, to be sure, but nonetheless rarely achieved. I am thinking especially of the solution brought to the problem of bilingualism inherent in a co-production. *M. Ripois* is probably the first example of a co-production that succeeds without camouflaging its origins. Up to now, this constraint was almost always catastrophic, barely managing on occasion to go unnoticed. The film's subject, the life of a Frenchman in London, called for a bilingual co-production. However, the same version could not have been released in the two countries in question: just a few words in French would be too exotic for the English, and vice versa. I saw the two versions within a few weeks of each other, and I have a hard time trying to figure out exactly what the differences were between them: that's how skillful and believable the interweaving of the respective portions of dialogue in the two languages was. The antipodal nationalities of the lark and the horse seemed to me to be converging on the same goal, the same pudding-pâté, if you will. The prowess of each version was made possible mostly by the novelistic style of the film, by the free and flexible manner in which it is written, its quick and easy passage from facts to contemplation of those facts. Thus, realism and abstraction ceased to be contradictory: on the contrary, they developed a dialectical tension that was always resolved, to the point that even the realism of the language became relative.

Incidentally, Italian neorealism has witnessed a comparable evolution. The best version of *Stazione Termini* (a.k.a. *Indiscretion* or *Indiscretion of an American Wife*, 1953; dir. Vittorio De Sica) turned out to be the American one. I was also amazed to realize that the English version of *Europe '51* (a.k.a. *The Greatest Love*, 1952; dir. Roberto Rossellini) was superior to the Italian one, despite the fact that it was unbelievable to hear Ingrid Bergman speak the language of Shakespeare to underprivileged people on the streets of Rome. Credibility here was less important than truth, however, and there was more truth in Ingrid Bergman's speaking English than in hearing her dubbed in Italian. In view of this truth, the lack of social credibility in the secondary characters' language could be turned into a mere convention of narrative. Of course, this transformation could take place only in accordance with a *mise en scène* whose principle was the permanent transmutation into style of the most immediate, most direct reality. But we see, at least with a man like Rossellini, how neorealism, whose trademark was the respect for languages (as in *Paisan* [1946]), plainly reveals its latent abstraction today, when it permits itself to deploy that abstraction very freely. Make no mistake, however: it then becomes a convention completely justified by its stylistic integration into the world of social realism, which is exactly the contrary of the abstraction found in the pre-war Italian films that were inmates rather than interpreters of the Tower of Babel.

All the good things that I've said about *M. Ripois* should be sufficient, I think, to reveal how much I value this film. But it is true that this assessment is based more on what is aesthetically generalizable in the work than on its singular reality. I admire in this movie the invention of new artistic tools, of devices of *mise en scène* and narrative that enrich the novelistic means of cinema; however, I still believe that it is a failed filmic novel, whereas Hémon's was a successful printed one. I don't know whether I owe my disappointment to the film's excess of formal concerns, or to Clément's lack of sensitivity toward his protagonist. I'm afraid that the chink in Clément's armor is not around the heart; his temptation is the exercise of style. There's something of the egghead in him, of the academician of *mise en scène*, who is able more to solve difficult aesthetic problems (as in *The Glass Castle* [1950])[4] than to move us even at the cost of clumsiness. His two films that "move" more than any of the others are *Battle of the Rails* (1946) and *Forbidden Games* (1952), but they are also his less "well-made" ones, since both were originally medium-length works expanded into full-length ones. Perhaps the Resistance, to which everybody had an emotional connection, and childhood, for which Clément obviously has a peculiar weakness, were themes that deeply moved him. But it is also possible that everything dangerous and unpredictable in the course of these two filmic endeavors actually insured Clément against the excesses of his own talent, by keeping a place open for the artistic grace of God.

In any event, Clément and Queneau's André Ripois is very different from Hémon's Amédée Ripois, and I think that the former gained only psychological improbability in the process of his make-over. Hémon's Ripois solidly exists, and his psychological coordinates are clear. He is not a Don Juan, not even an affected one, but he is a "womanizer." If he has so many women, it is not at all because of his natural charm (at the very best, he has the gallant's prestige of a Frenchman in England), but because of the maniacal stubbornness with which he pursues them. Some of them, of course, fall into his trap, because he gladly resorts to the basest of lures. He is a petty go-getter who, above all else, is heartless. One would be very hard put, by contrast, to define the Ripois of the film psychologically as well as socially. Although he has Gérard Philippe's "French" charm, one can hardly believe that it is enough to seduce a beautiful, rich bluestocking like Catherine, especially after he has piteously revealed to her his blatant lack of education. Amédée Ripois was not very intelligent, but at least he had cunningly forced himself to read a few good authors so as to be able to discuss them with Aurora and thus seduce her with his knowledge of *belles-lettres*. The fact that the radically vulgar young man of the film so easily adapts to the life of the English aristocracy could not reasonably be explained solely by his physical appearance and his determined epicureanism. There is something incoherent, or rather non-existent, in this character, which troubles the attentive viewer. And this vacuum can't be passed off to the ambiguities of André Ripois's character, because ambiguity never penetrates that character; it remains exterior to it, on the level of mere demeanor or deportment, whereas it should be a psychological reality. What remains ambiguous is Clément's view of and insight into Ripois.

I understand that psychology is not the be-all and end-all of characterization. For instance, the protagonists and *Kind Hearts and Coronets* (a.k.a. *Noblesse Oblige*, 1949; dir. Robert Hamer) and (1947; dir. Charlie Chaplin), to which one can't help referring, could only be analyzed as psychological cases at the risk of misinterpreting them, since they take their justification from another level of aesthetic being. These works are intentionally built on the metaphysics of a character, whereas *M. Ripois* is too obviously built, not on the psychological make-up of a man, but on the physical appearance of Gérard Philippe. Besides, the moral credibility of Hémon's protagonist does not remain a prisoner of novelistic naturalism; the greatness of this little novel (which is said to be partly autobiographical) is that it leads naturally to tragedy. Clément has, out of honesty, deleted the Nemesis from the book's title, and he hasn't found a replacement for it in his film. For André Ripois's accidental paralysis, which makes him hopelessly prey to the sympathy of boring women, cannot seriously be considered as Venus's revenge. Amédée Ripois, in contrast, remains whole: simply, inexplicably, monstrously, on the occasion of a woman's death for which he is entirely at fault, a heart grows in him. Or rather the organ of his soul, which has remained insensate until then, starts aching in him like a wisdom tooth. Taking life in stride, Ripois has not taken the time to realize that he loved Ella, or even to ask if he was capable of loving her. But little by little, because of other failures, the memory of Ella grows in his conscience, and Ripois believes that all he has to do is retrace his steps in order to win her back, that she will forgive him as stupidly, as pitifully, as all the others. Except that Ella is dead, and Amédée Ripois will remain alone with a memory he can't forget. Oh, but it's not remorse! This is simply the birth of a heart, and Ripois goes back to France more miserable than when he had left it, "after he has understood that a being whose soul awakens can no longer be happy." One sees that it is a far cry indeed from the book's simple and sincere moral tale, to which the character's literary originality gave new life and truth, to the entomological aridity of André Ripois, whose soul and destiny elude us.

Clément's film is a comedy. I said earlier that the proportion of the respective languages in the two versions did not change the taste of the dish, but I was wrong on at least one point: the English version had given me the impression of a tragic film, whereas that impression became comical in the French version. This was probably because my English wasn't good enough! Deprived of a clear understanding of the film's dialogue as I heard it, I naturally returned in my mind to the novel that I had read, which is to say *M. Ripois*-with-Nemesis. But Queneau's screenplay removes any doubt about its comic intentions and we can't be mistaken any longer. Although I am not in favor of a hierarchy of genres, I must say that I regret the movie's passage to comedy, in that it is much more difficult to achieve success in a work whose heartless protagonist likewise demands no heartfelt response from the viewing public.

NOTES TO CHAPTER 20

M. Ripois, *with or Without Nemesis*

(All notes have been provided by the Editor.)

This article was first published in French in *Esprit* (Aug.–Sept. 1951), then reprinted in Vol. 2 ("Le Cinéma et les autres arts") of Bazin's four-volume *Qu'est-ce que le cinéma?* (Paris: Éditions du Cerf, 1958–62), pp. 55–67.

1. Raymond Queneau, Hugh Mills, and René Clément adapted their script from Louis Hémon's novel *M. Ripois et la Némésis* (1951). *Monsieur Ripois* is known as *Lovers, Happy Lovers* in the United States and *Knave of Hearts* in Great Britain.

2. Viollet-le-Duc, *Eugène Emmanuel*, (1814–1879) was a French architect and writer. He studied architecture in Paris and began his career by restoring minor medieval buildings in the south of France. In the 1840s, he restored the Sainte Chapelle in Paris and the Cathedral of Notre Dame, building a new spire over the crossing and a new pulpit. Among his other restorations, Viollet-le-Duc worked on the cathedrals at Laon and Amiens, the town walls of Carcassonne, and the Château de Pierrefonds.

3. A famous street in Nice, located along the beach and therefore frequented by many tourists, the British prominent among them.

4. French title: *Le Château de Verre*, based on a bestseller by Vicki Baum and starring Michèle Morgan and Jean Marais. I assume that the problem Clément solved here was the adaptatioᵒn of Baum's unexceptional novel to film, which he managed with some strikingly inventive visual touches.

CHAPTER 21

T *wo Cents' Worth of Hope*

The Italian critics have said that neorealism doesn't exist, and the French critics that it won't last. I think that in reality only Cesare Zavattini and Rossellini have unabashedly embraced the term, although each has attached a different meaning to it. If you want to hurt any other Italian filmmaker, all you have to do is congratulate him on his contribution to neorealism. In truth the Italians are more irritated than pleased with the success they have had under this generic label; consequently, each one defends himself against the term's suggestion of a unified movement. There are probably two related reasons for this. The first is completely psychological and quite understandable: the irritation of any artist who is conscious of his uniqueness, which the critics attempt to smother with an historical classification. Neorealism throws apples and oranges into the same bag. There is at least as much difference, for example, among Alberto Lattuada, Luchino Visconti, and De Sica as there is among Marcel Carné, Renoir, and Jacques Becker. Yet with the term "neorealism," the critics often seem to be implying that Italian film exists as a movement, as a collective sensibility, rather than as a series of individual talents. One can understand the filmmakers' reaction.

But more important still than these natural reactions of artistic pride, it seems to me, is the bias against "realism." When neorealism first astonished the world, critics praised everything that was documentary about it, its sense of social reality—in short, everything that made it look like a news report. The Italian filmmakers rightly realized the danger that lay in that kind of praise. The prestige of a documentary could only be accidental and minor. Once the exoticism of authentic documentaries, on the

Two Cents' Worth of Hope (1951, dir. Renato Castellani. Museum of Modern Art, New York.

one hand, and the bias in their favor due to the war, on the other, had worn off, the popularity of Italian film would not have lasted if it had been grounded only in realism. Indeed, art aims to go beyond reality, not to reproduce it. And this is even truer of film because of its technical realism, its ability to reproduce reality so easily. The Italian directors, then, continue to resist as much as they can when the critics try to place the yoke of neorealism around their necks.

We often marveled in France at the success of Italian film production during the years 1946 and 1947, as if it were a sort of miracle, or at the very least the dazzling result of favorable, though precarious, circumstances: the sudden fertilization by the Liberation of an old and minor tendency in Italian film.[1] But such unforeseen brilliance could only be that of a nova, and as such couldn't last. Besides, a type of filmmaking that would lay more stress on the material photographed than on the subject treated, on the pictorial rather than on the narrative—that would substitute reality for the imagination—would sooner or later have to lose its luster. *Bicycle Thieves* was the first great work to prove, not only that neorealism could survive very well without the themes of the Liberation, that its subject matter was by no means directly linked to the war or its aftermath, but also that neorealism's apparent lack of "story," of plot or action, was not in the least a sign of its inferiority to the structures of classical film narrative. De Sica and Zavattini's film has at once the accidental freedom of life seen through a window and the relentless force of ancient tragedy.

For those who still have doubts about the present and future vigor of neorealism, Renato Castellani's *Two Cents' Worth of Hope*, which received the Grand Prize this year at the Cannes Film Festival, presents another irrefutable argument. This pure masterpiece, although its tone is quite different from that of *Bicycle Thieves*, proves once again that the Italian cinema has managed to discover a new relationship between the realistic calling of film and the eternal demands of dramatic poetry.

Two Cents' Worth of Hope is the story of an unemployed Romeo by the name of Antonio. After being discharged from military service, he goes back to his native village, where his mother and young sisters are as poverty-stricken as when he left them. With fierce determination he looks for work, but life is tough and unemployment is the common lot of many men his age. Because he is ready to take anything, even the dirtiest of jobs, he will from time to time find employment; most often it will be for a very short period, although sometimes there's a chance it will last. But then there is Juliet. Her name is Carmela, she is fifteen or sixteen years old, and she is the daughter of a respectable firecracker manufacturer who doesn't want to hear about the possibility of an unemployed son-in-law. In fact, though, Antonio has only a very slight weakness for this girl who is enamored of him. He had forgotten her while he was in the army. He tries to get rid of her, since he has enough worries for the moment trying to feed his family. But Carmela clings to Antonio with incredible patience and cunning; she looks for every opportunity to arouse him and to compromise them both in the eyes of the village and her parents. The principal result of her plotting is that Antonio loses the jobs he had so painfully managed to find, among them a peculiar one as the private blood donor to the anemic child of a Neapolitan bourgeoise. Thus, not only does Antonio not want Carmela t all, but also her indiscreet attentions to him jeopardize the marriage she dreams of, since, without a job, Antonio can't even think of marrying her.

Carmela's love strategy has paradoxical results, however. Even though he has many reasons to hate her, Romeo finally begins to be attracted to Juliet. He's not going to let it be said that his life has been poisoned to such an extent by a girl he does not even love. So many problems at least deserve a wife, but her father, the firecracker manufacturer, refuses to give his blessing. He accuses Antonio of trying to force his way into an honorable and relatively well-off family. Mad with wounded dignity, Antonio strips Carmela bare on the village square: he will take her naked, just as she was born; her only dowry will be the two cents' worth of hope that enable poor people to go on living. One can see that this story doesn't have the tragic ending of *Romeo and Juliet*.[2] But one cannot help thinking of their love story in connection with this film, not only because of certain precise analogies, such as the antagonism between the families, but also, and above all, because of the extraordinary poetry of the sentiments and the passions, the thoroughly Shakespearean imagination that inspires them.

One can easily understand why and how neorealism has managed to triumph over its aesthetic contradictions in this marvelous film. Castellani is one of those whom the label "neorealist" irritates. And yet, his film completely observes the canons of neorealism: it is a remarkable report on rural unemployment in the Vesuvian region of contemporary Italy. All the characters are naturally drawn from the premises (especially Antonio's

Two Cents' Worth of Hope (1951), dir. Renato Castellani. Museum of Modern Art, New York.

mother, an incredible gossip who is toothless, loud, and delightfully sly). The script's structure, for its part, is typically neorealistic: the episodes are not causally connected, or, in any event, they lack dramatic necessity. The narrative is rhapsodic, and the film would last two more hours with no effect whatsoever on its unity. This is because the events don't stretch along an a priori continuum; they follow one another accidentally, like events in real life. But it goes without saying that the reality of *Two Cents' Worth of Hope* is that of poetry itself, and that freer, less obvious harmonies are substituted in this tale for dramatic necessities. I mean "tale" here in the Oriental sense, which suggests a simple, leisurely story, more or less loosely organized. Thus, Castellani perfectly realizes the paradox of giving us one of the most beautiful, most pure love stories in the history of film, evoking Marivaux and Shakespeare in the process, while at the same time he gives us the most exact account, the most ruthless indictment, of Italian rural poverty in 1951.

Two Cents' Worth of Hope

(All notes have been provided by the Editor.)

This review was first published in French in *France-Observateur* (July 1952), then reprinted in Vol. 4 ("Une Esthétique de la réalité: le néoréalisme") of Bazin's four-volume *Qu'est-ce que le cinéma?* (Paris: Éditions du Cerf, 1958–62), pp. 68–72.

1. The origins of neorealism are traceable to the realist or "verismo" style cultivated in the Italian cinema between 1913 and 1916, when films inspired by the writings of Verga and Zola dealt with working people's problems in natural settings. This was the subject matter to which the neorealists of the forties returned, reacting against the banality that had long been the dominant mode of Italian films and against prevailing social conditions. Examples of this cinema: *Sperduti nel buio* (dir. Nino Martoglio, 1914); *Assunta Spina* (dir. Gustavo Serena, 1915); *Cenere* (dir. Febo Mari, 1916). This brief flowering of realistic cinema was devastated by the economic and political aftermath of World War I.

   The term "neorealism" was first applied by the critic Antonio Pietrangeli to Visconti's *Ossessione* (1942), and the style came to fruition in the mid-to-late forties in the films of Rossellini and De Sica. With minimal resources, the neorealist filmmakers worked in real locations using local people as well as professional actors, and their films conveyed a powerful sense of the plight of ordinary individuals oppressed by political events. Neorealism was, in fact, not only a cinematic style but also a whole social, moral, and political philosophy. It was gradually phased out of the Italian cinema in the early 1950s, as economic conditions improved and film producers succumbed to the growing demand for escapist entertainment. But the movement's effects have been far-reaching. Its influence can be traced across the world from Hollywood, where stylistic elements in films about social and political problems echoed those of the neorealists, to India, where Satyajit Ray adopted a typically neorealist stance in his early films. In Italy itself neorealist principles have been perpetuated by, among others, Ermanno Olmi, with his compassionate studies of working-class life, and Francesco Rosi, with his vigorous attacks on the misuse of power.

2. Renato Castellani (1913–1985) went on to make a film of *Romeo and Juliet* in 1954: *Guilietta e Romeo*. Here are his major films: *The Pistol Shot* (1941); *Under the Roman Sun* (1948); *Springtime in Italy* (1949); *Two Cents' Worth of Hope* (1951).

CHAPTER 22

The Profound Originality of *I Vitelloni*

Without question, few films in the history of cinema have captured their era and exercised their influence more subtly than *I Vitelloni* (1953). Chaplin's films operated through the miraculously universal character of the Tramp. Films like *The Threepenny Opera* (1931) owe their audience, and the mark they have left on an entire generation, in part to the particularly successful marriage of music and cinema. By contrast, nothing in *I Vitelloni* seemed capable of impressing itself on the viewer's memory: no famous actors; not even, as in *La Strada* (1954), a poetically original and picturesque character around which the film is built; no story, or almost none. And yet the term "vitelloni" has become a common word: it now designates an international human type, and what is more, some of the best films each year remind us of Fellini's own (most recently, *La Nuit des maris*).

Recently I saw *I Vitelloni* again, and I was deeply struck right away by the fact that, despite some minor weaknesses, the film had not only not aged, it had even matured with time, as if its message hadn't been able upon initial release to reveal the full scope of its richness, and as if we had needed some time to gauge its importance. Of course, it is true that three subsequent Fellini films have helped to give the earlier one more trenchancy, depth, and nuance.[1] But I think that everything was already contained in *I Vitelloni* and set out there with magisterial genius.

Much has been written about this film's message and its moral and spiritual significance; so I'd prefer to underline what the repercussions of this message are, not exactly for film form (never has the distinction between form and content been revealed to be more artificial than in *I*

Vitelloni), but for the idea of cinematic "spectacle." From this point of view, the profound originality of *I Vitelloni* seems to me to reside in its negation of the norms of storytelling on the screen. In almost all films, our interest is aroused not only by the plot or the action, but also by the development of the characters and the relationship of that development to the chain of events. Granted, neorealism had already changed things by succeeding in interesting us in small events that seemed to have no dramatic import (as in *Bicycle Thieves* [1948] and *Umberto D.* [1952]). Still, the action was carefully portioned out and the main character, whose personality was otherwise given or was determined by his environment, did *evolve* toward a denouement.

With Fellini, it's different. His protagonists don't "evolve"; they mature. What we see them do on the screen is not only frequently without dramatic value, but also without logical meaning in the narrative chain. Most of the time it is pointless "agitation," which is the opposite of action: stupid strolls along beaches, absurd divagations, ridiculous jokes. And yet, it is through these gestures and activities, which appear so marginal that they are cut in most films, that the characters reveal themselves to us in their innermost essence. Not that they reveal to us what we conventionally call "a psychology." The Fellinian protagonist is not a "character," he is a mode of being, a way of living. This is why the director can define him thoroughly through his behavior: his walk, his dress, his hairstyle, his mustache, his dark glasses. Such anti-psychological cinema goes farther and deeper than psychology, however: it goes to the protagonist's soul. This cinema of the soul thus focuses most exclusively on appearances; it is a cinema in which the viewer's gaze is most important. Fellini has made positively ridiculous a certain analytical and dramatic tradition of filmmaking by substituting for it a pure phenomenology of being in which the most commmonplace of man's gestures can be the beacons of his destiny and his salvation.

NOTES TO CHAPTER 22

The Profound Originality of I Vitelloni

This review was first published in French in *Radio-Cinéma-Télévision* (Oct. 1957), then reprinted in Vol. 4 ("Une Esthétique de la réalité: le néoréalisme") of Bazin's four-volume *Qu'est-ce que le cinéma?* (Paris: Éditions du Cerf, 1958–62), pp. 143–45.

2. Editor's note: *La Strada* (1954), *Il Bidone* (*The Swindle*, 1955), and *The Nights of Cabiria* (1957).

CHAPTER 23

O n *Why We Fight:* History, Documentation,
and the Newsreel[1]

War and the apocalypse it brings are at the heart of a decisive new reevaluation of documentary reporting. The reason is that, during a war, facts have an exceptional amplitude and importance. They constitute a colossal *mise en scène* compared with which that of *Caesar and Cleopatra* (1945; dir. Gabriel Pascal) or *Intolerance* (1916; dir. D. W. Griffith) looks as though it were the set for a small show touring the provinces. But these facts also constitute a real *mise en scène*, which is used only once. The drama also takes place "for real," for the protagonists have agreed to die at the same time as they are shot by the camera, like enslaved gladiators in the circus arena. Thanks to film, the world is cleverly saving money on the cost of its wars, since the latter are used for two purposes, history *and* cinema, thus reminding us of those less-than-conscientious producers who shoot a second film on the overpriced set of the first one. In this case, however, the world is right. War, with its harvest of dead bodies, its immense destructiveness, its countless migrations, its concentration camps, and its atomic bombs, leaves far behind the creative art that aims at reconstituting it.

The craze for war reports seems to me to derive from a series of psychological and perhaps also moral exigencies. Nothing suits us better than the unique event, shot on the spot, at the very moment of its creation. Such a theater of operations, when compared with the other one, has the invaluable dramatic superiority of inventing the play as it spontaneously unfolds. It is a kind of *commedia dell'arte* in which the scenario itself is always being reworked. As far as the technical means are concerned, there is no need to insist on their unerring efficiency. I would simply like to underline the fact that these means reach a cosmic scale and that they need fear only earthquakes,[2] volcanic eruptions, tidal waves, and the Apocalypse itself. I say this without irony, because I think that the number one broadcast in the series *News from Heaven* will certainly be devoted to a lengthy report on the Last Judgment, compared to which the report on the Nuremberg trials will somehow look like the Lumières' *Workers Leaving the Factory* (1895). If I were pessimistic, I would add a slightly Freudian psychological factor that I would call the "Nero complex" and define as the pleasure experienced at the sight of urban destruction. If I were optimistic, I would allude to the aforementioned moral factor and say that the cruelty and violence of war have taught us to respect—almost to make a cult of—actual facts, in comparison with which any reconstitution, even made in good faith, seems dubious, indecent, and sacrilegious.

But the war report above all fulfills another need, which explains its extreme popularity. The taste for such documentary news, combined with that for the cinema, reflects nothing if not modern man's will to be there, his need to observe history-in-the-making, not only because of political evolution, but also because of the evolution as well as irremediable intermingling of the technological means of communication and destruction. The days of total war are fatally matched by those of total History. The governments of the world have understood this very well; this is why they try to show us film reports of all their historical acts, such as the signing of treaties or the meetings of the various superpowers. As History is not at all a ballet that is fixed in advance, it is necessary to plant along the way as many cameras as possible so as to be able to film it in the act (in the historical act, of course). Thus nations at war have made provisions for the film equipment of their armies, just as they have made provisions for the truly military equipment of those armies. The camera operator accompanies the bomber on its mission or the infantrymen during their landing. The armament of the fighter-bomber contains an automatic camera placed between its two machine guns. The cameraman runs as many risks as the soldiers, whose death he is supposed to film even at the cost of his own life (but who cares, as long as the footage is saved!).

Most military operations now include a detailed filmic preparation. Who, then, is able to say to what extent strictly military efficiency differs from the cinematically effective spectacle that we expect from it? In a lecture on the art of the documentary, Roger Leenhardt imagined that, next time, Commander Humphrey Bogart or Sergeant Spencer Tracy, playing the parts we have come to expect of them, would be the protagonists of some grand semi-fictionalized report. A crew of cameramen would be responsible for filming the course of the actual military operations that

Bogart or Tracy would really command at the patriotic peril of his life. Shall we say that we haven't reached this point yet? I ask you to think about the bombing of the Bikini atoll[3] and about the naval theater boxes nearby, to which only special guests had access (somewhat as they do for live programs on television) while numerous cameras were filming for you and me the sensational moments. I ask you also to think about the Nuremberg trials, which took place under the spotlights, as though they were the enactment of some murder trial in a detective film.

We live more and more in a world stripped bare by film, a world that tends to peel off its own image. Hundreds of thousands of screens make us watch, during the news broadcasts, the extraordinary shedding performed each day by tens of thousands of cameras. As soon as it forms, history's skin peels off again. Before the war a filmed news report used to be called "the eye of the world." Today this title is hardly pretentious as countless Bell-and-Howell lenses, placed all over the world where important events take place, prey on the picturesque, bizarre, or terrible signs of our destiny.

Among the American films released in France right after the Liberation, the only ones that have elicited unanimous approval and inspired a boundless admiration are those in the series *Why We Fight*. They had the merit not only of introducing a new tone into the art of propaganda, a measured tone that convinced without violence, at once didactic and pleasant; but also, although they consisted only of newsreels, they knew how to capture attention like a detective novel. I think that, for the film historian, *Why We Fight* has created a new genre: the edited ideological documentary. I don't mean that such a use of editing is new. The great German or Soviet editors have long since demonstrated the use one could make of it in documentaries, but the Capra films display a new originality: none of the images of which they are composed (except for a few connecting shots) were photographed for these films. The editing thus aims not so much at showing as at making a point. There are abstract, purely logical films that paradoxically use the most historical and the most concrete kind of document: the newsreel. They have established for good, with a perfection that will probably never be surpassed, that the a posteriori editing of film shot for other purposes can achieve the flexibility and precision of language. The best-edited documentaries up to now have been only narratives; those under consideration are speeches.

The films in the series *Why We Fight* (along with a few other American and Russian documentaries) have been made possible only by the enormous accumulation of documentary footage from the war; they are the result of the search for people and events, which more and more has become an official institution. To make these films, an enormous selection of newsreels from international archives was necessary, and these archives had to be complete enough to contain an event as intimate in its historical nature as Hitler's war dance at the Rethondes Crossroads (in northern France). One can conclude from this that Dziga Vertov's theory of the Cine-Eye is beginning to be confirmed in a sense that even the Soviet theoretician had not foreseen.[4] But the camera, unique as it is among the picture hunters of the world, could not have reached this omnipresence in space and time by itself—an omnipresence that today permits us to catch in our nets an enormous number of documentary images. Naturally, human intervention was necessary.

It has been said how good these films are as much from a strictly cinematic point of view as from a political one. However, it turns out that probably not enough time has been spent on an analysis of the intellectual and psychological mechanism to which they owe their pedagogical efficiency. This mechanism is well worth examining, though, because its main force seems to me to be particularly dangerous for the future of the human spirit and should therefore not be excluded from any careful study of the rape of the masses.

The principle behind this type of documentary essentially consists in giving to the images the logical structure of language, and in giving to language itself the credibility and proof of photographic images. The viewer has the illusion of watching a visual demonstration, whereas this demonstration is in reality only a succession of equivocal facts held together merely by the cement of the words that accompany them. The essential part of the film is not in its projection but in the soundtrack. Shall we say that this is nothing new and that every single elucidation of a visual text, every single pedagogical documentary, does the same? I don't think so, because, in the case of the pedagogical documentary, preeminence is given either to the pictures or to the language. By contrast, a documentary on trawl fishing or on the building of a bridge shows *and* explains. There isn't any intellectual deception in the process; the intrinsic and distinct values of the words and of the pictures are preserved. Here, however, the film rests on the absolute opposite: the subordination of the events pictured on screen. Please, understand me well: I am not posing the problem of content but of form. I am denying neither the rightness of the arguments nor that the right people have to try and convince us, but solely the honesty of the method used. These films, which start with a favorable a priori, that of using logic, reason, and the evidence of the facts, in actuality rest on a grave confusion of values, on the manipulation of psychology, credulity, and perception.

One could closely analyze a scene like the battle before Moscow (the fifth film in the series) for evidence of what I am saying. The comments on the soundtrack clearly explain the facts: the retreat of the Russians, German offensive, Russian resistance, stabilization of the front line around the latest lines of retreat, Russian counteroffensive. It is evident that a battle of this size could not be filmed *in toto*. One could pull from it only extremely fragmentary shots. The work of the editor has been essentially to choose shots from German newsreels, which supposedly had been taken right outside Moscow and which gave the impression of a victorious German offensive: rapid movement of soldiers, tank attacks, and Russian corpses in the snow. Then, in the Russian counteroffensive, the editor found impressive scenes of soldiers rushing forward, being careful, of course, to position them on screen in the opposite direction from the Nazi infantrymen in the preceding shots. The mind makes of these apparently concrete elements an abstract outline and reconstitutes an ideal battle, since it has the indubitable illusion of seeing this battle as a kind of duel. I have chosen on purpose a sequence in which such a concrete schematization was inevitable and in this case completely justified, since the Germans did indeed lose the battle. But if we extrapolate this device, we understand that we can thus be convinced we are watching events whose outcome and meaning have been completely invented. Shall we say, then, that we should have at the very least a guarantee of the filmmaker's moral honesty? In any event, this honesty can bear only on the ends, since the very structure of the means renders them illusory.

The shots used in these films are in a way straight historical facts. We spontaneously believe in facts,[5] but modern criticism has sufficiently established that in the end they have only the meaning that the human mind gives to them. Up to the discovery of photography, the "historical fact" was reconstituted from written documents; the mind and human language came into play twice in such reconstitutions: in the reconstruction of the event and in the historical thesis it was adduced to support. With film, we can refer to the facts in flesh and blood, so to speak. Could they bear witness to something else other than themselves? To something else other than the narrative of which they form a part? I think that, far from moving the historical sciences toward more objectivity, the cinema paradoxically gives them the additional power of illusion by its very realism.

The invisible commentator, whom the viewer forgets while watching Capra's marvelously edited films, is tomorrow's historian of the masses, the ventriloquist of this extraordinary prosopopeia that is being prepared in all the film archives of the world and that wills the men and the events of another time back to life.

NOTES TO CHAPTER 23

On Why We Fight

This article was first published in French in *Esprit* (1946), then reprinted in Vol. 1 ("Ontologie et language") of Bazin's four-volume *Qu'est-ce que le cinéma* (Paris: Édition du Cerf, 1958–62), pp. 31–36.

1. Editor's note: *Why We Fight* series, 1942–1945:

    1. *Prelude to War*, dir. Frank Capra.

    2. *The Nazis Strike*, dir. Frank Capra.

    3. *Divide and Conquer*, dir. Frank Capra.

    4. *The Battle of Britain*, dir. Anthony Veiller.

    5. *The Battle of Russia*, dir. Anatole Litvak.

    6. *The Battle of China*, dir. Frank Capra, Anatole Litvak.

    7. *War Comes to America*, dir. Anatole Litvak.

    (All the films had editing by William Hornbeck, music by Dimitri Tiomkin, and commentary by Walter Huston.)

2. Bazin's note: Even more than that! An H-bomb today is equivalent to a hundred big earthquakes.

3. Editor's note: This atoll in the Marshal Islands was the site of atomic bomb tests in 1946.

4. Editor's note: In 1919 Vertov (1896–1954) published the Kinoks-Revolution manifesto, the first of several position papers in which he attacked the "impotence" and "backwardness" of fiction films and called for a new style of film reportage taken from real life. He expanded on these ideas in a 1922 magazine article, in which he introduced his theory of Kino-Glaz, or Kino-Oki (Cine-Eye or Kino-Eye). He spoke of the camera as an eye, more perfect that the human eye in its ability to move in time and space and perceive and record impressions: "I am eye. I am a mechanical eye. I, a machine, am showing you a world the likes of which only I can see. I free myself from today and forever from human immobility...I am an apparatus, maneuvering in the chaos of movements, recording one movement after another in the most complex combinations...My road is towards the creation of a fresh perception of the world. Thus I decipher in a new way the world unknown to you."

5. Bazin's note: But then again, with a very British sort of humor John Grierson has just revealed (in the newspapers of October 13, 1958) that he was the creator of Hitler's war dance at the Rethondes Crossroads. Hitler was simply lifting his leg. By redoubling the shot, as in the anti-Nazi burlesque entitled *The Lambeth Walk* (1939; dir. Albert de Courville), the famous English documentarian made Hitler dance his now famous Satanic jig, which has thus become "historical." See note 4, p. 37.

CHAPTER 24

The Road to Hope

The Road to Hope (1950) is one of the most beautiful postwar Italian films on the eminently epic, and hence cinematic, theme of the journey to the Promised Land. Some Sicilians, who have been reduced to unemployment by the closing down of the sulfur mines, leave with their families for France, where a crooked labor recruiter has promised them they will find work. The road is long, from the snows of Mount Etna to those of the Saint Gothard Pass.[1] Abandoned by their guide, hunted down by the police, chased by the farm workers whose strike they have unwittingly broken to earn a few lire, the survivors of this illegal emigration finally get to see the Promised Land from the top of a pass in the Alps, which an officer of the Alpine police will compassionately allow them to descend.

This "European" happy ending should not mislead us as to the real ending called for by the film: Sisyphuses to their misery and their despair, these Sicilians cannot but be driven back once more up the symbolic slopes of Mount Etna because of the social chaos that awaits them below. Thus the Promised Land is in fact just an absurd paradise where only grapes of wrath can grow. One can only regret Pietro Germi's concessionary and timid attitude toward this wonderful subject, which he doesn't always treat with the necessary rigor. A nasty crime story, complete with sentimental complication, needlessly encumbers the film, apparently for the edification of all the housewives of the world. His only excuse for this strand, and almost a valid one, is the taciturn beauty of Elena Varzi, whose stubborn brow bears the mark of the saber of destiny.

Pietro Germi is a young director in whom some Italian critics would like to see a brilliant hope for the future. It's possible, if he isn't consumed

The Road to Hope (1950), dir. Pietro Germi. La Cinémathèque
Royale, Brussels.

first by formalism or by a harking back to Eisensteinian rhetoric, to which
Germi's *In the Name of the Law* (1952) and above all his recent *Il Brigante
di Tacca del Lupo* (1952) dangerously testify more than does *The Road to
Hope*. But if *The Road to Hope* is a far cry from the masterpieces of neorealism, it can at least pride itself on indicating more clearly than other films
the shift that has occurred in Italian filmmaking, the transformation from
a neorealism of war, if you will (*Rome, Open City* [1945], *Paisan* [1946],
Shoeshine [1946], and other films inspired by the Liberation and its aftermath), to a neorealism of peace, to which De Sica's *Bicycle Thieves* (1948)
stands as the unforgettable introduction.

The fact is that the social reality of postwar Italy remains essentially
dramatic, or even more precisely: tragic. The fear of misery because of
unemployment plays the role of a fateful menace in the lives of the people. Living means trying to escape from this predicament. Working and,
through work, keeping one's basic human dignity, the right to minimal
happiness and love—these are the sole concerns of the protagonists of
Renato Castellani's *Two Cents' Worth of Hope* (1951), just as they are of the

protagonists of *The Road to Hope* or *Bicycle Thieves*. Of this fundamental theme, upon which screenwriters can fashion a thousand variations, one could say that it is the negative of the theme that inspires perhaps more than half of all American films. Many scripts, most of them written for American comedies, are in fact built on the pursuit of wealth or at least on the obsession with success, which for women means the conquest of some Prince Charming who is the heir to an industrial tycoon. Conversely, the neorealistic protagonist does not dream at all of asserting himself through ambition: he simply tries not to let himself be overcome by misery. Because unemployment can make him lapse into nothingness, "two cents' worth of hope" are enough to buy his happiness. So, as one might have surmised, the documentary substance of Italian neorealism achieves the dignity of art only insofar as it rediscovers in itself the great dramatic archetypes upon which our empathy is, and always will be, founded.

The Road to Hope (1950), dir. Pietro Germi. La Cinémathèque Royale, Brussels.

The Road to Hope

This review was first published in French in *Cahiers du Cinéma*, no. 20 (Feb. 1952), then reprinted in Vol. 4 ("Une Esthétique de la réalité: le néoréalisme") of Bazin's four-volume *Qu'est-ce que le cinéma?* (Paris: Éditions du Cerf, 1958–62), pp.65–66.

1. Editor's note: A pass in the Alps on the border between France and Italy, famous today for the long tunnel through it.

CHAPTER 25

Battle of the Rails and Ivan the Terrible

Two films have emerged in the last few months from the ocean of mediocrity that constitutes commercial distribution (one wonders what the film buffs in Paris would do without film societies). These two works rank far above the best films from around the world that have been shown on French screens since the Liberation. The first is French: *Battle of the Rails* (1946); the second is Russian: *Ivan the Terrible* (Part I, 1944; Part II, 1946).

Battle of the Rails is a film about the Resistance that was made a short time after the Liberation by a team of young technicians. Originally, it was only a documentary of about 2,625 feet in length, on the underground struggle of French railwaymen during World War II; it was commissioned by the Cinema Cooperative and the Railroad-Resistance movement. But the quality of the result so impressed Jean Painlevé,[1] who was then director of the Cinema Cooperative, that he called for the project to be turned into a feature-length film. One of the small weaknesses of *Battle of the Rails* might in fact derive from this happy extension: namely, its structure (although, on closer examination, one can see that this structure isn't lacking in skillful, intelligent execution).

The film, whose genre is the reconstituted documentary, moves between a pure report of significant, factual events and a fictionalized account of history. It was difficult for the director to limit himself to "pure report" in a full-length film. In order to do so, he would have had to classify the facts according to a transcendent unity and a global view of man in the throes of the Resistance. If you will, he would have had to make the iron filings of events obey a metaphysical or poetic magnetic field, as Malraux had done in *Man's Hope* (1939), which *Battle of the Rails* often recalls. And René Clément almost succeeds in doing this at certain moments: the shooting of the hostages; the shot of the glowworm in the grass before the attack on the armored train; the German soldier's shooting of the wounded Resistance fighter crawling in the stream; the tank relentlessly driving the last Maquis out of the bushes; the ghost train speeding along some out-of-use tracks, while a frightened shepherd and his sheep watch it go by without a soul aboard. All these and a thousand other moments transcend the anecdotal; they aren't really part of the narrative, or rather they give the narrative a vertical, "poetic" dimension that a mere documentary wouldn't possess. Or they almost do! For one doesn't get a sense of spiritual convergence in Clément's artistic intentions; no doubt, such a convergence or unity could only be the product of cinematic genius. I must say, however, that Clément's "found images" are so full of intelligence, import, and resonance that when one searches for artists who could have given them the light shock necessary to their full vitalization, one comes up with names such as Malraux, Hemingway, and Faulkner. Certainly, *Battle of the Rails* does not recall the American novel, nor does it have anything literary about it, but it nevertheless reaches an aesthetic level that is only slightly inferior to that of the modern novel, whose practitioners are endowed with the keenest and most extended powers of observation. I must also say that this slight deficiency is crucial, because it prevents the film from being the masterwork whose seeds it contains. But René Clément and his collaborators should be content with the creation of this "work," since there aren't many filmmakers who can say they have achieved as much.

One of the main qualities of the film is its will to say everything in images. There is very little dialogue, and it occurs only after the camera has expressed all it possibly could through its own devices. Actually, the dialogue is merely one part of a larger action, or picture, photographed by the camera. This cinematic will, which is extremely rare today, not only adds to the artistic value of the film, but it also has the advantage of solving the problem of dialogue in a film about the Resistance—a subject that doesn't have a high tolerance for conversation. We can see this demonstrated by the dialogue in *Jéricho* (1946; dir. Henri Calef), which would perhaps be a good film if it were about anything else but the Resistance.

I don't know whether Clément will again be able to summon up such purity of inspiration. *Battle of the Rails* is only his first feature film, and it is the work of a craftsman working in cooperation with other craftsmen, his friends. The money for the project was donated by the railwaymen themselves (many of whom reenact their exploits in the film). It is possible that the modest nature of the project and its economic limitations gave the film its tone, which is both one of intelligent humility before its subject and extreme scrupulousness in the treatment of that subject. The morality of art fuses here with the morality of history. The greatness of this film and its spiritual bond with the cause of the Resistance are not unrelated to the purity of intention revealed by its means and its men. There is a lesson and a comfort in this.

It has been said, and it will be said again and again, that *Battle of the Rails* has the authentic and eloquent simplicity, the naturalness and the realism, of Soviet cinema. But which Soviet cinema are we talking about? One is tempted to think that the Russian school is artistically unified, whereas it is the school that is perhaps the richest in contradictory tendencies. *Ivan the Terrible*, the latest film by Eisenstein, obeys an aesthetic that is the absolute opposite of the one found in Clément's film, or for that matter in any Russian film that we have seen since the Liberation.

Battle of the Rails (1946), dir. René Clément. La Cinémathèque Royale, Brussels.

At the moment I'm writing this article, barely two weeks after the release of *Ivan the Terrible* at the Normandie Theater, the fate of this superproduction already seems decided. Most of the critics were extremely restrained. The public itself has not been restrained: at best, it cannot hide its disappointment and its surprise, and at worst, it sometimes laughs out loud. The film *cognoscenti* gloat scornfully and keep repeating that it would have been preferable for Russian prestige had the film not been released in France. I persist in believing, however, that *Ivan the Terrible* is a beautiful work that does the director of *The Battleship Potemkin* (1925) and *The General Line* (1929) proud.

On account of the German invasion, Eisenstein went as far as Asia to make his film, in the remote studios of Alma-Ata.[2] Should we therefore see in these geographical considerations the origin of the film's style? Eisenstein's genius and sensibility may be the most Western in Russian cinema. Yet, in spite of the fact that the action takes place in western Russia in the sixteenth century, Eisenstein obviously wanted to make an Asian film. This intention is discernible not only in the preponderantly Eastern extravagance of the sets and the costumes, but also in the very conception of the drama and its performance, both of which are so heavily stylized that they border on mime and dance. I think that it would be a mistake, however, to consider the exaggerated conception of character and the extreme expressivenes of the acting as some kind of return to silent cinema. The conventional and contrived aspect of the mimicry of silent films came from having to communicate with the viewer without the help of speech. In *Ivan the Terrible* it is a deliberate choice, a freely chosen style of expression. Yet this style is not easy to define. It certainly derives a good deal from *The Nibelungen* (1924) and *The Cabinet of Dr. Caligari* (1919), but it is singularly enriched by other elements that are psychological, plastic, and musical. Eisenstein is trying to achieve here, using the plasticity of cinema as his starting point, the same type of artistic synthesis that Wagner wanted to build around music. Time will tell if this synthesis is viable or if it is as unstable as Bayreuth's, the only element of which survives today is the music. Prokoviev's music is beautiful, but it is not the major component of Eisenstein's film: it is the image that determines, according to its dramatic composition, the design, the acting, and the music.

Eisenstein's attention to composition has never before been so evident, despite the fact that it has always been dominant in his work. His phenomenal eye for framing and for the right camera angle wonderfully sustained the action of *The Battleship Potemkin*, for example: one need only recall the legs of the soldiers descending the huge Odessa Steps. But in his previous films the plastic demands of the image didn't have an effect on the action itself. In *Ivan the Terrible*, by contrast, it is fair to say that the action is transformed to its very core by the style of the image. From this point of view, one could call *Ivan the Terrible* decadent. But this would be to judge the film only by its chosen form and not by the quality of its means, which don't seem to me to be inferior to or less assured than those of Eisenstein's other works.

The pictorial influences are numerous. The historical period of the action—Donatello has just died (1466), and the Russian court has established relations with the Italian states—allowed Eisenstein to make allusions to the Italian Renaissance, which had always had a strong influence on him. As for the Byzantine references, they are even more numerous: the battle for Kazan,[3] for instance, is treated as a miniature on a surface without perspective: the characters, who are either carefully isolated or arrayed in serpentine lines, seem to be pinned to the hill, upon which we can see the czar's tent. The pictures are composed with extreme care; they contain, as it were, plastic, internal rhymes, which then echo one another from image to image. Thus the wondrous eye of the icon has its echo in the half-moon windows that light up a hall. Everything in this film is calculated and conscious, subject to an extraordinary system of references, contrasts, harmonies, and counterpoints. But it would be wrong to say that the film is therefore nothing more than an album of artistic photographs. Eisenstein's art has always been rather static within the image itself. The photographic dynamics come from the editing, which does not limit itself to conferring a rhythm on the successive shots, but which also connects what motion there is within each shot to that of the shots which precede and follow it.

It is true that *Ivan the Terrible* deliberately turns its back on what used to be the best tradition in Russian cinema, a tradition that Eisenstein himself helped create. It is also true that this film returns to the most conventional aesthetics of silent film—the aesthetics of German expressionism in particular—thus renouncing fifteen years of realistic cinema. Contrary to Fritz Lang, who evolved from the total artificiality of *The Nibelungen* to the violent realism of *Fury* (1936), Eisenstein followed a course that led him in *Ivan the Terrible* to deny nature even the briefest of appearances. But we must make a distinction between the value of the style as such and the quality of its individual execution. One may detest opera, one may think that it is a dying art form, while also recognizing the quality of Wagner's music. One may detest verse drama, one may think that it is a dying hybrid, but would one go as far as to condemn Racine's tragedies because they are not written in prose? In the cinema, we are not accustomed to making distinctions among styles. One could, of course, respond that cinema is different from the other arts, whose audiences are perhaps more expert and also smaller in number. By contrast, filmmakers address the anonymous masses. These people don't care about aesthetics or theories of film: they want to see "movies." Wouldn't it be a betrayal, then, to introduce the aesthetic categories of the "cultural" arts into this wonderfully "popular" form, from which American and Russian film-making had gradually managed to banish all pretensions to high art? One is certainly entitled to consider the path Eisenstein takes in *Ivan the Terrible* as an offensive return to a dangerous aestheticism, which every-body believed had been eliminated from all considerations of cinema's destiny. But such a hypothesis doesn't in itself give us leave to disregard the extraordinary mystery of this titan of the cinema, the genius of his camera in this, his latest film.[4]

I haven't said very much about the plot, because it is easy to set it aside or to see in it only a pretext for Eisenstein's stylistic configurations. The film's subject does pose a problem, however, and it would be dis-honest to ignore it. We all know that, since *Peter the Great*,[5] Russian cin-ema has been singing the praises of the great czars, who are presented both as pioneers of the union of all Russian peoples and as enemies of the feudalism that for so long oppressed the masses. The analogies are far too obvious for me to go through the trouble of pointing them all out. Therefore it would be silly to be shocked by just one: if you're going to compare General de Gaulle with Joan of Arc, then you have to compare Ivan the Terrible with Stalin. We never fail to find historical justifications for the political present; the real problem lies far more in the political ideals whose value is thus asserted: autocracy and nationalism. I'll leave it to the political analysts to judge *Ivan the Terrible* from this point of view, and I'll limit myself to discussing the manner in which Eisenstein sets out his thesis. *Ivan the Terrible* respects rather scrupulously the main histori-cal events, but naturally it assigns to them the meaning Eisenstein desires. The film doesn't for a moment try to avoid the baldest didacticism, clearly distinguishing between the good and the bad, between virtue and vice. I'll state a hypothesis here without being able to prove it: in yielding to the demands of propaganda, Eisenstein may have consciously chosen a style for his film that rejected psychological realism from the start and that required for its own aesthetic realization the systematic magnification of a thesis, that is, the elaboration of a thesis without benefit of nuance.

NOTES TO CHAPTER 25

Battle of the Rails *and* Ivan the Terrible

(All notes have been provided by the Editor.)

Bazin's reviews appeared in the April issue of *Esprit*, 14, no. 121 (1946), pp. 667–671.

1. French documentarist, born 1902 in Paris. He began directing scientific shorts in 1925 and has since turned out numerous such films of both educational and artistic merit.
2. Capital of the Kazakh Soviet Socialist Republic, in the southeastern part.
3. City in the west of the Russian Soviet Federated Socialist Republic, on the Volga.
4. And, as it turned out, Eisenstein's last. He died of a heart attack in 1948 at the age of fifty.
5. Directed by Vladimir Petrov (Part I, 1937; Part II, 1939).

CHAPTER 26

A Saint Becomes a Saint Only After the Fact
(*Heaven Over the Marshes*)

Italian film not only has good directors, it also has excellent cinematographers, among whom Aldo Tonti (a.k.a. G. R. Aldo) is probably one of the best in the world. To be sure, a cinematographer's art may lie in the direction of self- effacement, and Tonti has given us evidence of this. But it seems that in the last few years, more and more plastic composition has become the rule. This has become a way of integrating into realism a vivid and ornate theatricality, which is no less characteristic not only of Italian film but also of Italian artistic sensibility in general. One could even argue that this synthesis is more radically new than the neorealism of *Bicycle Thieves* (1948), which has always been present, as we know, in Italian film, even if not to so great an extent. Opposed to it was the public's more pronounced taste for spectacles with magnificent sets and mammoth crowds. In *La Terra Trema* (1948), for instance, one sees very well how Luchino Visconti, whose wonderful *Ossessione* (1942) had initiated the rebirth of Italian realistic cinema, strives to create a necessarily grand synthesis between the most rigorous verisimilitude, on the one hand, and the most plastic composition, on the other—a plasticity that necessarily completely transforms the verism. Whereas the taste for spectacular grandeur expressed itself in the past through the fame of the star, the magnitude of the set, or the number of wild animals deployed, it has come today to be totally subordinate to the most modest, down-to-earth subject matter. Visconti's fishermen are real fishermen, but they have the bearing of tragic princes or operatic leads, and the cinematography confers on their rags the aristocratic dignity of Renaissance brocade.

Using the same cinematographer as Visconti did in *La Terra Trema*—the amazing Aldo, whom the French studios have let get away[1]—Augusto

[*Heaven over the Marshes*] (1949), dir. Augusta Genina. Museum of
Modern Art, New York.

Genina has been no less concerned to play the game of realism in
Heaven over the Marshes (1949). His peasants are as authentic as were
Georges Rouquier's in *Farrebique* (1947). Whereas three quarters of
Italian films, even those made in studios with professional actors, are
post-synchronized, Genina recorded the sound on the spot, and his
peasants really say...what they say. When one considers the enormous
difficulty of getting nonprofessional actors to speak as naturally as they
behave (see, for example, *Farrebique*), one can appreciate the additional
amount of work that Genina imposed on himself in order to obey the
dictates of realism, right down to the least discernible details. If this
were a minor work, one could regard these details as superfluous. But
they are, in fact, part of a coherent aesthetic whole whose essential elements are laid down in the initial script.

Heaven over the Marshes is a film about the circumstances that led to
the canonization of little Maria Goretti, who was murdered at the age of
fourteen by the boy whose sexual advances she had resisted. These factors

made me fear the worst. Hagiography is already a dangerous exercise in itself, but, granted, there are some saints made to appear on stained-glass windows and others who seem destined for the painted plaster of Saint-Sulpice,[2] whatever their standing in paradise might be. And the case of Maria Goretti doesn't seem to be a priori any more promising than that of Saint Thérèse of Lisieux.[3] Less even, for her biography is devoid of extraordinary events; hers is the life of a daughter of a poor family of farmhands in the Pontine marshes near Rome at the turn of the century. No visions, no voices, no signs from heaven: her regular attendance at catechism and the fervor of her first Holy Communion are merely the commonplace signals of a rather commonplace piety. Of course, there is her "martyrdom," but we have to wait until the last fifteen minutes of the film before it occurs, before "something finally happens."

And even this martyrdom: what is it when you take a close look at it and judge the psychological motives behind it? A banal sex crime, a trivial news item devoid of dramatic originality: "Young Peasant Stabs Unwilling Girl to Death." And why? There is not a single aspect of this crime that doesn't have a natural explanation. The resistance of the girl is perhaps nothing but an exaggerated physiological response to the violation of her sense of decency, the reflex action of a frightened little animal. It's true that she invokes divine will and the threat of hellfire to resist Alessandro. However, it is not necessary to have recourse to the subtleties of psychoanalysis to understand how the imperatives of catechism and the mysticism of first Holy Communion could kindle the imagination of a frightened adolescent. Even if we take for granted that Maria's Christian upbringing can't be made to substitute for her real, unconscious motives in determining behavior, that behavior still isn't convincing, for we sense that she does indeed love Alessandro. So why all this resistance, which can only have tragic consequences? Either it is a psychological reaction that is stronger than the heart's desire, or it really is the obedience to a moral precept; but isn't this taking morality to an absurd extreme, since it leads to the downfall of two beings who love each other? Moreover, before she dies, Maria asks Alessandro to forgive her for all the trouble she has caused him, i.e., for driving him to kill her.

It should not be surprising, therefore, that, at least in France, this saint's life has disappointed the Christians even more than it has the nonbelievers. The former don't find in it the requisite religious apologetics, and the latter don't find in it the necessary moral apologetics. All that we have here is the senseless crushing of a poor child's life—there are no unusual mitigating circumstances. Maria Goretti is neither Saint Vincent de Paul, nor Saint Teresa of Avila, nor even Bernadette Soubirous.[4] But it is to Genina's credit that he made a hagiography that doesn't prove anything, above all not the sainthood of the saint. Herein lies not only the film's artistic distinction but also its religious one. *Heaven over the Marshes* is a rarity: a good Catholic film.

What was Genina's starting point? It was not simply to reject all the ornament that comes with the subject matter—the religious symbolism and, it goes without saying, the supernatural element of traditional hagiographies (a film such as *Monsieur Vincent*[5] also avoids these stumbling blocks). He set out to achieve much more than this: his goal was to create a phenomenology of sainthood. Genina's *mise en scène* is a systematic refusal not only to treat sainthood as anything but a fact, an event occurring in the world, but also to consider it from any point of view other than the external one. He looks at sainthood from the outside, as the ambiguous manifestation of a spiritual reality that is absolutely impossible to prove. The apologetic nature of most hagiographies supposes, by contrast, that sainthood is conferred a priori. Whether it be Saint Thérèse of Lisieux or Saint Vincent de Paul, we are told the life of a saint. Yet, good logic dictates, as does good theology, that a saint becomes a saint only after the fact: when he is canonized; during his lifetime, he is simply *Monsieur Vincent*. It is only by the authoritative judgment of the Holy See that his biography becomes a hagiography. The question raised in film as in theology is the retroactiveness of eternal salvation, since, obviously, a saint does not exist as a saint in the present: he is simply a being who becomes one and who, moreover, risks eternal damnation until his death. Genina's bias in favor of realism made him go as far as to prohibit in any of his images the supposition of his protagonist's "sainthood," so afraid was he of betraying the spirit of his endeavor. She is not, and she must not be, a saint whose martyrdom we witness, but rather the little peasant girl Maria Goretti, whose life we see her live. The camera lens is not the eye of God, and microphones could not have recorded the voices heard by Joan of Arc.

This is why *Heaven over the Marshes* will be disconcerting to viewers who are used to an apologetics that confuses rhetoric with art and sentiment with grace. In a way, Genina plays devil's advocate by playing servant to the only filmic reality possible. But just as canonization hearings are won against the public prosecutor Satan, Maria Goretti's sainthood is served in the only valid manner possible by a film that expressly sets out not to demonstrate it. In short, Genina tells us: "This is Maria Goretti, watch her live and die. *On the other hand*, you know she is a saint. Let those who have eyes to see, read by transparence the evidence of grace in her life, just as you must do at every moment in the events of your own lives." The signs that God sends to his people are not always supernatural. A serpent in a bush is not the devil, but the devil is still there as well as everywhere else.

NOTES TO CHAPTER 26

A Saint Becomes a Saint Only After the Fact

(All notes have been provided by the Editor.)

This review was first published in French in *Cahiers du Cinéma*, no. 2 (May 1951), then reprinted in Vol. 4 ("Une Esthétique de la réalité: le néoréalisme) of Bazin's four-volume *Qu'est-ce que le cinéma?* (Paris: Éditions du Cerf: 1958–1962), pp. 60–64.

1. Aldo (born Aldo Graziati, 1902–1953) went to France in 1921 to become an actor and trained there as a cameraman. In 1947 he returned to Italy with the crew of a French production and stayed to become one of Italy's most distinguished postwar cinematographers.

2. Church in Saint-Germain, Paris.

3. French Carmelite nun, 1873–1897. Her saint's day is October 3rd.

4. Saint Vincent de Paul was a French priest (1580?–1660) who founded charitable orders; his saint's day is July 19th. Saint Teresa of Avila was a Spanish Carmelite nun (1515–1582); her saint's day is October 12th. The story of Saint Bernadette Soubirous (1844–1879), a peasant girl who had a vision of the Virgin Mary at what has become the shrine of Lourdes, was made into a film, *The Song of Bernadette*, in 1943 (dir. Henry King from the novel by Franz Werfel). See note 4, p. 72

5. A film of the life of Saint Vincent de Paul, directed by Léon Carré from a script by Jean-Bernard Luc and Jean Anouilh (1947). Pierre Fresnay starred and Claude Renoir did the cinematography.

CHAPTER 27

A Bergsonian Film: *The Picasso Mystery*

The first observation I have to make is that *The Picasso Mystery* (1956; a.k.a. *The Mystery of Picasso*) "doesn't explain anything." If we are to judge from some of his statements and from the prologue to the film, Henri-Georges Clouzot seems to think that showing the making of the paintings will make them understandable to the uninitiated. If he really believes that, he's wrong, as the public's reaction seems to have demonstrated: the fans become even more fanatical, and those who don't like Picasso have their dislike confirmed. *The Picasso Mystery* radically departs from the more or less didactic films about art that are still being made up to this very day. In fact, Clouzot's film does not explain Picasso: it shows him, and the lesson to be learned, if there is one, is that watching an artist work cannot give us the key to his art, not to mention to his genius. Of course, watching the work at its intermediate stages might in some cases reveal the evolution of the thinking behind it or show us a few tricks of the trade, but these are at best merely idiosyncratic secrets from which no larger meaning can be derived. Take, for instance, the slow movement, even tentativeness, of Matisse's brush in François Campaux's film.[1] Such small satisfactions are in any case denied the student of Picasso, who himself put the essence of his art in a nutshell: "I don't *look* for anything; I find it." If anybody still doubted the aptness and profundity of this statement, he would no longer be able to do so after seeing Clouzot's film. For during this work not a single stroke, not one patch of color appears—"appears" is the right word—in any way to be predictable. And conversely, this unpredictability implies the inexplicability of the compound—in this case the composition—by the simple isolation of its elements. This is so true that the whole idea of the film as a spectacle, and even more precisely as a kind of thriller, rests on our anticipation, on unceasing suspense. Each of Picasso's strokes is a creation that leads to further creation, not as a cause leads to an effect, but as one living thing engenders another. This process is particularly evident in the first stages of the paintings, when Picasso is still working on the sketching. Since the hand and the pencil are invisible, nothing gives away their place but the line or the dot that appears, and, very quickly, the mind is trying more or less consciously to guess what will come next; but each time Picasso's decision completely defeats our expectation. When we think his hand is on the right, the stroke appears on the left. When we expect a stroke, we get a patch; when we look for a patch, a dot appears. Very often the same holds true for the subjects: the fish becomes a bird and the bird a faun. This phenomenon of unpredictability in turn implies another that I'm going to examine now: that of pictorial duration.

The Picasso Mystery constitutes the second revolution in films about art. I have attempted to show the importance of the first, as it was initiated by the films of Emmer and Gras[2] and so beautifully developed in all its ramifications by Alain Resnais.[3] This revolution lay in the abolition of the frame, whose disappearance makes us equate the pictorial universe with the universe itself in all its tangibility. To be sure, once it had penetrated "into" the paintings, the camera would have taken us along on a descriptive or dramatic journey of a certain duration. The real novelty, however, was not at all temporal in nature but rather exclusively spatial. It is true that the eye also takes its time as it analyzes, but the dimensions and borders of the painting—despite the camera's abolition of the latter—remind it of the autonomy of the pictorial microcosm, which is forever crystallized outside time.

What *The Picasso Mystery* reveals is not that creation takes a certain amount of time, which we already knew, but that duration may be an integral part of the work itself, an additional dimension, which is foolishly ignored once a painting has been completed. More accurately, all we knew until now were "canvases," vertical sections of a creative flow more or less arbitrarily decided upon by the painter himself, in sickness and in health. What Clouzot at last reveals is the painting itself, i.e., a work that exists in time, that has its own duration, its own life, and sometimes—as at the end of the film—a death that precedes the extinction of the artist.

I must further insist on this point here, for the aforementioned idea might be confused with a rather similar one: the idea that it is interesting and instructive—pleasant, too—to watch *how* the painter has achieved *what* he has achieved in his painting. This ontogenetic concern can be found in many previous films about art, good and bad. It is acceptable but banal, and its nature is not aesthetic but pedagogic. In *The Picasso Mystery*, by contrast, the intermediate stages are not subordinate and inferior realities, parts of a process that will result in a final product: they are already the work itself, but a work that is destined to devour itself, or rather to metamorphose, until the painter wants to stop. This is what Picasso perfectly expresses when he says: "One should be able to show the paintings that are underneath the paintings"; he doesn't say the "sketches," or "the process by which one completes the painting." Indeed, for him, even if he was guided by the idea of perfecting his work (as in *La Plage de la Garoupe*), the different layers that he covered over were also paintings in their own right, although these had to be sacrificed in order to get to the next painting.

To be sure, this temporal aspect of painting has always manifested itself in what can be called a larval manner, i.e., in books of sketches, in "studies," and in engravers' etchings. But temporality turned out to be a more demanding mistress in modern painting. When he paints over *The Rumanian Blouse* (1940) several times, what does Matisse do but spread out his creative inspiration in space, that is to say in implied time, as one would do in a game of solitaire? One can clearly see how the notion of a painting subordinates itself here to the more integral notion of the art of painting, in which the final painted work takes up only one of many moments. We know the importance of "series" in the work of Picasso— as a matter of fact, they are more important in his work than in anybody else's. Let me remind you, for example, of the famous evolution undergone by his bull. But only film could radically solve the problem of a "series" within one work itself, could realize the passage from the gross approximations of the discontinuous to the temporal realism of a continuous vision; only film could make us see duration itself.

Certainly, in these matters, nobody is ever the very first to do anything, and the idea upon which the whole of Clouzot's film rests is not absolutely new. One could find traces of this idea in several films about art, although I can think of only one film where this idea is episodically used with a comparable efficiency: Frédérique Duran's *Braque* (in the sequence of the sculpted pebbles). Similarly, the idea of painting by transparency— so that canvases can be filmed from behind—was crudely rendered here in the scene of the painting on a piece of transparent or translucent glass. But Clouzot's genius lies in the fact that he took these devices and ideas and made them pass from an experimental, episodic, or embryonic stage to a fully formed, spectacular one. There's more to *The Picasso Mystery*, however, than simply its perfection of process, or its difference in degree from everything on this subject we have seen so far. The contemplation of the work during its creation, of the "work in progress," was never anything but a relatively short episode in any other instructive documentary that used many approaches to, and points of view on, its subject, at the same time that it always stayed within the limits of a short or medium-length film. But it is precisely on such a "working" episode that Clouzot bases his entire film: the seed planted at random in the garden of documentary has become his forest. My purpose is not to dwell on the extraordinary audacity of this project, but I must nevertheless underline it in passing for fairness' sake. Furthermore, *The Picasso Mystery* does not limit itself to being a feature-length film in a field where others dare not go beyond fifty minutes: it is the extension of only a few of these minutes into almost eighty through the elimination of all descriptive and informative biographical elements. Thus Clouzot deliberately gave up the trump card that everybody else would have retained in such a difficult game: variety.

The reason is that, in his mind, the artistic creation is the only authentic spectacular element, the only cinematic one, because it is essentially temporal. Creation is pure waiting and uncertainty; it is "suspense," in that the absence or incompleteness of subject creates anticipation in the viewer. This is probably what seduced Clouzot to make this film, whether consciously or not. *The Picasso Mystery* is his most revealing work, for this filmmaker's genius appears here in its purest state by taking itself to the limit. "Suspense" in this film could, in fact, no longer be confused with a form of dramatic progression, with a certain ordering of the action, or with its explosion in violence. Literally, nothing happens here, nothing but the carrying out over time of the artistic process, the performance of the painter's work itself more than the fulfillment of his subject. The action, if there is indeed any, has nothing to do with the stock dramatic situations. This is a pure and free metamorphosis that is at root the direct apprehension of the freedom of the mind, made visible through art. It is also the evidence that this freedom lies in duration. The spectacle as such, then, is the fascination created by the appearance of free forms in a nascent state.

Clouzot's discovery unexpectedly ties in with the most interesting tradition in animated films, the one that was initiated by Emile Cohl (with *The Merry Microbes* [1909] especially) but that found its liveliest expression only in the work of Oskar Fischinger, Len Lye, and above all Norman McLaren.[4] This tradition does not make of the animated film an a posteriori animation of a drawing that has a virtually autonomous existence. Rather, it turns such a film into the evolution of the drawing itself or, more accurately, its metamorphosis. Animation here is not the mere logical transformation of space: it is the temporal transformation of that space as well. It is a germination, a budding; form engenders form without ever justifying its existence. That *The Picasso Mystery* reminds us of McLaren is therefore not surprising. I beg André Martin's pardon, but here is a kind of animated film or painting that owes nothing to the image in itself. Instead of starting from motionless drawings that the projector is going to animate through an optical illusion, the canvas exists as a screen, which must then be photographed for the length of the artistic or painterly process.

I know that some people are going to protest here and take exception to the liberties that Clouzot has apparently taken with the duration of artistic creation. I can hear them say that he had no right to "accelerate" the making of the paintings, to manipulate the duration of the original event as he did during the editing. It is true that this audacious initiative on his part is debatable; nevertheless, I shall attempt to justify it.

Clouzot rightly denies that he "accelerated" Picasso's work. Indeed, the speed of the shooting remained constant at twenty-four frames per second. But isn't he using an equally unacceptable special effect during the editing when he cuts at will the dull or long passages, thus making two juxtaposed strokes appear as if they have been made one right after the other? My answer is no. We must make a distinction between special effect and falsification. First, Clouzot is not trying to deceive us. Only the absentminded, the foolish, or those who don't know the first thing about cinema may be unaware of the device of accelerating editing. Just to be sure, Clouzot has Picasso refer expressly to this device during the film. Second, and most important, we must make a radical distinction between the length of the final edited print and the actual time it took to shoot the film. The former is abstract, intellectual, imaginary, and spectacular; only the latter is concrete. The whole of filmmaking rests on the free dividing up or parceling out of time through editing, although each of the fragments of the mosaic is projected at the realistic shooting speed of twenty-four frames per second. Clouzot carefully refrained from showing us—and should be warmly congratulated for doing so—the classical flower painting, blooming like the plants displayed in accelerated scientific films. He understood and felt, as a filmmaker should, the necessity for a spectacle of some duration. So he decided to use for his own purposes the concrete length of time it took to shoot the film as well as the concrete length of footage he had gathered as a result—without, however, changing the essential nature of his material. This is why, among other reasons, it would be ridiculous to deny the film any merit as a documentary. There isn't any less mastery of the film idiom in *The Picasso Mystery* than in *The Wages of Fear* (1953). But there may be more audacity. It is precisely because Clouzot made, not a "documentary" in the most narrow and pedagogic sense of the word, but a "real film," that he could, indeed had to, take the duration of spectacle into account. Film here is not the mere moving photography of an a priori, external reality. It is legitimately and intimately organized in aesthetic symbiosis with the events pictured.

If I had been one of the members of the Cannes jury, I would have voted for *The Picasso Mystery*, if only to reward Clouzot for one discovery of his that is well worth the success of two or three dramatic films. I'd like to talk now about the film's use of color. Clouzot had an idea here that only a great filmmaker could have had. I barely hesitate to call it an idea of genius, and this idea is all the more extraordinary since it is almost invisible to most viewers. Indeed, ask somebody who has just seen *The Picasso Mystery* if the film is in black and white or color. Nine times out of ten, the person will answer, after a slight hesitation, "in color." But nobody, or almost no one, will tell you that the film rests on an incredible contradiction, and gets away with it simply because this contradiction seems to partake of the very nature of things. For, materially, *The Picasso Mystery* is a black-and-white film printed on color stock, except, and exclusively, when the screen is occupied by Picasso's painting. Come to think of it, of course, this choice was as obvious as the succession of night and day, but you have to be a great filmmaker to reinvent night and day. Clouzot makes us thus accept (so implicitly that only some serious reflection reveals it to us) as a natural reality that the real world is in black and white, "except for paintings." The chemical permanence of the positive color film gives the whole its necessary and substantial unity. One then naturally thinks that the reverse-angle shot of the painter, who appears in black and white next to his painting, is in color. In fact, if we want to get to the bottom of the matter, it would be wrong to say that the film is both in black and white and in color. It would be better to consider *The Picasso Mystery* as the first color film made at a second remove.

Here is what I mean. Let's suppose that Clouzot shot the whole film in color. The painting would then exist plastically on the same plane of reality as the painter. The blue color on the canvas would be the same on screen as the blue of Picasso's eyes; the red color on the same canvas would be identical to the red of Clouzot's shirt. So, in order to make spectacularly visible the imaginary or aesthetic mode of existence of the colors on the canvas, in opposition to those of reality, the filmmaker would have had to create coloring at a second remove, that is, he would have had, mathematically speaking, to square the red and blue on the canvas. This impossible aesthetic problem was solved by Clouzot with the elegance of the great mathematicians. He understood that, whereas he couldn't square the colors on canvas, he could very well divide those off canvas by themselves. Thus, since natural reality is merely form multiplied by color, it can be reduced by division to form alone, i.e., black and

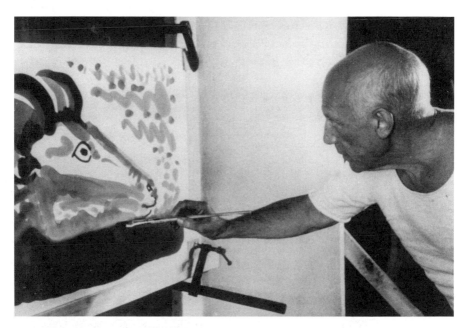

The Picasso Mystery (1956), dir. Henri-Georges Clouzot, Le Cinémathèque Royale, Brussels.

white, whereas the painting, which is in fact color superimposed upon the color of the real world, keeps its aesthetic chromaticism. And the viewer barely realizes the contrast, as the actual relations or proportions of reality have not been modified. When we look at a painting, we perceive that its colors are essentially different from those of the wall or the easel itself. What we do then is virtually annihilate the natural colors from our field of vision to the benefit of those in the pictorial creation. It is this mental process that Clouzot reconstitutes without our realizing it. In other words, *The Picasso Mystery* is not "a black-and-white film, except when the screen is occupied by Picasso's painting": on the contrary, it is essentially a color film, reduced to black and white for all non-pictorial moments.

Only spite or blindness could make one argue therefrom that the film is not Clouzot's but rather Picasso's. Of course, the painter's genius is inherent in the principle of the film, not only for his a priori quality as a painter of genius, but also for other qualities attached to his genius that no doubt made the conception and production of the film materially possible. Yet, underlining the decisive creative role played by Clouzot would not amount to diminishing Picasso's. The unbearable music by Georges Auric is the only concession that the filmmaker thought fit to make to the anecdotal and the picturesque, but, then again, he had already discarded with often amazing audacity a great many psychological tricks that could have made his job easier if not more rewarding.

NOTES TO CHAPTER 27

A Bergsonian Film: The Picasso Mystery

(All notes have been provided by the Editor.)

This article was first published in French in *Cahiers du Cinéma*, no.60 (June 1956), then reprinted in Vol. 2 ("Le Cinéma et les autres arts") of Bazin's four-volume *Qu'est-ce que le cinéma?* (Paris: Éditions du Cerf, 1958–62), pp. 133–142.

1. *Henri Matisse, Paul Langevin, Louis de Broglie* (1945).

2. In collaboration with Enricho Gras, Luciano Emmer wrote and directed an innovative series of short documentaries on art and artists, notable for their mood and pace, often achieved through the dynamic editing of stills. Among them are *Racconto da un Fresco* on Giotto (1941), *Il Paradiso Terrestre* on Bosch (1946), *Leonardo da Vinci* (1952), and *Picasso* (1954).

3. In 1947 Resnais embarked on a series of short 16-mm documentaries in which he attempted to take "paintings out of the dusty setting of the museums." There were "visits to" Lucien Coutaud, Félix Labisse, Hans Hartnung, César Doméla, and Max Ernst, and a "portrait" of Henri Goetz, all made in 1947. The problem Resnais set out to solve in these art films, he says, "was to find out if painted trees, painted hous-

es, and painted characters could, by way of montage, fulfill the roles of real objects and if, in this case, it was possible to substitute, for the observer, the interior world of an artist for the world that photography revealed." In terms of Resnais's apprenticeship these movies, as James Monaco writes, "were important and invaluable experiments in the crucial relationship of montage and *mise en scène*."

The films are: *Visite à Lucien Coutaud* (1947); *Visite à Félix Labisse* (1947); *Visite à Hans Hartnung* (1947); *Visite à César Doméla* (1947); *Portrait d'Henri Goetz* (1947); *Journée naturelle/Visite à Max Ernst* (1947); *Malfray* (1947); *Van Gogh* (1948); *Gauguin* (1948); *Guernica* (1950, with Robert Hessens); and *Les Statues meurent aussi* (1953, with Chris Marker).

4. **Len Lye** (1901–1980): He began experimenting with film animation in 1929 in London, breaking new ground in this area in 1939 by inventing a technique for painting directly on film. The abstract short *Color Box* was the first film in which he utilized this technique, which was later to influence the work of Norman McLaren. The New Zealand-born Lye became an American citizen in 1947.

Norman McLaren (1914–1987): A gifted innovator and a meticulous craftsman, McLaren (who was born in Scotland but emigrated to the U.S. in 1939) pioneered in many areas of animation, but his greatest contribution was in developing and perfecting the techniques of drawing directly on film, a cameraless method of animation originated by Len Lye. McLaren also experimented with three-dimensional animation and with the conversion of animated drawings into synthetic sound waves.

Emile Cohl (1857–1938): Utilizing the American invention of stop-motion photography (one-turn, one picture), the Parisian Cohl made some one-hundred brief animated films between 1908 and 1918, drawing every frame of his films himself. His drawing was simple and schematic, almost primitive, but he infused his characters with much life and humor. He is credited with being the first to develop a regular cartoon character, Fantoche, a little man who "appeared" in many of his films.

Oskar Fischinger (1900–1967): An avant-garde painter, the German Fischinger had begun toying with the idea of creating abstract visual interpretations of poetry and music at the age of nineteen and became involved in film animation in the course of diagramming the emotional movements in a Shakespearean play. He made his first animated shorts in 1920 with the help of a wax-cutting machine of his own design. In 1926 he presented the first of a series of "absolute film" shorts, which he named *Study 1*, *Study 2*, etc. These "studies" gained in impact after the advent of sound, when they could be shown to the accompaniment of classical music and jazz. In 1933 he began exploring color with a special process he had helped to develop and in 1935 won a prize at the Venice Festival for his *Komposition in Blau* (*Composition in Blue*). The following year he went to Hollywood, where he made the animated short *Allegretto* to the tune of a jazz theme. He won the Grand Prix at the Brussels Exhibition of 1949 for his *Motion Painting No. 1*, in which he used intricate designs and geometric forms to the accompaniment of Bach's Brandenburg Concerto No. 3.

CHAPTER 28

I*l Bidone*, or the Road to Salvation Reconsidered

When I heard one of my colleagues cleverly sneer, "It's a swindle!" to a countryman after the screening of this film at the Venice Festival, I didn't feel very proud of being a French critic. But these "wise guys" weren't as harsh as most Italian critics, for I have also heard the most esteemed among them declare that *Il Bidone* (*The Swindle* or *The Swindlers*, 1955) definitely proved that those who had praised *La Strada* (1954) had been mistaken. For my part, I admit that the Venice screening left me perplexed because I don't understand Italian: some long sequences therefore appeared to me to be doubly questionable. But, far from negating my admiration for *La Strada*, *Il Bidone* seemed to me to confirm the genius that was manifested in it. Even if Fellini's latest film was relatively unsuccessful, it still suggested a power of invention, a poetic and moral vision, that was by no means inferior to that of *La Strada* or even *I Vitelloni* (1953).

But *Il Bidone* is not an unsuccessful film. I realize this today after seeing it for the third time, subtitled at last, and rid of a few scenes, which were indeed unnecessary. Not that they were unjustified from a certain point of view. In fact, the film is now too short, for Fellini had intended to develop these scenes further, which would have been useful to a full understanding of the characters' destinies; but he finally gave up on doing so. So the excised scenes were superfluous, and it was better to cut too much than not enough. This is not at all comparable, fortunately, to the mutilations undergone at a certain point by a print of *La Strada*, nor is it comparable, even more fortunately, to the mutilations allegedly intended for *Il Bidone* by the French distributor: these were supposed to do nothing less than radically transform the meaning of the denouement.

Augusto, the protagonist of the film, does indeed die for having tried to con his two pals into believing that he has taken pity on the paralyzed girl whose parents the three of them have just swindled. In fact, he wants to keep the money for himself, so that he can help his own daughter pursue her studies. The other swindlers beat him up in revenge and leave him to die alone on a stony hillside. We can see that if Augusto had really let himself be moved by the poor peasant girl, he would have been redeemed and would have died an innocent man, much to the great satisfaction of the Manichaeism that presides over all commercial happy endings.

Does his behavior make him fundamentally good or evil? Fortunately, Fellini never places himself on the level of such moral psychology. His universe dramaturgically remaps the road to salvation. People are what they are—beings—and what they *become*, not what they do; their actions, whether good or evil or filled with purity of intention, don't permit them to be judged any more objectively than subjectively. The purity of the man lies deeper: for Fellini, it is essentially defined by the transparency or the opacity of the soul, or even, if you will, by a certain perviousness to grace. Naturally, those who are perfectly transparent and open to other people's love want to do good and generally do so (although this type of "good" often has very little to do with morality in the strictest sense); but we are dealing here with the consequences of essence, not the causes of action. So, we may believe that Augusto is saved, just like Zampanò in *La Strada*, even though he has intended and done evil right up to the end, because he has at least died in a state of anxiety. His conversation with the paralyzed girl did not move him at all in the psychological sense of the word. Far from making him comprehend the shame of betraying a child's confidence, it doubtless gave him, on the contrary, the courage and determination to swindle his accomplices. At the same time, however, his conversation with the paralyzed girl introduced turmoil to his soul; it made him see, finally, not so much the accidental lie of his actions as the essential imposture of his life.

By contrast, Picasso (whose story was abbreviated in the final version) is a nice, sensitive, sentimental man, always full of good intentions and always ready to take pity on others or on himself. But for all this, Picasso's salvation is probably hopeless. Why does he steal? Because he "looks like an angel"; with a face like his, he couldn't be suspected of anything. Incapable of truly responding to his internal fissures, of bridging them, Picasso is doomed to darkness and to ultimate downfall, despite the gentleness and love he displays toward his wife and child. Picasso's actions do not make him evil, but he *is* lost, just as Augusto is probably saved, despite the fact that he is incapable of pity.

I haven't used this Christian vocabulary intentionally—although a Christian inspiration is certainly undeniable in Fellini's work—but such a vocabulary is undoubtedly the one that best conveys the nature of the realities that are the object of a film like *Il Bidone*. Whether construed as metaphors or as metaphysical truths, the terms salvation or damnation, darkness or transparency of the soul, are the ones that impose themselves on me as I write, since they most accurately express the state of ultimate urgency in which our being is suspended as we otherwise conduct our lives.

Of these swindlers Fellini has said, I think, that they are aging *vitelloni* (overgrown calves, from Fellini's film *I Vitelloni* [1953]). The phrase perfectly describes these second-rate con men whose art resides solely in their huckster's gift of gab; they can't even get rich off their work, unlike the former colleague of theirs who is now a drug dealer and who invites them to celebrate New Year's Eve at his luxurious apartment. This extraordinary sequence, in which the chief device of contemporary cinema, the surprise party, is once again to be found, is the climax of the film. If there can be talk of symbolism at the precise moment in *Il Bidone* where realism is at its peak, then one can say that Fellini doubtless wanted to construct an image of hell, and a rather scorching one at that, for these poor devils who will not be able to endure its fire for very long.

I realize that I haven't told much of the "story." This is probably because I surmised that the reader had already read several summaries of it. One reason above all others is that the film doesn't much encourage plot summary. Although full of strange and funny episodes, it goes beyond the merely picturesque. If I dwelt on that aspect, I'd only be treating the accessories. *Il Bidone* is built, or rather created, like a novel: from the very inside of the characters. Fellini has certainly never conceived a situation for its narrative logic, nor even less for its dramatic necessity, and he doesn't do so here. The events happen all of a sudden: they are totally unpredictable, yet somehow inevitable, as the ones would have been that Fellini could have substituted for them.

If I had to compare this world to the world of a well-known novelist, it would unquestionably be that of Dostoyevsky, despite all the particulars that separate the two. In the Russian novelist's work, as in Fellini's, events are in fact never anything but the completely accidental instruments through which human souls feel their way, and nothing ever happens that is fundamentally connected with their salvation or damnation. Good and evil, happiness and anguish, are from this point of view nothing more than relative categories in comparison with the absolute alternative in which these protagonists are trapped, and that I can't help but call, even if only metaphorically, salvation or damnation.

NOTES TO CHAPTER 28

Il Bidone, *or the Road to Salvation Reconsidered*

This review was first published in French in *France-Observateur* (March 1956), then reprinted in Vol. 4 ("Une Esthétique de la réalité: le néoréalisme") of Bazin's four-volume *Qu'est-ce que le cinéma?* (Paris: Éditions du Cerf, 1958–62), pp. 129–133.

CHAPTER 29

High Infidelity (*The Bridge on the River Kwai*)

I saw *The Bridge on the River Kwai* (1957) after some delay, so I had plenty of time to get preconceived notions, first from the massive publicity that preceded its commercial release, second from a careful reading of the reviews, and third from the reading of Pierre Boulle's book. In short, I finally went to the Normandie Theater somewhat resigned, for I was convinced that I knew everything in advance about the film and its action. This review will first of all be an analysis and explanation of my relative surprise. Within the artistic limits that I shall try to define, David Lean's film, all things considered, seemed to me to be far more worthy than I had been able to gather from the orgasmic praise of some and the guarded reservations of others.

First, I must observe that the film is far superior to the book. This, by the way, is not meant to take anything away from the author, since Pierre Boulle wrote the screenplay as well. But we clearly find ourserves here in a very peculiar situation, where the usual relationship between novel and film is reversed. It is well-known that the aesthetic length of a film corresponds somewhat to that of a short story. Even when the filmic adaptation has no desire to flatten the novel's characters emotionally and to reduce its world intellectually—and most adaptations *do* have such a desire—the temporal contingencies of cinematic spectacle condemn the adaptation to be a simplification, if not a devaluation, of the original. Yet, for once, what was fated to occur has not occurred: no doubt due to the courage and determination of the people in charge—the producer and the director—but also and above all because the aesthetic relationship between the novel and the film is reversed. Of the two, the novel is the one that is in fact a short story and the film is the one that is a novel. However long and sweeping the narrative created by Pierre Boulle may be, it is so in a perfunctory and minimally descriptive way. It is merely the logical development, in almost abstract terms, of a situation set within a historical and geographical framework. As for the characters, their personal psychology is limited simply to what's needed for the full working out of the initial situation. Colonel Nicholson is nothing but a stick-in-the-mud draped in British dignity, only he's a little more stubborn and stupid than most of his fellow officers; he is also a little more courageous, but the former traits do not necessarily preclude the latter one. In any case, he leaves in one's memory merely the schematic image of a sociological and moral type, and not the rich image of an intimate and familiar acquaintance that is proper to the protagonist of a novel.

Because of its simplicity and monotony, the action of the novel had to be thickened and diversified for the film adaptation; but above all, the characters could not be left in their semi-anonymous state. The act of giving them a face forced the director to give them in addition a psychology, which the book did not do. He had to give one to Nicholson first, naturally, and then to the crowd of English soldiers, whose attachment to their colonel had to be justified, explained, and given some nuance. Next, there were the saboteurs, whose role almost inevitably had to be expanded, not only for the purpose of dramatic symmetry, but also to take advantage of the opportunity they presented to vary location and action, which, again, was not done in the novel. One could not deny here the intelligence of the creation of the American character, whose personality gives us, through contrast, perspective on and relief from the personalities of the English. This is a screenwriter's trick, but it is justified by the success of the result.

So *The Bridge on the River Kwai*, which is taken from a 150-page novel, seems to whoever hasn't read the book to be the adaptation of a work that is three times longer. Of course, length is not automatically synonymous with quality, and the result could have been bad, even in these circumstances. I don't think it is, because this elaboration, this thickening of the initial plot, was for once accomplished with the intent of respecting, not the conventional lines of commercial filmmaking, but rather the logic of the story and of the characters, and, wherever possible, the writer's freedom. I know that this particular adaptation has been challenged by many, and that Pierre Boulle himself has discreetly expressed some regrets about the ending of the film; but, upon reflection, it doesn't seem to me that the criticisms are completely justified. I shall examine only the two principal grounds for complaint: the love affairs with the native girls and, above all, the final destruction of the bridge, which is caused when Nicholson, who has just been shot to death, falls on the device that triggers the explosives.

Certainly I shall not deny for a moment that there is something a bit conventional in the sentimental relationship between the girls, who are being used as porters in the building of the bridge, and two of the soldiers of the sabotage unit (William Holden and the young Canadian). This little business clearly allows the director to introduce an erotic note, for which this otherwise virile script did not leave much room. I shall also concede that the physical beauty of the two village girls is so exotic that it may seem needlessly provocative. But the requisition by the Japanese of able-bodied men for the construction of the bridge is a clever justification for the use of these women, who had to be young in order to resist the hardships of the heavy work. Finally, I have to admit that *all* the Burmese young women in the film are very pretty, which is after all credible. In any event, and even if David Lean is stretching things here a bit, this stylization is justified by the psychological and dramatic usefulness of an erotic aura, which serves as a prelude to the heroes' death. The idea is not simply to satisfy the viewer's libido, but to give him relief from the sacrifice of the two young fellows, as if the shadow of this sacrifice were being projected on this side of life. I think, then, that not only was the screenwriter not wrong to sketch in these love affairs, but he also would have been mistaken not to do so.

The question of the ending is subtler, but it is even more indicative of the inherent requirements of the cinematic image. First, how could you blame a director for identifying with his viewers in deeming it impossible not to destroy a bridge that has cost so much to build? The physical realization of the famous bridge by the filmmakers puts the viewer in a state of mind that is different from the situation that has been created in the imagination of the reader. At the end of the film, the bridge really spans the River Kwai; it is not a studio model. Can it survive the film without thus creating a second absurdity that both rules out the one intended by the script—the blowing up of the bridge—and engulfs the entire work, in the same way that two negative charges cancel each other and in the process destroy the electrical current? A choice had to be made: the absurdity either had to be *in* the film or it had, finally, to be the film *itself.* Acting out of instinct, and for reasons that are less than intellectual, the director was right to deem necessary the destruction of the bridge.

I'd even say that he hasn't gone far enough in his infidelity to the book. It is obvious that the screenwriter, the director, or the producer has agreed to a concession that his conscience had told him was unworthy of the audacity of this undertaking. In Boulle's novel, Nicholson dies without self-knowledge and the bridge is not blown up. Even in hell, the colonel will be oblivious to the foolishness of his behavior. I think that this ontological perseverance in the absurdity of his being would have been unbearable in the cinema—that is to say, implausible. Alec Guinness' remarkable acting in the long final scene underlines this palpable truth. It is possible for a writer to elude psychology for the sake of writing a moral tale: all he has to do is proceed by ellipsis and refrain from describing too precisely the realities that he wants to put into play. But writing about Colonel Nicholson in a novel is one thing; embodying him on film is quite another. One cannot at the same time impose his existence on us, bring us face to face with him, and deny the conclusions that this visible existence finally implies. I myself experienced as a necessity— a physical as well as a psychological one—Nicholson's final flash of lucidity, and I don't at all think that it cancels in retrospect the absurdity of his actions. At any rate, Nicholson is incorrigible: he can but understand too late, for himself and for the others.

At this point, however, David Lean found himself stuck in a contradiction. As long as (1) the bridge had to be blown up and (2) Nicholson finally realized his foolishness, the only logical conclusion was that the colonel himself had to press the detonator. But this denouement evidently appeared to Lean to be a kind of commercial happy ending, which contradicted the emotional austerity and intellectual rigor of the adaptation at the same time that it increased the infidelity to the novel. This is why he opted in the end for a compromise that adds up to the disadvantages of both concession and implausibility: Nicholson will blow up his bridge, but involuntarily, by dropping dead on the detonator.

I don't believe, then, that one can seriously criticize David Lean's film on the basis of the changes he has made to the book. First, because these changes generally enhance the original, and second, because they are, in fact, demanded by the additional psychological realism supplied by the image, even though they may appear to soften the impact of Boulle's novel.

Must we therefore conclude that *The Bridge on the River Kwai* is a masterpiece and consider it the ideal in filmmaking? This is not at all the view that my defense of it is intended to foster. But being fair and defining exactly the shortcomings as well as the virtues of such a film is indeed difficult. *The Bridge on the River Kwai* is in fact of extraordinarily high quality for the film industry—there are very few examples each year of cinematic enterprises that are carried out with such intelligence and above all with such care. But the quality of this film must ultimately be put in its artistic place, and that place is not the highest.

It has been said that this is an "adult" film, and the adjective is valid if one means by it the rejection of certain conventions in the script or in David Lean's direction. To judge by its manifest themes, *The Bridge on the River Kwai* is simultaneously an adventure film and a war movie. Certainly the latter genre has produced some thoughtful works deserving of praise, but I don't think that any of these contains fewer dramatic conventions than Lean's film. I can especially see an illustration of this point in the final slaughter, which dispatches most of the characters in whom the viewer has taken an interest during the film. Of course, having the hero die is not startlingly original, but such a death generally occurs only after some preparation, which at the same time foretells it and makes it dramatically necessary. Nothing of the kind happens here: the death of two of the three saboteurs is simply the logical outgrowth of the immediate situation. These protagonists are made to die without regard for the moral relationships that have been created between them and the audience. It is undeniable that, in any traditional script, at least one of the two saboteurs would have survived, so as to allow the transfer to the survivor of the potential for sympathy released by the death of the other saboteur, according to a law of emotional compensation that is always respected. Here, to the contrary, we are deprived of each of the two most appealing characters, after their lives have been made even more precious to us by a sentimental love story. We are left in the sole company of a survivor to whom we are emotionally indifferent: the Englishman in charge of the expedition. To cut a long story short, and to explain the phenomenon in different terms, the script possesses from beginning to end the same freedom from convention and internal rigor as Boulle's novel.

The rigor of the script is matched and strengthened by the equally rigorous *mise en scène*. By this I mean, not that the directing is anything more than precise and conscientious, but that, being shot almost entirely on location, the film rejects the ease and obviousness of the studio: instead, it embraces the complexity and richness of the natural world. This solely photographic attribute gives *The Bridge on the River Kwai* an exceptional tonality. In the end, if one compares David Lean's intent with his execution, one has to admit, first, that it is indeed unusual when the ambition of a film reaches such a level, but beyond this, that it is even more unusual when there is so little difference between the quality of this ambition and the quality of its realization. In other words, I am happy to report that we have here the best conceivable film that could be made from a certain type of script.

But, then, it is just this script that we must judge. And my judgment tells me that I value far more the artistry of other kinds of film, even if they unfortunately offer few examples of such a perfect equation between ambition and execution. And since this has all been about the adaptation of a novel to film, let me add that we must naturally prefer Bernanos to Rudyard Kipling, let alone to Pierre Boulle, just as we prefer Renoir or Fellini to David Lean.

NOTES TO CHAPTER 29

High Infidelity (The Bridge on the River Kwai)

1. First published in French in *Cahiers du Cinéma*, 14, no. 80 (February 1958), pp. 50–53.

CHAPTER 30

The Technique of *Citizen Kane*

Well, then, let's talk once more about *Citizen Kane* (1941).[1] Today, as the last echoes from the critics seem to have faded away, we can take stock of their judgments. I'll leave aside those who have understood nothing, and I'll challenge the testimony of the film's assistant directors, cameramen, and designers, who could barely contain themselves in the face of such a provocative achievement. For the rest, the opinions range between these two extremes: Orson Welles reinvents filmmaking, *Citizen Kane* is as important as *Greed* (1925, dir. Erich von Stroheim), and Welles is a great man; nonetheless, however talented he may be, his film is only an intelligent bluff. Georges Sadoul, for example, talks about some monstrous puffball that probably owes its existence to a deluge of dollars during one of those long Hollywood nights. He can't see anything new in the style; on the contrary, he finds

> an excess of feebly assimilated reminiscences. The film is an ency-
> clopedia of old techniques. One can find in it all of the following:
> the simultaneous clarity of the foregrounds and the most distant
> backgrounds, as in Louis Lumière's *Arrival of a Train in the Station
> at La Ciotat* (1895); Méliès' taste for special effects and cardboard
> sets; the mixing of accelerated montage and superimposition, which
> was the latest fashion in 1920; the acrobatics of the traveling shot,
> which goes back to 1935; the sets with ceilings taken over from
> *Greed*..., the newsreel montage invented by Dziga Vertov...One
> senses that Welles is intoxicated with the apparent novelty of his
> means and technique.[2]

All of Sadoul's comparisons are accurate except one, whose importance is in fact paramount: to equate Gregg Toland's special lenses with
Louis Lumière's fixed lenses seems wrong to me. The depth of field in the
shot of the train's arrival could easily be obtained in full sunlight by a simple reduction of the size of the diaphragm. The interesting thing about
Welles's depth of field is that it is created *in the studio*, where lighting can
vary tremendously depending on the scene. And it is the very sharpness
of the deep-focus shots that contributes to *Citizen Kane*'s significance,
provided one sees in this work not only a series of recipes and effects, but
also the perfectly conscious use of all the resources of filmmaking in order
to achieve a meaningful style. In this respect, the accusation of plagiarism
could very well be extended to the film's use of panchromatic film or its
exploitation of the properties of gelatinous silver halide without taking
anything away from Welles's originality.

In an article published by *L'Écran Français* long before the release of
Citizen Kane in France, Jean-Paul Sartre also disputes the technical originality of Welles's *mise en scène*, acknowledging its intelligence but regret-
ting its intellectualism.[3] In addition, he makes an ingenious analysis of
time in the film's narrative—an analysis that has hardly been taken up by
other critics:

> There is a strange effect that gives certain images a quality of gen-
> eralization. In fact even in prose fiction we say, "He was forcing his
> wife to sing on all the stages in America," which condenses into a
> single sentence a great number of events.... [In *Citizen Kane*]
> Welles excels at this kind of *generalizing* shortcut... This device is
> well known, but up to now it has been used as a footnote to the
> action in order to inject a political opinion or to reveal the influ-
> ence of some course of events on the narrative as a whole, or to
> supply a simple transition. In *Citizen Kane*, it is a *part* of the action,
> it is the action itself, it provides the foundation of the plot, and the
> scenes with dates are for once the exceptions. It is as if the narrator
> were saying, "He *forced* her to sing everywhere; she *had had* enough
> of it; *one time* she tried to tell him, etc." (p. 4)

In any event, the true originality of the film doesn't derive from its
devices. For ten years now, the language of filmmaking has been fully
defined (at least until the advent of 3-D); the novelty of language, cinematic or otherwise, must be understood from the point of view of style,
not from the point of view of vocabulary or syntax. Flaubert did not

invent the imperfect tense, nor did Gide invent the simple past, or Camus the present perfect: their use of these tenses is personal, and it is one component of their prose styles. However, even if Welles did not invent the cinematic devices employed in *Citizen Kane*, one should nevertheless credit him with the invention of their *meaning*. His way of "writing" a film is undeniably his own. I don't mean by this the mere architecture of the story, although the novelty of the ordering of the film's scenes is itself worthy of our consideration. In this sense, the connection between *Citizen Kane* and the novels of Dos Passos is obvious. The insertion of the newsreel extracts probably has nothing to do with Dziga Vertov, contrary to what Sadoul writes, but it does owe quite a lot to the author of *The 42nd Parallel* (1930) and *Big Money* (1936). The substitution for the chronological story of a kind of jigsaw puzzle, whose pieces are provided by the memories of a series of witnesses, can hardly be traced, however, to *The Power and the Glory* (1933) or even *Marie-Martine* (1943).[4]

Still, in my opinion, this does not amount to "reinventing filmmaking." It is fitting that, after having directly or indirectly influenced the novel, the cinema should in turn be influenced by it. But what is even more important is that the cinema not limit itself to the more or less skillful imitation of fiction; it is to Welles's credit that he managed to accomplish a revolution in film language that was necessary to his thematic purpose. All the effects of *Citizen Kane*'s *mise en scène*, whether borrowed from the past or created from scratch, are now material for a new conception of filmmaking.

Most of the critics have pointed out the use of lenses with great depth of field in this film, and Roger Leenhardt has explained the main consequence of such use: "The acting takes place in depth [from the foreground to the background], so tracking and editing become unnecessary."[5] This simple sentence requires some elaboration once one recalls that the cinema has been based for the last thirty years or so on the idea of the edited or reassembled scene. The *mise en scène* has consisted of decomposing the action into fragments (the shots), whose arrangement or sequence is meant to be grasped by the viewer's mind as the story itself. This cutting, which I would call analytical, tends never to show two things on screen at the same time. The dialogue becomes a succession of shot-countershot in favor of one or the other speaker. The camera cuts according to the dramatic center of gravity of the scene, choosing for us what we must see at the moment when it must be seen. The cutting of the camera can be compared to the compulsory movement of one's head, and the change of shot to the refocusing of one's crystalline lens, as if it were inescapably coupled to the lens of the camera. Leenhardt also observed that the apparent wholeness of the action in such a sequence corresponded less to the physical proximity of people and things to one another than to the degree of our attentiveness or absorption (which explains why we don't react to the material impossibility of the shot changes). The story is thus reconstituted on the screen along a melodic visual line that closely follows all the sinuosities of the action. Oh, Minotaur, here you will find Ariadne's thread: it is the editor's scissors.[6]

Welles builds most of his sequences in a completely different way. Let's take Susan Alexander Kane's suicide attempt as an example: we get it in a single shot on a level with the bed. In the left-hand corner, on the night table, are the enormous glass and the teaspoon. A little farther back, in shadow, we sense rather than see the woman's face. The presence of drama and its nature, already suggested by the glass, are revealed to us on the soundtrack: by a raspy groan and the snore of a drugged sleeper. Beyond the bed: the empty room, and completely in the background, even farther away because of the receding perspective created by the wide-angle lens: the locked door. Behind the door, we hear on the soundtrack Kane's calls and his shoulder bumping against the wood. This single shot, then, is built in depth around two dramatic centers of gravity, each consisting of sonorous and visual elements. One sees immediately the use Welles has made of his lens by putting the desert of the bedroom between the bed and the door. It is difficult, if one hasn't seen the film, to imagine the internal dynamism of this image, stretched between two poles, with its monstrous foreground pressed against the viewer's face and this little rectangle of sound far away in which one can divine Kane's fear and anger. But let's continue: the door gives way and Kane appears and rushes to the bed. Along with him, it's the whole dramatic background that comes toward us. The two nuclei of the action, which were irresistibly attracting each other, are coming together. The tension that was dividing the image, and doubling the action of the story with its own plastic drama, dissolves; it broke with the door from the force of Kane's shoulder. Then the dramatic overload of the image suddenly dissipates as Welles changes shots.

One can easily imagine what classical or analytical cutting would have made of this scene: four or five different shots would have been necessary to relate to us the same event. Clearly, we would not have been spared the parallel montage of shots taken inside and outside the room until the inevitable reverse-angle shot of the room at the moment the door breaks open. I won't insist on giving twenty more examples of this kind from the film. I'll recall only the scene of Kane's falling out with Jed Leland and the banquet celebrating the hiring of the *Chronicle*'s staff as well as the declaration of war against Spain, during which the director makes sure that we don't lose sight of Kane by keeping his reflection in a windowpane when the camera has to make a cut. Talking about montage and cutting in relation to these dramatic blocks has little meaning other than a metaphoric one; what matters is less a succession of images and their relationship to each other than the interior structure of the image, the attractions or currents that are created within the dramatic space, which is at last used in its three dimensions. It is not the lens that makes the arrangements for our eye, it's our mind that is compelled to follow the dramatic spectrum in its entirety within this uniformly visible space.

The extraordinary richness of the acting in Welles's films is a natural consequence of this technique. When a character becomes secondary in the course of a scene, classical cutting automatically takes him off the screen. While keeping him there, Welles makes sure that his acting doesn't stop being as precise as if he were still the center of attention, thus always running the risk of splitting the viewer's focus. We must constantly be attentive in order to avoid having the main event take place behind our backs, as it were. The deliberate aim here is complete realism, a way of considering reality as if it were homogeneous and indivisible, as if it had the same density at all coordinates on the screen. The whole set and all the actors are, in the totality of the image, offered up equally to our eyes; if something remains off screen, it's simply a coincidence that is as unpredictable as an exception to the rule of great numbers.

The leitmotif of the jigsaw puzzle that dominates the end of the film is also the symbol of its aesthetics, whether we are referring to the rough fragments of the newsreels, where by definition an event is cut up at random by the editor's hand, or to the more sophisticated dramatic segments, in which the frame of the screen is used as an open window ideally situated for the action to develop plastically all of its elements. But, just as a jigsaw puzzle cuts up a picture that has previously been whole, Welles's cutting fragments reality along selected lines instead of analyzing it into its component parts, as cinema usually does according to a completely conventional mechanism. Thus Welles sometimes comes back twice to the same scene—that of opening night at the Chicago Opera House, for example, as remembered initially by Jed Leland and then by Susan Alexander Kane herself. The first time, we see the heroine from the front of the house; the second time, from the back of the stage. These two points of view on the same event fit together as closely as two contiguous pieces of a jigsaw puzzle, even though the second has not been placed immediately after the first. The same holds true for the scene of Susan's departure: it is resumed during Raymond the butler's testimony exactly at the point where the camera had left it in Susan's story.

Necessarily, I have given only a few, representative examples in this brief analysis. *Citizen Kane* is not entirely built according to these principles; often, even within the most characteristically photographed segments, Welles does not hesitate to employ classical cutting. It remains to be seen why this return to a traditional method of storytelling does not destroy the overall style of the film. Doesn't Welles in fact manage to incorporate, even into his quick cuts, the essence of the realistic technique found in his long takes? Even supposing that we could draw this conclusion, there would probably remain a significant portion of the film unexplained—a portion that the less friendly critics would ascribe to a deliberate taste for paradox, to the compulsion for being nonconformist at all costs. Whether we put into this category the sets with ceilings or the sets that were built instead of using more economical transparencies, is in the end not very important. I'd only observe that these little by-products are far from being negligible and that the artistic mileage we could get from them would be enough to make the reputation of many a film. The systematic use of techniques other than the accepted ones, when it's done with talent, always has the effect of revealing forgotten truths. We had come to believe that the faces of beautiful women, when we look at them from up close, are naturally lit by various, judiciously arranged sources; we had come to believe that people don't turn their backs when saying important things, and that ceilings never confine our existence. By reminding us of all this, Welles has given the cinema a theoretical restoration. He has enriched his filmic repertory with new or forgotten effects that, in today's artistic context, take on a significance we didn't know they could have.

I'll leave to more philosophical minds the task of defining the metaphysics, to use Sartre's word,[7] of Welles's technique. I'd simply like to remark, in conclusion, that the mutual influence that literature and cinema have on each other, which seems obvious, does not diminish the uniqueness of their respective means of expression. We persist in France in "adapting" to the screen the novels of Dostoyevsky, Gide, and Balzac in a quasi-uniform language that tries in vain to respect the original prose style through childish artifices of set or lighting design. However, men like Orson Welles, William Wyler, and Preston Sturges don't adapt: they write or rewrite their story in film language and never doubt thereby to achieve, each in his own way, the artistic revolution required, just as James Joyce, for instance, managed to do it in literature. Although the connections between American fiction and American cinema appear to be more and more numerous, far from leading to a literary kind of filmmaking, they have instead reaffirmed each of these arts in its own technique. Fiction and filmmaking do not engage in mutual imitation; they only adopt common purposes, they fulfill the same aims, without copying each other.

To detail, as Sadoul does, the previous use of certain devices in order to deny their appropriation by Welles, is to forget that the invention belongs to the man who can master it. D. W. Griffith himself did not invent the close-up, which you can find here and there years before he used it, but he did invent analytical cutting—i.e., the last thirty years of filmmaking—by systematically changing shots for the sake of clarifying his narrative. Even if *Citizen Kane* had merely been one of the most brilliant examples of the alchemy of modern cinematic language, Welles would deserve more than just the attention of film snobs. If he doesn't "reinvent filmmaking," at least he reinvents his own cinema, just as Malraux, Hemingway, and Dos Passos reinvent language for their own purposes. Perhaps Welles's endeavor was fully possible only beyond the standardized, transparent cinema of the studio system, in an arena where no more resistance is offered to the artist's intention than to the novelist's pen. What is significant is that we owe the most audacious film in the last ten years to a young man of twenty-five who had nothing to recommend him except his ideas.

NOTES TO CHAPTER 30

The Technique of Citizen Kane

"The Technique of *Citizen Kane*" was first published in French in *Les Temps Modernes*, II, no. 17 (1947), pp. 943-949. See also the following:
(All notes have been provided by the Editor.)

1. *André Bazin, *Orson Welles: A Critical View*, trans. Jonathan Rosenbaum (New York: Harper and Row, 1978): "*Citizen Kane*," pp. 53-59; "The Technique of Wide Angles," pp. 74–75; "Construction in Depth," pp. 75–80; and "A Style That Creates Meaning," pp. 81–82.

*André Bazin, "The Evolution of the Language of Cinema," in *What is Cinema?*, I, trans. Hugh Gray (Berkeley: Univ. of Calif. Press, 1967), pp. 23-40, where Bazin discusses depth-of-field shooting versus montage in *Citizen Kane* on pp. 33-37.

*André Bazin, "An Aesthetic of Reality: Neorealism," in *What is Cinema?* II, trans. Hugh Gray (Berkeley: Univ. of Calif. Press, 1971), pp. 16–40, which has a section entitled "From *Citizen Kane* to *Farrebique*" on pp. 27–30.

*André Bazin and Jean-Charles Tacchella, "Les Secrets d'Orson Welles" (Interview), *L'Écran Français*, no. 169 (21 Sept. 1948), pp. 3-4.

*André Bazin, "L'Apport d'Orson Welles," *Ciné-Club*, no. 7 (May 1948).

*André Bazin and Charles Bitsch, "Entretien avec Orson Welles," *Cahiers du Cinéma*, no. 84 (June 1958).

*André Bazin, Charles Bitsch, and Jean Domarchi, "Nouvel Entretien avec Orson Welles," *Cahiers du Cinéma*, no. 87 (Sept. 1958), pp. 2-27.

*André Bazin, "Orson Welles, la télévision et le magnétophone," *France-Observateur*, 12 June 1958.

*André Bazin, "Orson Welles chez les Jivaros," *Cahiers du Cinéma*, no. 88 (Oct. 1958).

*André Bazin, 'Le Pour et le Contre (Orson Welles)," *Cahiers du Cinéma*, no. 4 (July-Aug. 1951), pp. 46–51.

*André Bazin, "Buñuel et Orson Welles justifient le (Cannes) Festival officieux," *Le Parisien libéré*, 5 May 1956.

*André Bazin, "*Citizen Kane*," *Le Parisien libéré*, July 5, 1946.

2. Georges Sadoul, "Le Cinéma: Hypertrophie du cerveau" (Review of *Citizen Kane*), *Les Lettres françaises*, no. 115 (5 July 1946), p. 9. Sadoul (1904–1967) was a French film critic and historian. In 1945 he became general secretary of the Fédération Française de Ciné-Clubs and began his weekly film review in *Les Lettres françaises*, which he continued until his death. He also contributed to *L'Écran Français*. From 1945 until the mid-1950s, Sadoul stood with André Bazin as the main figure and inspiration of French film criticism; his chief contribution in later years was calling attention to the newly emerging cinema of Third-World countries. He wrote the first large-scale history of film, *Histoire générale du cinéma* in six volumes (1946–1952), left unfinished at his death, together with a number of other books such as *Dictionary of Films* and *Dictionary of Film Makers* (both published in French in 1965 and translated in 1972), *French Film* (published first in English in 1953, then in French in 1962), *Georges Méliès* (1961), and *Louis Lumière* (1964).

3. Jean-Paul Sartre, "Quand Hollywood veut faire penser...*Citizen Kane*, Film d'Orson Welles," *L'Écran Français*, no. 5 (1 August 1945), pp. 3-5, 15. Hereafter cited by page number. *Citizen Kane* opened in Paris in July 1946.

4. Sartre claims the opposite in his article on *Citizen Kane*, that "[The narrative structure of *Citizen Kane*] is not unfamiliar to us: recall *Thomas Garner* and *Marie-Martine*" (p. 4). Keep in mind that even though *Marie-Martine* was made after *Citizen Kane*, it was released in France before Welles's film.

The Power and the Glory was known as *Thomas Garner* in France and tells the flashback story of a tycoon who rose from nothing, only to be corrupted by power. William K. Howard directed the film, which starred Spencer Tracy, Colleen Moore, Ralph Morgan, and Helen Vinson. *Marie-Martine* is a comedy-drama about a young woman with a turbulent past, which a writer wants to exploit in his new novel. The film was directed by Albert Valentin and starred Renée Saint-Cyr, Jules Berry, Bernard Blier, Marguerite Deval, Saturnin Fabre, and Jean Dubucourt.

5. Roger Leenhardt, "Le génie d'Orson Weles, dans un pamphlet social d'une audace inconnue: *Citoyen Kane*," *L'Écran Français*, no. 53 (3 July 1946), p. 7. Leenhardt (1903–1985) was a French director and film critic. He began to write film criticism in 1933 and from 1936 to 1939 contributed an extremely influential column to the review *Esprit*. The most eminent of his disciples was André Bazin, who regarded Leenhardt as the first serious film critic and as the subtlest of them all. He was described in Bazin's magazine *Cahiers du Cinéma* as the "spiritual father of the New Wave" and the formulator of its principles.

Leenhardt was the first serious European critic to champion the American cinema; Bazin shared Leenhardt's admiration for some Hollywood directors and joined him in his advocacy of deep-focus cinematography and the moving camera. After the war, when Bazin succeeded his master as *Esprit*'s regular film columnist, Leenhardt said that Bazin's work "was a continuation of what I was doing and he took it beyond what I was trying to do." Leenhardt wrote regularly on film for *Les Lettres françaises* from 1944 to 1946, and also contributed to *Fontaine*, *Cahiers du Cinéma*, and *L'Écran Français*. His criticism was collected after his death in *Chroniques de Cinéma*, ed. Jean Narboni and Alain Bergala (Paris: Éditions de l'Étoile, 1986).

The strength of Leenhardt's criticism derives partly from the fact that he knew the problems and possibilities of filmmaking at first hand. He began making documentary shorts in the mid-1930s and, as a documentarist, is best known for his perceptive biographies of writers and artists, including *Victor Hugo* (1951); *François Mauriac* (1954); *Jean-Jacques* (1957), about Rousseau; *Daumier* (1958); *Paul Valéry* (1959); *L'Homme à la pipe* (1962), about Gustave Courbet; and *Corot* (1965). In addition to over fifty shorts, Leenhardt directed two feature films of some quality: *Les Dernières Vacances* (*The Last Vacation*, 1947), his most famous work, and *Le Rendez-vous de minuit* (*Rendezvous at Midnight*, 1962). See Bazin's review of *The Last Vacation*, translated in this volume.

6. Greek mythology: Ariadne, King Minos's daughter, gave Theseus the thread by which he found his way out of the labyrinth after killing the Minotaur, a monster with the body of a man and the head of a bull.

7. Sartre had written in reference to Faulkner and Dos Passos that every novelistic technique necessarily relates back to a metaphysics. See Jean-Paul Sartre, "American Novelists in French Eyes," trans. Evelyn de Solis, *Atlantic Monthly*, 178, no. 2 (Aug. 1946), pp. 114–18; "*Sartoris* par William Faulkner," *La Nouvelle Revue française*, no. 293 (Feb. 1938), pp. 323–28; and "À propos de John Dos Passos et de *1919*," *La Nouvelle Revue Française*, no. 299 (Aug. 1938), pp. 292–301. The last two articles are collected in Jean-Paul Sartre, *Literary and Philosophical Essays*, trans. Annette Michelson (London: Rider, 1955; New York: Criterion, 1966).

A BAZIN BIBLIOGRAPHY

BOOKS BY BAZIN IN FRENCH

Bazin, André. *Cinéma de la cruauté* Ed. François Truffaut. Paris: Flammarion, 1975.
—————. *Jean Renoir.* Paris: Èditions Champs Libre, 1971.
—————. *Le Cinéma de l'occupation et de la résistance.* Paris: Union Générale d'éditions, 1975.
—————. *Orson Welles.* Paris: Èditions du Cerf, 1972.
—————. *Qu'est-ce que le cinéma?* In four volumes: I. Ontologie et langage (1958); II. Le Cinema et les autres arts (1959); III. Cinéma et sociologie (1961); IV. Une Esthétique de la réalité: le néoréalisme (1962). Paris: Èditions du Cerf, 1958–1962.
—————, and Eric Rohmer. *Charlie Chaplin.* Paris: Èditions du Cerf, 1972.

ARTICLES AND REVIEWS BY BAZIN IN FRENCH

1, 375 items total:
In *Le Parisien libéré: 625* items from issue #117 in 1944 to issue #4405 the day before he died in November 1958.
In *Esprit*: 52 items.
In *L'Observateur (France-Observateur)* : 275 items.
In *Cahiers du Cinéma*: 111 items.
In *Télérama (Radio-Cinéma-Télévision)* : 96 items.
In *Education Nationale*: 33 items.
In *Arts*: 9 items.
In *Peuple et Culture (DOC Education Populaire)* : 7 items.
In *Ècran Français*: 111 items.
Also: 56 miscellaneous items (including pieces from his student period) in magazines such as *Les Temps Modernes, Ciné-Club,* etc.; and in books such as the collective work titled *Sept ans de cinéma français (1945–1952)* [one chapter by Bazin; published by Editions du Cerf], J. L. Rieupeyrout's *Le Western ou le cinéma américain par excellence* [preface by Bazin; published by Editions du Cerf], *Cinéma 53 à travers le monde* [Italian chapter by Bazin; published by Editions du Cerf], and Pierre Leprohon's edited work *Contemporary Presences* [chapter on Welles by Bazin; published by Debressie].

What Is Cinema? Selected and translated by Hugh Gray from the first two volumes of
Qu'est-ce que le cinéma?. Preface by Jean Renoir. Berkeley: University of California
Press, 1967.

What Is Cinema? Volume II. Selected and translated by Hugh Gray from the last two volumes of *Qu'est-ce que le cinéma?*. Preface by François Truffaut. Berkeley: University of
California Press, 1971.

Jean Renoir. Translated by W. W. Halsey II and William H. Simon. Preface by François
Truffaut. New York: Simon and Schuster, 1973.

Orson Welles. Translated by Jonathan Rosenbaum. Preface by François Truffaut. New
York: Harper and Row, 1978.

French Cinema of the Occupation and Resistance: "The Birth of a Critical Esthetic". Translated by
Stanley Hochman. Preface by François Truffaut. New York: Frederick Ungar, 1981.

The Cinema of Cruelty . Translated by Sabine d'Estrée. Preface by François Truffaut. New
York: Seaver Books, 1982.

Essays on Chaplin. Translated by Jean Bodon. New Haven, Conn.: University of New
Haven Press, 1985.

WORKS ON BAZIN IN ENGLISH

BOOK REVIEWS

Of *What Is Cinema?*:

Michelson, Annette. In *Artforum*, VI, No. 10 (1968), pp. 66–71.
Kael, Pauline. "Behind the New Wave." *The New York Times*, 10 Sept. 1967, Sec. 7, p. 1.

Of *Jean Renoir*:

In *Afterimage*, 2 (April 1975), p. 9.
Sight and Sound, 44, No. 1 (Winter 1974–1975), pp. 16–18.
Film Comment, 12 (May-June 1976), pp. 60–61.
Cinema Journal, 13, No. 2 (1974), pp. 58–63.
Film Heritage, 9, No. 3 (1974), p. 37–40.
Focus on Film, #19 (Autumn 1974), p. 13.
Film Quarterly 27, No. 3 (1974), p. 25.

Of *Orson Welles*:

In *The American Scholar*, 48, No. 1 (1979), pp. 140–44.
Cineaste, 9, No. 2 (1978), pp. 52-53.
American Film, 4 (Oct. 1978), pp. 75–76.
Focus on Film, #31 (Nov. 1978), pp. 51–52.
The New York Times, 23 July 1978, Sec. 7, p. 9+.
Quarterly Review of Film Studies, 5, No. 3 (1980), pp. 377–382.

Of *French Cinema of the Occupation and Resistance*:

In *Films and Filming*, #329 (Feb. 1982), p. 38.
Wide Angle, 5, No. 2 (1983), pp. 78–79.
American Film, 8 (June 1983), pp. 66–67+.
Afterimage, 9 (Jan. 1982), p. 17.
Film Criticism, 6, No. 2 (1982), pp. 58–66.
Film Quarterly, 34, No. 4 (1981), p. 34.

Andrew, Dudley. "André Bazin." *Film Comment*, IX, No. 2 (March-April 1973), pp. 64–67.

——. "Realism and Reality in Cinema: The Film Theory of André Bazin and Its Source in Recent French Thought." Ph.D. dissertation, University of Iowa, 1972.

——. *André Bazin*. New York: Oxford University Press, 1978; Columbia Univ. Press, 1990.

——. "Bazin on Stalin." In *Movies and Methods*, Vol. 2. Ed. Bill Nichols. Berkeley: University of California Press, 1985, pp. 29–31.

——. "André Bazin." In Andrew's *The Major Film Theories*. New York: Oxford University Press, 1976, pp. 134–78.

——. "Cinematic Politics in Postwar France: Bazin before *Cahiers*." *Cineaste*, 12, No. 1 (1982), pp. 12-16.

Brubaker, David Adam. "André Bazin's Realism: The Metaphysics of Film Reception." Ph.D. dissertation, University of Illinois-Chicago, 1991.

——. "André Bazin on Automatically Made Images." *Journal of Aesthetics and Art Criticism*, 51, No. 1 (Winter 1993), pp. 59–67.

Cadbury, William. "The Cleavage Plane of André Bazin." *Journal of Modern Literature*, III, No. 2 (Spring 1973), pp. 253-67.

Carroll, Noël. "Cinematic Representation and Realism: André Bazin and the Aesthetics of Sound Film." Ch. 2 in his *Philosophical Problems of Classical Film Theory*. Princeton, New Jersey: Princeton University Press, 1988, pp. 93-171.

Gray, Hugh. "On Interpreting Bazin." *Film Quarterly*, 26, No. 3 (1973), pp. 58–59.

Harcourt, Peter "What, Indeed, Is Cinema?" *Cinema Journal*, VI, No. 1 (Fall 1968), pp. 22-28.

Henderson, Brian, "Reply to Hugh Gray." *Film Quarterly*, 26, No. 3 (1973), pp. 59–61.

——. "The Structure of André Bazin's Thought." *Film Quarterly*, 25, No. 4 (Summer 1972), pp. 15–27.

——. "Bazin Defended Against His Devotees." *Film Quarterly*, 32, No. 4 (1979), pp. 26– 37.

Lesses, Glenn. "Renoir, Bazin, and Film Realism." In *Purdue University's Seventh Annual Conference on Film*. Ed. Marshall Deutelbaum and Thomas P. Adler. West Lafayette Indiana: Dept. of English at Purdue University, 1983, pp. 147–52.

McConnell, F. "The Critic as Romantic Hero: André Bazin." *Quarterly Review of Film Studies*, 5, No. 1 (1980), pp. 109–13.

Michelson, Annette. "What Is Cinema?" *Performing Arts Journal*, 17 (May-Sept. 1995), pp. 20 29

Roud, Richard. "Face to Face: André Bazin." *Sight and Sound*, XXVIII, Nos. 3-4 (1959), pp. 176–79.

——. "André Bazin: His Rise and Fall." *Sight and Sound*, XXXVII, No. 2 (1968), pp. 94–96.

Sarris, Andrew. "The Aesthetics of André Bazin." In his *The Primal Screen*. New York: Simon and Schuster, 1973, pp. 87–90.

Staiger, J. "Theorist, yes, but what of? Bazin and History." *Iris*, 2, No. 2 (1984), pp. 99–109.

Trope, Zippora. "A Critical Application of André Bazin's *Mise en Scène* Theory." Ph.D. dissertation, University of Michigan, 1974.

Velvet Light Trap, 21 (Summer 1985). Special issue devoted to Bazin:
Bordwell, David. "Widescreen Aesthetics and *mise-en-scène* Criticism," pp. 18–25.
Spellerberg, James. "CinemaScope and Ideology," pp. 26–34. Plus several translations of essays by Bazin.

Wagner, J. "Lost Aura: Benjamin, Bazin, and the Realist Paradox." *Spectator*, 9, No. 1 (1988), pp. 56–69.

Wide Angle, 9, No. 4 (1987). Special issue devoted to Bazin:

    Andrew, Dudley. Preface, pp. 4–6.

    Belton, John. "Bazin Is Dead! Long Live Bazin!" pp. 74–81.

    Falkenberg, Pamela. "'The Text! The Text!': André Bazin's Mummy Complex, Psychoanalysis, and the Cinema," pp. 35–55.

    Narboni, Jean. "André Bazin's Style," pp. 56–60.

    Rosen, Philip. "History of Image, Image of History: Subject and Ontology in Bazin," pp. 7–34.

    Tacchella, Jean-Charles. "Andre Bazin From 1945 to 1950: The Time of Struggles and Consecration," pp.61–73.

Williams, Christopher. "Bazin on Neorealism." *Screen*, XIV, No. 4 (Winter 1973–1974), pp. 61-68.

——————, ed. *Realism and the Cinema*. London: Routledge and Kegan Paul, 1980, pp. 35–54, 246–49, et passim.

Wolfe, Charles. "Fictional Realism: Watt and Bazin on the Pleasures of Novels and Films." *Literature/Film Quarterly*, 9, No. 1 (1981), pp. 40–50.

INDEX